Get the eBook FREE!
(PDF, ePub, Kindle, and liveBook all included)

We believe that once you buy a book from us, you should be able to read it in any format we have available. To get electronic versions of this book at no additional cost to you, purchase and then register this book at the Manning website.

Go to https://www.manning.com/freebook and follow the instructions to complete your pBook registration.

That's it!
Thanks from Manning!

Classic Computer Science Problems in Java

Classic Computer Science Problems in Java

DAVID KOPEC

MANNING

SHELTER ISLAND

For online information and ordering of this and other Manning books, please visit
www.manning.com. The publisher offers discounts on this book when ordered in quantity.
For more information, please contact

    Special Sales Department
    Manning Publications Co.
    20 Baldwin Road
    PO Box 761
    Shelter Island, NY 11964
    Email: orders@manning.com

Manning Publications Co.
20 Baldwin Road
PO Box 761
Shelter Island, NY 11964

Development editor:	Jenny Stout
Technical development editor:	Frances Buontempo
Review editor:	Aleks Dragosavljević
Production editor:	Deirdre S. Hiam
Copy editor:	Andy Carroll
Proofreader:	Katie Tennant
Technical proofreader:	Jean-François Morin
Typesetter:	Dennis Dalinnik
Cover designer:	Marija Tudor

ISBN: 9781617297601
Printed in the United States of America

To Xingben Chen of SUNY Suffolk and Wei Kian Chen of Champlain College,
who gave me the opportunity and mentorship to be a teacher.

brief contents

contents

acknowledgments

I would like to thank everyone at Manning who helped in the development of the book. I would especially like to thank development editor Jenny Stout for her kindness and for being there when it mattered during the most difficult of circumstances for me out of our three books together; technical development editor Frances Buontempo for her attention to detail; acquisition editor Brian Sawyer for believing in the *Classic Computer Science Problems* series and always being a voice of reason; copy editor Andy Carroll for catching my errors better than I catch them myself these past few years; Radmila Ercegovac for helping me promote the series throughout the world; and technical reviewer Jean-François Morin for finding ways to make the code more clean and modern. Also, I would like to thank Deirdre Hiam, my project editor; Katie Tennant, my proofreader; and Aleks Dragosavljević my reviewing editor. There are at least a dozen more people at Manning in management, graphics, typesetting, finance, marketing, reviews, and production who worked in various stages of the book's development that I didn't get to know as well, but I thank them for their part.

Thank you, Brian Goetz, for being generous with your time, and for providing an interview that will be sure to delight and inform readers. It was an honor to interview you.

Thank you, my wife, Rebecca, and my mom, Sylvia, for your unwavering support during an unpleasant year.

Thank you, all the reviewers: Andres Sacco, Ezra Simeloff, Jan van Nimwegen, Kelum Prabath Senanayake, Kimberly Winston-Jackson, Raffaella Ventaglio, Raushan

Jha, Samantha Berk, Simon Tschöke, Víctor Durán, and William Wheeler. Your suggestions helped make this a better book. I appreciate the care and time you put into your reviews.

Thank you, most importantly: the readers who have supported the *Classic Computer Science Problems* series. If you enjoy this book, leave a review. It really does help.

about this book

liveBook discussion forum

Purchase of *Classic Computer Science Problems in Java* includes free access to a private web forum run by Manning Publications where you can make comments about the book, ask technical questions, and receive help from the author and from other users. To access the forum, go to https://livebook.manning.com/#!/book/classic-computer-science-problems-in-java/discussion. You can also learn more about Manning's forums and the rules of conduct at https://livebook.manning.com/#!/discussion.

Manning's commitment to our readers is to provide a venue where a meaningful dialogue between individual readers and between readers and the author can take place. It is not a commitment to any specific amount of participation on the part of the author, whose contribution to the forum remains voluntary (and unpaid). We suggest you try asking him some challenging questions lest his interest stray! The forum and the archives of previous discussions will be accessible from the publisher's website as long as the book is in print.

about the author

 DAVID KOPEC is an assistant professor of Computer Science & Innovation at Champlain College in Burlington, Vermont. He is the author of *Classic Computer Science Problems in Python* (Manning, 2019), *Classic Computer Science Problems in Swift* (Manning, 2018), and *Dart for Absolute Beginners* (Apress, 2014). He is also a software developer and podcaster.

about the cover illustration

The figure on the cover of *Classic Computer Science Problems in Java* is captioned "Dame de la Côte de Barbarie dans tout saparure," or "Full dress of a lady of quality in Barbary, in 1700." The illustration is taken from Thomas Jefferys' *A Collection of the Dresses of Different Nations, Ancient and Modern* (four volumes), London, published between 1757 and 1772. The title page states that these are hand-colored copperplate engravings, heightened with gum arabic. Thomas Jefferys (1719–1771) was called "Geographer to King George III." He was an English cartographer who was the leading map supplier of his day. He engraved and printed maps for government and other official bodies and produced a wide range of commercial maps and atlases, especially of North America. His work as a map maker sparked an interest in local dress customs of the lands he surveyed and mapped, which are brilliantly displayed in this collection.

Fascination with faraway lands and travel for pleasure were relatively new phenomena in the late eighteenth century, and collections such as this one were popular, introducing both the tourist as well as the armchair traveler to the inhabitants of other countries. The diversity of the drawings in Jefferys' volumes speaks vividly of the uniqueness and individuality of the world's nations some 200 years ago. Dress codes have changed since then, and the diversity by region and country, so rich at the time, has faded away. It's now often hard to tell the inhabitants of one continent from another. Perhaps, viewing it optimistically, we've traded a cultural and visual diversity for a more varied personal life—or a more varied and interesting intellectual and technical life.

At a time when it's difficult to tell one computer book from another, Manning celebrates the inventiveness and initiative of the computer business with book covers based on the rich diversity of regional life of two centuries ago, brought back to life by Jefferys' pictures.

Introduction

Thank you for purchasing *Classic Computer Science Problems in Java*. Java has been one of the most popular programming languages in the world for around two decades. It is arguably the dominant language in the enterprise space, higher education, and Android app development. In this book I hope to take you beyond using Java as a means to an end. Instead, I hope to bring you to a place where you are thinking about Java as a tool for computational problem solving. The problems in this intermediate book will help seasoned programmers refresh themselves on ideas from their CS education while learning some advanced features of the language. Students using Java in school and self-taught programmers will accelerate their CS education by learning generally applicable problem-solving techniques. This book covers such a diversity of problems that there is truly something for everyone.

This book is not an introduction to Java. There are numerous excellent books from Manning and other publishers in that vein. Instead, this book assumes that you are already an intermediate or advanced Java programmer. Although this book uses features from a fairly recent version of Java (Java 11), mastery of every facet of the latest version of Java is not assumed. In fact, the book's content was created with the assumption that it would serve as learning material to help readers achieve such mastery. On the other hand, this book is not appropriate for readers completely new to Java.

Some say that computers are to computer science as telescopes are to astronomy. If that's the case, then perhaps a programming language is like a telescope lens. In any event, the term "classic computer science problems" is used here to mean "programming problems typically taught in an undergraduate computer science curriculum."

There are certain programming problems that are given to new programmers to solve and that have become commonplace enough to be deemed classic, whether in a classroom setting during the pursuit of a bachelor's degree (in computer science, software engineering, and the like) or within the confines of an intermediate programming textbook (for example, a first book on artificial intelligence or algorithms). A selection of such problems is what you will find in this book.

The problems range from the trivial, which can be solved in a few lines of code, to the complex, which require the buildup of systems over multiple chapters. Some problems touch on artificial intelligence, and others simply require common sense. Some problems are practical, and other problems are fanciful.

Who should read this book

Java is used in pursuits as diverse as mobile app development, enterprise web development, computer science education, finance software, and much more. Java is sometimes criticized for being verbose and lacking some modern features, but it has possibly touched more people's lives since its inception than any other programming language. There must be a reason for its popularity. Java was originally imagined by its creator, James Gosling, as a better C++: a language that would offer the power of object-oriented programming, while introducing safety features and streamlining some of C++'s more frustrating edges. In this regard Java has succeeded with flying colors, in my opinion.

Java is a great general-purpose object-oriented language. However, many people get into a rut, whether they be Android developers or enterprise web developers, where most of their time with the language feels like "API mashup." Instead of working on solving interesting problems, they find their time being spent learning every corner of an SDK or library. This book aims to offer those programmers a respite. And there are also programmers out there who have never received an education in computer science that teaches them all of the powerful problem-solving techniques available to them. If you are one of those programmers who knows Java but does not know CS, this book is for you.

Other programmers learn Java as a second, third, fourth, or fifth language after a long time working in software development. For them, seeing old problems they've already seen in another language will help them accelerate their learning of Java. For them, this book may be a good refresher before a job interview, or it might expose them to some problem-solving techniques they had not previously thought of exploiting in their work. I would encourage them to skim the table of contents to see if there are topics in this book that excite them.

This book is for both intermediate and experienced programmers. Experienced programmers who want to deepen their knowledge of Java will find comfortably familiar problems from their computer science or programming education. Intermediate programmers will be introduced to these classic problems in the language of their choice: Java. Developers getting ready for coding interviews will likely find this book to be valuable preparation material.

In addition to professional programmers, students enrolled in undergraduate computer science programs who have an interest in Java will likely find this book helpful. It makes no attempt to be a rigorous introduction to data structures and algorithms. *This is not a data structures and algorithms textbook.* You will not find proofs or extensive use of big-O notation within its pages. Instead, it is positioned as an approachable, hands-on tutorial to the problem-solving techniques that should be the end product of taking data structure, algorithm, and artificial intelligence classes.

Once again, knowledge of Java's syntax and semantics is assumed. A reader with zero programming experience will get little out of this book, and a programmer with zero Java experience will almost certainly struggle. In other words, *Classic Computer Science Problems in Java* is a book for working Java programmers and computer science students.

How this book is organized: A roadmap

Chapter 1 introduces problem-solving techniques that will likely look familiar to most readers. Things like recursion, memoization, and bit manipulation are essential building blocks of other techniques explored in later chapters.

This gentle introduction is followed by chapter 2, which focuses on search problems. Search is such a large topic that you could arguably place most problems in the book under its banner. Chapter 2 introduces the most essential search algorithms, including binary search, depth-first search, breadth-first search, and A*. Search algorithms are used throughout the rest of the book.

In chapter 3, you will build a framework for solving a broad range of problems that can be abstractly defined by variables of limited domains that have constraints between them. This includes such classics as the eight queens problem, the Australian map-coloring problem, and the cryptarithmetic SEND+MORE=MONEY.

Chapter 4 explores the world of graph algorithms, which to the uninitiated are surprisingly broad in their applicability. In this chapter, you will build a graph data structure and then use it to solve several classic optimization problems.

Chapter 5 explores genetic algorithms, a technique that is less deterministic than most covered in the book but that sometimes can solve problems traditional algorithms cannot solve in a reasonable amount of time.

Chapter 6 covers k-means clustering and is perhaps the most algorithmically specific chapter in the book. This clustering technique is simple to implement, easy to understand, and broadly applicable.

Chapter 7 aims to explain what a neural network is and to give the reader a taste of what a very simple neural network looks like. It does not aim to provide comprehensive coverage of this exciting and evolving field. In this chapter, you will build a neural network from first principles, using no external libraries, so you can really see how a neural network works.

Chapter 8 is on adversarial search in two-player perfect information games. You will learn a search algorithm known as minimax, which can be used to develop an artificial opponent that can play games like chess, checkers, and Connect Four well.

Chapter 9 covers interesting (and fun) problems that did not quite fit anywhere else in the book.

Finally, chapter 10 is an interview with Brian Goetz, the Java Language Architect at Oracle, who guides the development of the language. Brian has some sage advice for readers about programming and computer science.

About the code

The source code in this book was written to adhere to version 11 of the Java language. It utilizes features of Java that only became available in Java 11, so some of the code will not run on earlier versions of Java. Instead of struggling and trying to make the examples run in an earlier version, please just download the latest version of Java before starting the book. I chose version 11 because it was the most recent LTS (long-term support) version of Java released at the time of writing. All of the code should work on more recent (and future) versions of Java. In fact, a significant amount of the code would work on Java versions going all the way back to Java 8. I know that many programmers are still stuck on Java 8 for various reasons (cough Android), but I wanted to use a more recent version of Java to provide additional value by teaching a couple of the language's newer features.

This book uses only the Java standard library, so all of the code in this book should run on any platform where Java is supported (macOS, Windows, GNU/Linux, and so on). The code in this book was tested against only OpenJDK (the main Java implementation available from http://openjdk.java.net), although it is unlikely any of the code would have a problem running in an alternative implementation of Java.

This book does not explain how to use Java tools like editors, IDEs, and debuggers. The book's source code is available online from the GitHub repository: https://github .com/davecom/ClassicComputerScienceProblemsInJava. The source code is organized into folders by chapter. As you read each chapter, you will see the name of a source file in the header of each code listing. You can find that source file in its respective folder in the repository.

Note that the repository is organized as an Eclipse workspace. Eclipse is a popular free Java IDE that is available for all three major operating systems and is available from eclipse.org. The easiest way to use the source code repository is to open it as an Eclipse workspace after downloading it. You can then expand the src directory, expand the package representing a chapter, right-click (or control-click on a Mac) a file containing a `main()` method, and select Run As > Java Application from the pop-up menu to run an example problem's solution. I will not be providing a tutorial on Eclipse because I think it would come across as filler to most intermediate programmers, who should find getting started with it quite straightforward. In addition, I expect many programmers will choose to use this book with alternative Java environments.

Since it is all just standard Java, you can also run any of the source code from this book in your IDE of choice, be that NetBeans, IntelliJ, or some other environment that you are comfortable with. If you choose to do that, take note that I cannot offer support importing the projects into your chosen environment, although that should be fairly trivial. Most IDEs can import from Eclipse.

In short, if you are starting from scratch, then the easiest way to get your computer set up with the source code from this book is to do the following:

1 Download and install Java 11 or later from openjdk.java.net.
2 Download and install Eclipse from eclipse.org.
3 Download the book's source code from the repository at https://github.com/davecom/ClassicComputerScienceProblemsInJava.
4 Open the entire repository as a workspace in Eclipse.
5 Right-click a source code file you want to run and select Run As > Java Application.

There are no examples in this book that produce graphical output or that make use of a graphical user interface (GUI). Why? The goal is to solve the posed problems with solutions that are as concise and readable as possible. Often, doing graphics gets in the way or makes solutions significantly more complex than they need to be to illustrate the technique or algorithm in question.

Further, by not making use of any GUI framework, all of the code in the book is eminently portable. It can as easily run on an embedded distribution of Java running on a command-line interface under Linux as it can on a desktop running Windows. Also, a conscious decision was made to use only packages from the Java standard library instead of any external libraries, as many advanced Java books do. Why? The goal is to teach problem-solving techniques from first principles, not to "install a solution." By having to work through every problem from scratch, you will hopefully gain an understanding about how popular libraries work behind the scenes. At a minimum, using only the standard library makes the code in this book more portable and easier to run.

This is not to say that graphical solutions are not sometimes more illustrative of an algorithm than text-based solutions. It simply is not the focus of this book. It would add another layer of unnecessary complexity.

Other online resources

This is the third book in a series titled *Classic Computer Science Problems* published by Manning. The first book was *Classic Computer Science Problems in Swift*, published in 2018, which was followed by *Classic Computer Science Problems in Python*, published in 2019. In each book in the series, we aim to provide language-specific insight while teaching through the lens of the same (mostly) computer science problems.

If you enjoy this book and plan to learn another language covered by the series, you may find going from one book to another an easy way to improve your mastery of that language. For now, the series covers Swift, Python, and Java. I wrote the first three books myself, because I have significant experience in all of those languages, but we are already discussing plans for future books in the series coauthored by people who are experts in other languages. I encourage you to look out for them if you enjoy this book. For more information about the series, visit https://classicproblems.com/.

Small problems

To get started, we will explore some simple problems that can be solved with no more than a few relatively short functions. Although these problems are small, they will still allow us to explore some interesting problem-solving techniques. Think of them as a good warm-up.

1.1 The Fibonacci sequence

The Fibonacci sequence is a sequence of numbers such that any number, except for the first and second, is the sum of the previous two:

```
0, 1, 1, 2, 3, 5, 8, 13, 21...
```

The value of the first Fibonacci number in the sequence is 0. The value of the fourth Fibonacci number is 2. It follows that to get the value of any Fibonacci number, n, in the sequence, one can use the formula

```
fib(n) = fib(n - 1) + fib(n - 2)
```

1.1.1 A first recursive attempt

The preceding formula for computing a number in the Fibonacci sequence (illustrated in figure 1.1) is a form of pseudocode that can be trivially translated into a *recursive* Java method. (A recursive method is a method that calls itself.) This mechanical translation will serve as our first attempt at writing a method to return a given value of the Fibonacci sequence.

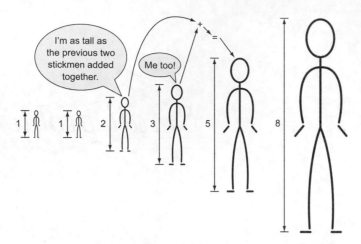

Figure 1.1 **The height of each stickman is the previous two stickmen's heights added together.**

Listing 1.1   Fib1.java

```java
package chapter1;

public class Fib1 {

    // This method will cause a java.lang.StackOverflowError
    private static int fib1(int n) {
        return fib1(n - 1) + fib1(n - 2);
    }
}
```

Let's try to run this method by calling it with a value.

Listing 1.2   Fib1.java continued

```java
    public static void main(String[] args) {
        // Don't run this!
        System.out.println(fib1(5));
    }
}
```

Uh-oh! If we try to run Fib1.java, we generate an exception:

```
Exception in thread "main" java.lang.StackOverflowError
```

The issue is that fib1() will run forever without returning a final result. Every call to fib1() results in another two calls of fib1() with no end in sight. We call such a circumstance *infinite recursion* (see figure 1.2), and it is analogous to an *infinite loop*.

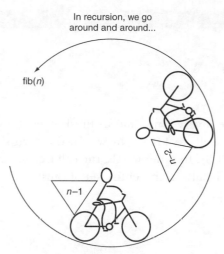

In recursion, we go around and around...

fib(*n*)

Figure 1.2   The recursive function `fib(n)`
calls itself with the arguments `n-1` **and** `n-2`.

1.1.2   Utilizing base cases

Notice that until you run `fib1()`, there is no indication from your Java environment that there is anything wrong with it. It is the duty of the programmer to avoid infinite recursion, not the compiler. The reason for the infinite recursion is that we never specified a base case. In a recursive function, a base case serves as a stopping point.

In the case of the Fibonacci sequence, we have natural base cases in the form of the special first two sequence values, 0 and 1. Neither 0 nor 1 is the sum of the previous two numbers in the sequence. Instead, they are the special first two values. Let's try specifying them as base cases.

Listing 1.3   Fib2.java

```java
package chapter1;

public class Fib2 {
    private static int fib2(int n) {
        if (n < 2) { return n; }
        return fib2(n - 1) + fib2(n - 2);
    }
}
```

NOTE   The `fib2()` version of the Fibonacci method returns 0 as the zeroth number (`fib2(0)`), rather than the first number, as in our original proposition. In a programming context, this kind of makes sense because we are used to sequences starting with a zeroth element.

`fib2()` can be called successfully and will return correct results. Try calling it with some small values.

Listing 1.4   Fib2.java continued

```java
public static void main(String[] args) {
    System.out.println(fib2(5));
    System.out.println(fib2(10));
}
}
```

Do not try calling `fib2(40)`. It may take a very long time to finish executing! Why? Every call to `fib2()` results in two more calls to `fib2()` by way of the recursive calls `fib2(n - 1)` and `fib2(n - 2)` (see figure 1.3). In other words, the call tree grows exponentially. For example, a call of `fib2(4)` results in this entire set of calls:

```
fib2(4)  -> fib2(3), fib2(2)
fib2(3)  -> fib2(2), fib2(1)
fib2(2)  -> fib2(1), fib2(0)
fib2(2)  -> fib2(1), fib2(0)
fib2(1)  -> 1
fib2(1)  -> 1
fib2(1)  -> 1
fib2(0)  -> 0
fib2(0)  -> 0
```

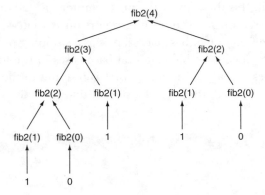

Figure 1.3   Every non-base-case call of `fib2()` results in two more calls of `fib2()`.

If you count them (and as you will see if you add some print calls), there are 9 calls to `fib2()` just to compute the 4th element! It gets worse. There are 15 calls required to compute element 5, 177 calls to compute element 10, and 21,891 calls to compute element 20. We can do better.

1.1.3   *Memoization to the rescue*

Memoization is a technique in which you store the results of computational tasks when they are completed so that when you need them again, you can look them up instead of needing to compute them a second (or millionth) time (see figure 1.4).[1]

---

[1]   Donald Michie, a famous British computer scientist, coined the term *memoization*. Donald Michie, *Memo Functions: A Language Feature with "rote-learning" Properties* (Edinburgh University, Department of Machine Intelligence and Perception, 1967).

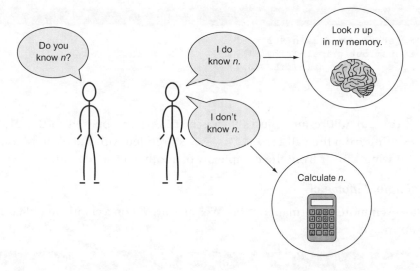

Figure 1.4　The human memoization machine

Let's create a new version of the Fibonacci method that utilizes a Java map for memoization purposes.

Listing 1.5　Fib3.java

```java
package chapter1;

import java.util.HashMap;
import java.util.Map;

public class Fib3 {

    // Map.of() was introduced in Java 9 but returns
    // an immutable Map
    // This creates a map with 0->0 and 1->1
    // which represent our base cases
    static Map<Integer, Integer> memo = new HashMap<>(Map.of(0, 0, 1, 1));

    private static int fib3(int n) {
        if (!memo.containsKey(n)) {
            // memoization step
            memo.put(n, fib3(n - 1) + fib3(n - 2));
        }
        return memo.get(n);
    }
}
```

You can now safely call fib3(40).

Listing 1.6   Fib3.java continued

```
    public static void main(String[] args) {
        System.out.println(fib3(5));
        System.out.println(fib3(40));
    }
}
```

A call to fib3(20) will result in just 39 calls of fib3() as opposed to the 21,891 of fib2() resulting from the call fib2(20). memo is prefilled with the earlier base cases of 0 and 1, saving fib3() from the complexity of another if statement.

1.1.4   *Keep it simple, Fibonacci*

There is an even more performant option. We can solve Fibonacci with an old-fashioned iterative approach.

Listing 1.7   Fib4.java

```
package chapter1;

public class Fib4 {

    private static int fib4(int n) {
        int last = 0, next = 1; // fib(0), fib(1)
        for (int i = 0; i < n; i++) {
            int oldLast = last;
            last = next;
            next = oldLast + next;
        }
        return last;
    }

    public static void main(String[] args) {
        System.out.println(fib4(20));
        System.out.println(fib4(40));
    }
}
```

The gist is, last is being set to the previous value of next, and next is being set to the previous value of last plus the previous value of next. A temporary variable, oldLast, facilitates the exchange.

With this approach, the body of the for loop will run n - 1 times. In other words, this is the most efficient version yet. Compare 19 runs of the for loop body to 21,891 recursive calls of fib2() for the 20th Fibonacci number. That could make a serious difference in a real-world application!

In the recursive solutions, we worked backward. In this iterative solution, we work forward. Sometimes recursion is the most intuitive way to solve a problem. For example, the meat of fib1() and fib2() is pretty much a mechanical translation of the original Fibonacci formula. However, naive recursive solutions can also come with significant performance costs. Remember, any problem that can be solved recursively can also be solved iteratively.

1.1.5 Generating Fibonacci numbers with a stream

So far, we have written methods that output a single value in the Fibonacci sequence. What if we want to output the entire sequence up to some value instead? It is easy to convert fib4() into a Java stream using the generator pattern. When the generator is iterated, each iteration will spew a value from the Fibonacci sequence using a lambda function that returns the next number.

Listing 1.8   Fib5.java

```java
package chapter1;

import java.util.stream.IntStream;

public class Fib5 {
    private int last = 0, next = 1; // fib(0), fib(1)

    public IntStream stream() {
        return IntStream.generate(() -> {
            int oldLast = last;
            last = next;
            next = oldLast + next;
            return oldLast;
        });
    }

    public static void main(String[] args) {
        Fib5 fib5 = new Fib5();
        fib5.stream().limit(41).forEachOrdered(System.out::println);
    }
}
```

If you run Fib5.java, you will see 41 numbers in the Fibonacci sequence printed. For each number in the sequence, Fib5 runs the generate() lambda once, which manipulates the last and next instance variables that maintain state. The limit() call ensures that the potentially infinite stream stops spewing numbers when it reaches its 41st item.

1.2   Trivial compression

Saving space (virtual or real) is often important. It is more efficient to use less space, and it can save money. If you are renting an apartment that is bigger than you need for your things and family, you could "downsize" to a smaller place that is less expensive. If you are paying by the byte to store your data on a server, you may want to compress it so that its storage costs you less. *Compression* is the act of taking data and encoding it (changing its form) in such a way that it takes up less space. *Decompression* is reversing the process, returning the data to its original form.

If it is more storage-efficient to compress data, then why is all data not compressed? There is a trade-off between time and space. It takes time to compress a piece of data and to decompress it back into its original form. Therefore, data compression only makes sense in situations where small size is prioritized over fast execution. Think of large files being transmitted over the internet. Compressing them makes sense because it will take longer to transfer the files than it will to decompress them once received. Further, the time taken to compress the files for their storage on the original server only needs to be accounted for once.

The easiest data compression wins come about when you realize that data storage types use more bits than are strictly required for their contents. For instance, thinking low-level, if a signed integer that will never exceed 32,767 is being stored as a 64-bit long in memory, it is being stored inefficiently. It could instead be stored as a 16-bit short. This would reduce the space consumption for the actual number by 75% (16 bits instead of 64 bits). If millions of such numbers are being stored inefficiently, it can add up to megabytes of wasted space.

In Java programming, sometimes for the sake of simplicity (which is a legitimate goal, of course), the developer is shielded from thinking in bits. The vast majority of Java code in the wild uses the 32-bit int type for storing integers. There is really nothing wrong with that for the vast majority of applications. However, if you are storing millions of integers, or you need integers of a certain precision, then it may be worth considering what the appropriate type for them is.

> **NOTE** If you are a little rusty regarding binary, recall that a bit is a single value that is either a 1 or a 0. A sequence of 1s and 0s is read in base 2 to represent a number. For the purposes of this section, you do not need to do any math in base 2, but you do need to understand that the number of bits that a type stores determines how many different values it can represent. For example, 1 bit can represent two values (0 or 1), 2 bits can represent four values (00, 01, 10, 11), 3 bits can represent eight values, and so on.

If the number of possible different values that a type can represent is less than the number of values that the bits being used to store it can represent, it can likely be more efficiently stored. Consider the nucleotides that form a gene in DNA. Each nucleotide can only be one of four values: *A*, *C*, *G*, or *T*. Yet, if the gene is stored as a Java String, which can be thought of as a collection of Unicode characters, each nucleotide will be represented by a character, which generally requires 16 bits of storage in Java (Java uses the UTF-16 encoding by default). In binary, just 2 bits are needed to store a type with four possible values: 00, 01, 10, and 11 are the four different values that can be represented by 2 bits. If *A* is assigned 00, *C* is assigned 01, *G* is assigned 10, and *T* is assigned 11, the storage required for a string of nucleotides can be reduced by 87.5% (from 16 bits to 2 bits per nucleotide).

Instead of storing our nucleotides as a String, we can store them as a *bit string* (see figure 1.5). A bit string is exactly what it sounds like: an arbitrary-length sequence of 1s and 0s. Fortunately, the Java standard library contains an off-the-shelf construct for

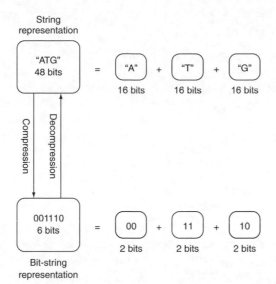

Figure 1.5 Compressing a
`String` representing a gene into
a 2-bit-per-nucleotide bit string

working with bit strings of arbitrary length called `BitSet`. The following code converts a `String` composed of *A*s, *C*s, *G*s, and *T*s into a string of bits and back again. The string of bits is stored within a `BitSet` via the `compress()` method. We will also implement a `decompress()` method to convert back into a `String`.

Listing 1.9 CompressedGene.java

```java
package chapter1;

import java.util.BitSet;

public class CompressedGene {
    private BitSet bitSet;
    private int length;

    public CompressedGene(String gene) {
        compress(gene);
    }
```

A `CompressedGene` is provided a `String` of characters representing the nucleotides in a gene, and it internally stores the sequence of nucleotides as a `BitSet`. The constructor's main responsibility is to initialize the `BitSet` construct with the appropriate data. The constructor calls `compress()` to do the dirty work of actually converting the provided `String` of nucleotides into a `BitSet`.

Next, let's look at how we can actually perform the compression.

Listing 1.10 CompressedGene.java continued

```java
private void compress(String gene) {
    length = gene.length();
```

```java
        // reserve enough capacity for all of the bits
        bitSet = new BitSet(length * 2);
        // convert to upper case for consistency
        final String upperGene = gene.toUpperCase();
        // convert String to bit representation
        for (int i = 0; i < length; i++) {
            final int firstLocation = 2 * i;
            final int secondLocation = 2 * i + 1;
            switch (upperGene.charAt(i)) {
            case 'A': // 00 are next two bits
                bitSet.set(firstLocation, false);
                bitSet.set(secondLocation, false);
                break;
            case 'C': // 01 are next two bits
                bitSet.set(firstLocation, false);
                bitSet.set(secondLocation, true);
                break;
            case 'G': // 10 are next two bits
                bitSet.set(firstLocation, true);
                bitSet.set(secondLocation, false);
                break;
            case 'T': // 11 are next two bits
                bitSet.set(firstLocation, true);
                bitSet.set(secondLocation, true);
                break;
            default:
                throw new IllegalArgumentException("The provided gene String
    contains characters other than ACGT");
            }
        }
    }
```

The compress() method looks at each character in the String of nucleotides sequentially. When it sees an *A*, it adds 00 to the bit string. When it sees a *C*, it adds 01, and so on. For the BitSet class, the Boolean values true and false serve as markers for 1 and 0, respectively.

Every nucleotide is added using two calls of the set() method. In other words, we continually add two new bits to the end of the bit string. The two bits that are added are determined by the type of the nucleotide.

Finally, we will implement decompression.

Listing 1.11   CompressedGene.java continued

```java
public String decompress() {
    if (bitSet == null) {
        return "";
    }
    // create a mutable place for characters with the right capacity
    StringBuilder builder = new StringBuilder(length);
    for (int i = 0; i < (length * 2); i += 2) {
        final int firstBit = (bitSet.get(i) ? 1 : 0);
        final int secondBit = (bitSet.get(i + 1) ? 1 : 0);
```

```java
        final int lastBits = firstBit << 1 | secondBit;
        switch (lastBits) {
        case 0b00: // 00 is 'A'
            builder.append('A');
            break;
        case 0b01: // 01 is 'C'
            builder.append('C');
            break;
        case 0b10: // 10 is 'G'
            builder.append('G');
            break;
        case 0b11: // 11 is 'T'
            builder.append('T');
            break;
        }
    }
    return builder.toString();
}
```

decompress() reads two bits from the bit string at a time, and it uses those two bits to determine which character to add to the end of the String representation of the gene, which is built using a StringBuilder. The two bits are composed together in the variable lastBits. lastBits is made by shifting the first bit back one place, and then ORing (| operator) the result with the second bit. When a value is shifted, using the << operator, the space left behind is replaced with 0s. An OR says, "If either of these bits are a 1, put a 1." Therefor ORing secondBit with a 0 will always just result in the value of secondBit. Let's test it out.

Listing 1.12 CompressedGene.java continued

```java
public static void main(String[] args) {
    final String original =
    "TAGGGATTAACCGTTATATATATATAGCCATGGATCGATTATATAGGGATTAACCGTTATATATATATAGC
    CATGGATCGATTATA";
    CompressedGene compressed = new CompressedGene(original);
    final String decompressed = compressed.decompress();
    System.out.println(decompressed);
    System.out.println("original is the same as decompressed: " +
    original.equalsIgnoreCase(decompressed));
    }

}
```

The main() method does a compression and a decompression. It checks whether the final result is the same as the original String using equalsIgnoreCase().

Listing 1.13 CompressedGene.java output

```
TAGGGATTAACCGTTATATATATATAGCCATGGATCGATTATATAGGGATTAACCGTTATATATATATAGCCATGGA
    TCGATTATA
original is the same as decompressed: true
```

1.3   *Unbreakable encryption*

A one-time pad is a way of encrypting a piece of data by combining it with meaningless random dummy data in such a way that the original cannot be reconstituted without access to both the product and the dummy data. In essence, this leaves the encrypter with a key pair. One key is the product, and the other is the random dummy data. One key on its own is useless; only the combination of both keys can unlock the original data. When performed correctly, a one-time pad is a form of unbreakable encryption. Figure 1.6 shows the process.

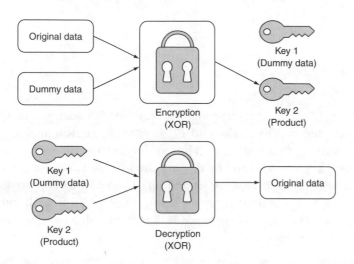

Figure 1.6   A one-time pad results in two keys that can be separated and then recombined to re-create the original data.

1.3.1   *Getting the data in order*

In this example, we will encrypt a `String` using a one-time pad. One way of thinking about a Java `String` is as a sequence of UTF-16 characters (with UTF-16 being a Unicode character encoding). Every UTF-16 character is 16 bits (hence the 16) and can be further subdivided into 2 bytes (8 bits each). A `String` can be converted into an array of bytes, represented as an array of the `byte` type, through the `getBytes()` method. Likewise, an array of bytes can be converted back into a `String` using one of the built-in constructors on the `String` type. We will need an intermediary form to store the key pair, which will consist of two arrays of `byte`. That is the purpose of the `KeyPair` class.

Listing 1.14   KeyPair.java

```java
package chapter1;

public final class KeyPair {
    public final byte[] key1;
    public final byte[] key2;
```

```
KeyPair(byte[] key1, byte[] key2) {
    this.key1 = key1;
    this.key2 = key2;
}
}
```

There are three criteria that the dummy data used in a one-time-pad encryption operation must meet for the resulting product to be unbreakable. The dummy data must be the same length as the original data, truly random, and completely secret. The first and third criteria are common sense. If the dummy data repeats because it is too short, there could be an observed pattern. If one of the keys is not truly secret (perhaps it is reused elsewhere or partially revealed), then an attacker has a clue. The second criterion poses a question all its own: can we produce truly random data? The answer for most computers is no.

In this example we will use the pseudo-random data-generating function `nextBytes()` from the standard library's `Random` class. Our data will not be truly random, in the sense that the `Random` class is using a pseudo-random number generator behind the scenes, but it will be close enough for our purposes. Let's generate a random key for use as dummy data.

Listing 1.15 UnbreakableEncryption.java

```java
package chapter1;

import java.util.Random;

public class UnbreakableEncryption {
    // Generate *length* random bytes
    private static byte[] randomKey(int length) {
        byte[] dummy = new byte[length];
        Random random = new Random();
        random.nextBytes(dummy);
        return dummy;
    }
```

This method creates a `byte` array filled with `length` random bytes. Ultimately, the bytes will serve as the "dummy" key in our key pair.

1.3.2 *Encrypting and decrypting*

How will the dummy data be combined with the original data that we want to encrypt? The *XOR* operation will serve this purpose. XOR is a logical bitwise (operates at the bit level) operation that returns `true` when one of its operands is true but returns `false` when both are true or neither is true. As you may have guessed, XOR stands for *exclusive or*.

In Java, the XOR operator is `^`. In the context of the bits of binary numbers, XOR returns 1 for 0 ^ 1 and 1 ^ 0, but 0 for 0 ^ 0 and 1 ^ 1. If the bits of two numbers are combined using XOR, a helpful property is that the product can be recombined with either of the operands to produce the other operand:

```
C = A ^ B
A = C ^ B
B = C ^ A
```

This key insight forms the basis of one-time-pad encryption. To form our product, we will simply XOR bytes from our original String with the randomly generated bytes of the same length (as produced by randomKey()). Our returned key pair will be the dummy key and the product key, as depicted in figure 1.6.

Listing 1.16   UnbreakableEncryption.java continued

```java
public static KeyPair encrypt(String original) {
    byte[] originalBytes = original.getBytes();
    byte[] dummyKey = randomKey(originalBytes.length);
    byte[] encryptedKey = new byte[originalBytes.length];
    for (int i = 0; i < originalBytes.length; i++) {
        // XOR every byte
        encryptedKey[i] = (byte) (originalBytes[i] ^ dummyKey[i]);
    }
    return new KeyPair(dummyKey, encryptedKey);
}
```

Decryption is simply a matter of recombining the key pair we generated with encrypt(). This is achieved once again by doing an XOR operation between each and every bit in the two keys. The ultimate output must be converted back to a String. This is accomplished using a constructor from the String class that takes a byte array as its lone argument.

Listing 1.17   UnbreakableEncryption.java continued

```java
public static String decrypt(KeyPair kp) {
    byte[] decrypted = new byte[kp.key1.length];
    for (int i = 0; i < kp.key1.length; i++) {
        // XOR every byte
        decrypted[i] = (byte) (kp.key1[i] ^ kp.key2[i]);
    }
    return new String(decrypted);
}
```

If our one-time-pad encryption truly works, we should be able to encrypt and decrypt the same Unicode string without issue.

Listing 1.18   UnbreakableEncryption.java continued

```java
public static void main(String[] args) {
    KeyPair kp = encrypt("One Time Pad!");
    String result = decrypt(kp);
```

```
        System.out.println(result);
    }
}
```

If your console outputs `One Time Pad!` then everything worked. Try it out with your own sentences.

1.4   Calculating pi

The mathematically significant number pi (π or 3.14159…) can be derived using many formulas. One of the simplest is the Leibniz formula. It posits that the convergence of the following infinite series is equal to pi:

```
π = 4/1 - 4/3 + 4/5 - 4/7 + 4/9 - 4/11...
```

You will notice that the infinite series' numerator remains 4 while the denominator increases by 2, and the operation on the terms alternates between addition and subtraction.

We can model the series in a straightforward way by translating pieces of the formula into variables in a function. The numerator can be a constant 4. The denominator can be a variable that begins at 1 and is incremented by 2. The operation can be represented as either –1 or 1 based on whether we are adding or subtracting. Finally, the variable `pi` is used in listing 1.19 to collect the sum of the series as the `for` loop proceeds.

Listing 1.19   PiCalculator.java

```java
package chapter1;

public class PiCalculator {

    public static double calculatePi(int nTerms) {
        final double numerator = 4.0;
        double denominator = 1.0;
        double operation = 1.0;
        double pi = 0.0;
        for (int i = 0; i < nTerms; i++) {
            pi += operation * (numerator / denominator);
            denominator += 2.0;
            operation *= -1.0;
        }
        return pi;
    }

    public static void main(String[] args) {
        System.out.println(calculatePi(1000000));
    }
}
```

TIP Java `doubles` are 64-bit floating-point numbers, and they offer more precision than the 32-bit type `float`.

This function is an example of how rote conversion between formula and programmatic code can be both simple and effective in modeling or simulating an interesting concept. Rote conversion is a useful tool, but we must keep in mind that it is not necessarily the most efficient solution. Certainly, the Leibniz formula for pi can be implemented with more efficient or compact code.

> **NOTE** The more terms in the infinite series (the higher the value of nTerms when calculatePi() is called), the more accurate the ultimate calculation of pi will be.

1.5   *The Towers of Hanoi*

Three vertical pegs (henceforth "towers") stand tall. We will label them *A, B,* and *C.* Doughnut-shaped discs are around tower A. The widest disc is at the bottom, and we will call it disc 1. The rest of the discs above disc 1 are labeled with increasing numerals and get progressively narrower. For instance, if we were to work with three discs, the widest disc, the one on the bottom, would be 1. The next widest disc, disc 2, would sit on top of disc 1. And finally, the narrowest disc, disc 3, would sit on top of disc 2. Our goal is to move all of the discs from tower A to tower C given the following constraints:

- Only one disc can be moved at a time.
- The topmost disc of any tower is the only one available for moving.
- A wider disc can never be atop a narrower disc.

Figure 1.7 summarizes the problem.

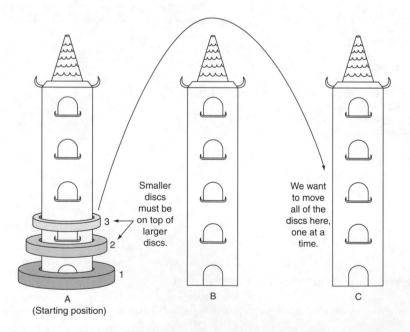

Figure 1.7   The challenge is to move the three discs, one at a time, from tower A to tower C. A larger disc may never be on top of a smaller disc.

1.5.1 *Modeling the towers*

A stack is a data structure that is modeled on the concept of Last-In-First-Out (LIFO). The last thing put into it is the first thing that comes out of it. Think of a teacher grading a stack of papers. The last paper put on top of the stack is the first paper that the teacher will remove from the stack to grade. The two most basic operations on a stack are push and pop. A *push* puts a new item into a stack, whereas a *pop* removes and returns the last item put in. The Java standard library includes a built-in class, `Stack`, that includes methods for push() and pop().

Stacks are perfect stand-ins for the towers in The Towers of Hanoi. When we want to put a disc onto a tower, we can just push it. When we want to move a disc from one tower to another, we can pop it from the first and push it onto the second.

Let's define our towers as `Stacks` and fill the first tower with discs.

Listing 1.20   Hanoi.java

```java
package chapter1;

import java.util.Stack;

public class Hanoi {
    private final int numDiscs;
    public final Stack<Integer> towerA = new Stack<>();
    public final Stack<Integer> towerB = new Stack<>();
    public final Stack<Integer> towerC = new Stack<>();

    public Hanoi(int discs) {
        numDiscs = discs;
        for (int i = 1; i <= discs; i++) {
            towerA.push(i);
        }
    }
}
```

1.5.2 *Solving The Towers of Hanoi*

How can The Towers of Hanoi be solved? Imagine we were only trying to move one disc. We would know how to do that, right? In fact, moving one disc is our base case for a recursive solution to The Towers of Hanoi. The recursive case is moving more than one disc. Therefore, the key insight is that we essentially have two scenarios we need to codify: moving one disc (the base case) and moving more than one disc (the recursive case).

Let's look at a specific example to understand the recursive case. Say we have three discs (top, middle, and bottom) on tower A that we want to move to tower C. (It may help to sketch out the problem as you follow along.) We could first move the top disc to tower C. Then we could move the middle disc to tower B. Then we could move the top disc from tower C to tower B. Now we have the bottom disc still on tower A and the upper two discs on tower B. Essentially, we have now successfully moved two discs from one tower (A) to another tower (B). Moving the bottom disc from A to C is our base case (moving a single disc). Now we can move the two upper discs from B to C with the same procedure that we did from A to B. We move the top disc to A, the middle disc to C, and finally the top disc from A to C.

> **TIP** In a computer science classroom, it is not uncommon to see a little model of the towers built using dowels and plastic doughnuts. You can build your own model using three pencils and three pieces of paper. It may help you visualize the solution.

In our three-disc example, we had a simple base case of moving a single disc and a recursive case of moving all of the other discs (two in this case), using the third tower temporarily. We could break the recursive case into three steps:

1 Move the upper *n*-1 discs from tower A to B (the temporary tower), using C as the step in between.
2 Move the single lowest disc from A to C.
3 Move the *n*-1 discs from tower B to C, using A as the step in between.

The amazing thing is that this recursive algorithm works not only for three discs, but for any number of discs. We will codify it as a method called move() that is responsible for moving discs from one tower to another, given a third temporary tower.

Listing 1.21 Hanoi.java continued

```java
private void move(Stack<Integer> begin, Stack<Integer> end, Stack<Integer>
    temp, int n) {
    if (n == 1) {
        end.push(begin.pop());
    } else {
        move(begin, temp, end, n - 1);
        move(begin, end, temp, 1);
        move(temp, end, begin, n - 1);
    }
}
```

Finally, a helper method, solve(), will call move() for all of the discs from tower A to tower C. After calling solve(), you should examine towers A, B, and C to verify that the discs were moved successfully.

Listing 1.22 Hanoi.java continued

```java
    public void solve() {
        move(towerA, towerC, towerB, numDiscs);
    }

    public static void main(String[] args) {
        Hanoi hanoi = new Hanoi(3);
        hanoi.solve();
        System.out.println(hanoi.towerA);
        System.out.println(hanoi.towerB);
```

```
        System.out.println(hanoi.towerC);
    }

}
```

You will find that they were. In codifying the solution to The Towers of Hanoi, we did not necessarily need to understand every step required to move multiple discs from tower A to tower C. But we came to understand the general recursive algorithm for moving any number of discs, and we codified it, letting the computer do the rest. This is the power of formulating recursive solutions to problems: we often can think of solutions in an abstract manner without the drudgery of negotiating every individual action in our minds.

Incidentally, the move() method will execute an exponential number of times as a function of the number of discs, which makes solving the problem for even 64 discs untenable. You can try it with various other numbers of discs by passing a different number of discs to the constructor for Hanoi. The exponentially increasing number of steps required as the number of discs increases is where the legend of The Towers of Hanoi comes from; you can read more about it in any number of sources. You may also be interested in reading more about the mathematics behind its recursive solution; see Carl Burch's explanation in "About the Towers of Hanoi," http://mng.bz/c1i2.

1.6   *Real-world applications*

The various techniques presented in this chapter (recursion, memoization, compression, and manipulation at the bit level) are so common in modern software development that it is impossible to imagine the world of computing without them. Although problems can be solved without them, it is often more logical or performant to solve problems with them.

Recursion, in particular, is at the heart of not just many algorithms, but even whole programming languages. In some functional programming languages, like Scheme and Haskell, recursion takes the place of the loops used in imperative languages. It is worth remembering, though, that anything doable with a recursive technique is also doable with an iterative technique.

Memoization has been applied successfully to speed up the work of parsers (programs that interpret languages). It is useful in all problems where the result of a recent calculation will likely be asked for again. Another application of memoization is in language runtimes. Some language runtimes (versions of Prolog, for instance) will store the results of function calls automatically (*auto-memoization*), so that the function need not execute the next time the same call is made.

Compression has made an internet-connected world constrained by bandwidth more tolerable. The bit-string technique examined in section 1.2 is usable for real-world simple data types that have a limited number of possible values, for which even a byte is overkill. The majority of compression algorithms, however, operate by finding patterns or structures within a data set that allow for repeated information to be eliminated. They are significantly more complicated than what is covered in section 1.2.

One-time pads are not practical for general encryption. They require both the encrypter and the decrypter to have possession of one of the keys (the dummy data in our example) for the original data to be reconstructed, which is cumbersome and defeats the goal of most encryption schemes (keeping keys secret). But you may be interested to know that the name "one-time pad" comes from spies using real paper pads with dummy data on them to create encrypted communications during the Cold War.

These techniques are programmatic building blocks that other algorithms are built on top of. In future chapters you will see them applied liberally.

1.7   *Exercises*

1 Write yet another function that solves for element n of the Fibonacci sequence, using a technique of your own design. Write unit tests that evaluate its correctness and performance relative to the other versions in this chapter.

2 The `BitSet` class in the Java standard library has a flaw: while it keeps track of how many total bits have been set `true`, it does not keep track of how many bits have been set in total, including bits that have been set `false` (that's why we needed the `length` instance variable). Write an ergonomic subclass of `BitSet` that keeps track of exactly how many bits have been set either `true` or `false`. Reimplement `CompressedGene` using the subclass.

3 Write a solver for The Towers of Hanoi that works for any number of towers.

4 Use a one-time pad to encrypt and decrypt images.

Search problems

"Search" is such a broad term that this entire book could be called *Classic Search Problems in Java*. This chapter is about core search algorithms that every programmer should know. It does not claim to be comprehensive, despite the declaratory title.

2.1 DNA search

Genes are commonly represented in computer software as a sequence of the characters *A*, *C*, *G*, and *T*. Each letter represents a *nucleotide*, and the combination of three nucleotides is called a *codon*. This is illustrated in figure 2.1. A codon codes for a specific amino acid that together with other amino acids can form a *protein*. A classic task in bioinformatics software is to find a particular codon within a gene.

2.1.1 Storing DNA

We can represent a nucleotide as a simple enum with four cases.

Listing 2.1 Gene.java

```java
package chapter2;

import java.util.ArrayList;
import java.util.Collections;
import java.util.Comparator;

public class Gene {

    public enum Nucleotide {
        A, C, G, T
    }
```

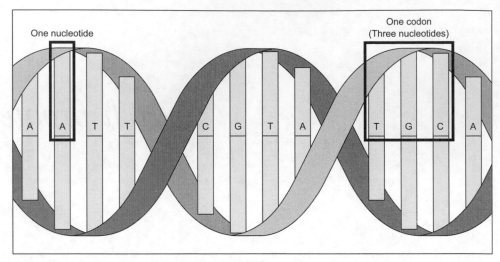

Part of a gene

Figure 2.1   A nucleotide is represented by one of the letters *A*, *C*, *G*, and *T*. A codon is composed of three nucleotides, and a gene is composed of multiple codons.

Codons can be defined as a combination of three `Nucleotides`. The constructor for the `Codon` class converts a `String` of three letters into a `Codon`. To implement search methods, we will need to be able to compare one `Codon` to another. Java has an interface for that, `Comparable`.

Implementing the `Comparable` interface requires the construction of one method, `compareTo()`. `compareTo()` should return a negative number if the item in question is smaller than the item being compared, a zero if the two items are equal, and a positive number if the item is larger than the item being compared. In practice you can often avoid having to implement this by hand and instead use the built-in Java standard library interface `Comparator`, as we do in the following example. In this example, the `Codon` will first be compared to another `Codon` by its first `Nucleotide`, then by its second if the firsts are equivalent, and finally by its third if the seconds are equivalent. They are chained using `thenComparing()`.

Listing 2.2   Gene.java continued

```
public static class Codon implements Comparable<Codon> {
    public final Nucleotide first, second, third;
    private final Comparator<Codon> comparator =
Comparator.comparing((Codon c) -> c.first)
        .thenComparing((Codon c) -> c.second)
        .thenComparing((Codon c) -> c.third);

    public Codon(String codonStr) {
        first = Nucleotide.valueOf(codonStr.substring(0, 1));
```

```
        second = Nucleotide.valueOf(codonStr.substring(1, 2));
        third = Nucleotide.valueOf(codonStr.substring(2, 3));
    }

    @Override
    public int compareTo(Codon other) {
        // first is compared first, then second, etc.
        // IOW first takes precedence over second
        // and second over third
        return comparator.compare(this, other);
    }
}
```

NOTE Codon is a static class. Nested classes that are marked static can be instantiated without regard to their enclosing class (you do not need an instance of the enclosing class to create an instance of a static nested class), but they cannot refer to any of the instance variables of their enclosing class. This makes sense for classes that are defined as nested classes primarily for organizational purposes instead of logistical purposes.

Typically, genes on the internet will be in a file format that contains a giant string representing all of the nucleotides in the gene's sequence. The next listing shows an example of what a gene string may look like.

Listing 2.3 Gene string example

```
String geneStr = "ACGTGGCTCTCTAACGTACGTACGTACGGGGTTTATATATACCCTAGGACTCCCTTT";
```

The only state in a Gene will be an ArrayList of Codons. We will also have a constructor that can take a gene string and convert it into a Gene (converting a String into an ArrayList of Codons).

Listing 2.4 Gene.java continued

```
private ArrayList<Codon> codons = new ArrayList<>();

public Gene(String geneStr) {
    for (int i = 0; i < geneStr.length() - 3; i += 3) {
        // Take every 3 characters in the String and form a Codon
        codons.add(new Codon(geneStr.substring(i, i + 3)));
    }
}
```

This constructor continually goes through the provided String and converts its next three characters into Codons that it adds to the end of a new Gene. It piggybacks on the constructor of Codon, which knows how to convert a three-letter String into a Codon.

2.1.2   *Linear search*

One basic operation we may want to perform on a gene is to search it for a particular codon. A scientist may want to do this to see if it codes for a particular amino acid. The goal is to simply find out whether the codon exists within the gene or not.

A linear search goes through every element in a search space, in the order of the original data structure, until what is sought is found or the end of the data structure is reached. In effect, a linear search is the most simple, natural, and obvious way to search for something. In the worst case, a linear search will require going through every element in a data structure, so it is of $O(n)$ complexity, where n is the number of elements in the structure. This is illustrated in figure 2.2.

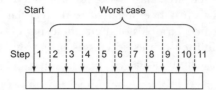

Figure 2.2   In the worst case of a linear search, you'll sequentially look through every element of the array.

It is trivial to define a function that performs a linear search. It simply must go through every element in a data structure and check for its equivalence to the item being sought. You can use the following code in `main()` to test it.

Listing 2.5   Gene.java continued

```java
public boolean linearContains(Codon key) {
    for (Codon codon : codons) {
        if (codon.compareTo(key) == 0) {
            return true; // found a match
        }
    }
    return false;
}

public static void main(String[] args) {
    String geneStr =
"ACGTGGCTCTCTAACGTACGTACGTACGGGGTTTATATATACCCTAGGACTCCCTTT";
    Gene myGene = new Gene(geneStr);
    Codon acg = new Codon("ACG");
    Codon gat = new Codon("GAT");
    System.out.println(myGene.linearContains(acg)); // true
    System.out.println(myGene.linearContains(gat)); // false
}

}
```

NOTE   This function is for illustrative purposes only. All of the classes in the Java standard library that implement the `Collection` interface (like `ArrayList` and

`LinkedList`) have a `contains()` method that will likely be better optimized than anything we write.

2.1.3 Binary search

There is a faster way to search than looking at every element, but it requires us to know something about the order of the data structure ahead of time. If we know that the structure is sorted, and we can instantly access any item within it by its index, we can perform a binary search.

A binary search works by looking at the middle element in a sorted range of elements, comparing it to the element sought, reducing the range by half based on that comparison, and starting the process over again. Let's look at a concrete example.

Suppose we have a list of alphabetically sorted words like `["cat", "dog", "kanga-roo", "llama", "rabbit", "rat", "zebra"]` and we are searching for the word "rat":

1 We could determine that the middle element in this seven-word list is "llama."
2 We could determine that "rat" comes after "llama" alphabetically, so it must be in the (approximately) half of the list that comes after "llama." (If we had found "rat" in this step, we could have returned its location; if we had found that our word came before the middle word we were checking, we could be assured that it was in the half of the list before "llama.")
3 We could rerun steps 1 and 2 for the half of the list that we know "rat" is still possibly in. In effect, this half becomes our new base list. These steps continually run until "rat" is found or the range we are looking in no longer contains any elements to search, meaning that "rat" does not exist within the word list.

Figure 2.3 illustrates a binary search. Notice that it does not involve searching every element, unlike a linear search.

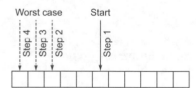

Figure 2.3   In the worst case of a binary search, you'll look through just lg(n) elements of the list.

A binary search continually reduces the search space by half, so it has a worst-case runtime of O(lg n). There is a sort-of catch, though. Unlike a linear search, a binary search requires a sorted data structure to search through, and sorting takes time. In fact, sorting takes O(n lg n) time for the best sorting algorithms. If we are only going to run our search once, and our original data structure is unsorted, it probably makes sense to just do a linear search. But if the search is going to be performed many times, the time cost of doing the sort is worth it, to reap the benefit of the greatly reduced time cost of each individual search.

Writing a binary search function for a gene and a codon is not unlike writing one for any other type of data, because the Codon type can be compared to others of its type, and the Gene type just contains an ArrayList of Codons. Note that in the following example we start by sorting the codons—this eliminates all of the advantages of doing a binary search, because doing the sort will take more time than the search, as described in the previous paragraph. However, for illustrative purposes, the sort is necessary, since we cannot know when running this example that the codons Array-List is sorted.

Listing 2.6   Gene.java continued

```java
public boolean binaryContains(Codon key) {
    // binary search only works on sorted collections
    ArrayList<Codon> sortedCodons = new ArrayList<>(codons);
    Collections.sort(sortedCodons);
    int low = 0;
    int high = sortedCodons.size() - 1;
    while (low <= high) { // while there is still a search space
        int middle = (low + high) / 2;
        int comparison = codons.get(middle).compareTo(key);
        if (comparison < 0) { // middle codon is less than key
            low = middle + 1;
        } else if (comparison > 0) { // middle codon is > key
            high = middle - 1;
        } else { // middle codon is equal to key
            return true;
        }
    }
    return false;
}
```

Let's walk through this function line by line.

```java
int low = 0;
int high = sortedCodons.size() - 1;
```

We start by looking at a range that encompasses the entire list (gene).

```java
while (low <= high) {
```

We keep searching as long as there is still a range to search within. When low is greater than high, it means that there are no longer any slots to look at within the list.

```java
int middle = (low + high) / 2;
```

We calculate the middle by using integer division and the simple mean formula you learned in grade school.

```java
int comparison = codons.get(middle).compareTo(key);
if (comparison < 0) { // middle codon is less than key
    low = middle + 1;
```

If the element we are looking for is after the middle element of the range we are looking at, we modify the range that we will look at during the next iteration of the loop by moving `low` to be one past the current middle element. This is where we halve the range for the next iteration.

```
} else if (comparison > 0) { // middle codon is greater than key
    high = middle - 1;
```

Similarly, we halve in the other direction when the element we are looking for is less than the middle element.

```
} else { // middle codon is equal to key
    return true;
}
```

If the element in question is not less than or greater than the middle element, that means we found it! And, of course, if the loop ran out of iterations, we return `false` (not reproduced here), indicating that it was never found.

We can now try running our binary search method with the same gene and codon. We can modify `main()` to test it.

Listing 2.7   Gene.java continued

```
public static void main(String[] args) {
    String geneStr = "ACGTGGCTCTCTAACGTACGTACGTACGGGGTTTATATATACCCTAGGACTCCCTTT";
    Gene myGene = new Gene(geneStr);
    Codon acg = new Codon("ACG");
    Codon gat = new Codon("GAT");
    System.out.println(myGene.linearContains(acg)); // true
    System.out.println(myGene.linearContains(gat)); // false
    System.out.println(myGene.binaryContains(acg)); // true
    System.out.println(myGene.binaryContains(gat)); // false
}
```

> **TIP**   Once again, like with linear search, you would never need to implement binary search yourself because there's an implementation in the Java standard library. `Collections.binarySearch()` can search any sorted `Collection` (like a sorted `ArrayList`).

2.1.4   A generic example

The methods `linearContains()` and `binaryContains()` can be generalized to work with almost any Java `List`. The following generalized versions are nearly identical to the versions you saw before, with only some names and types changed.

> **NOTE**   There are many imported types in the following code listing. We will be reusing the file GenericSearch.java for many further generic search algorithms in this chapter, and this gets the imports out of the way.

NOTE The extends keyword in T extends Comparable<T> means that T must be a type that implements the Comparable interface.

Listing 2.8   GenericSearch.java

```java
package chapter2;

import java.util.ArrayList;
import java.util.HashMap;
import java.util.HashSet;
import java.util.LinkedList;
import java.util.List;
import java.util.Map;
import java.util.PriorityQueue;
import java.util.Queue;
import java.util.Set;
import java.util.Stack;
import java.util.function.Function;
import java.util.function.Predicate;
import java.util.function.ToDoubleFunction;

public class GenericSearch {

    public static <T extends Comparable<T>> boolean linearContains(List<T>
      list, T key) {
        for (T item : list) {
            if (item.compareTo(key) == 0) {
                return true; // found a match
            }
        }
        return false;
    }

    // assumes *list* is already sorted
    public static <T extends Comparable<T>> boolean binaryContains(List<T>
      list, T key) {
        int low = 0;
        int high = list.size() - 1;
        while (low <= high) { // while there is still a search space
            int middle = (low + high) / 2;
            int comparison = list.get(middle).compareTo(key);
            if (comparison < 0) { // middle codon is < key
                low = middle + 1;
            } else if (comparison > 0) { // middle codon is > key
                high = middle - 1;
            } else { // middle codon is equal to key
                return true;
            }
        }
        return false;
    }

    public static void main(String[] args) {
        System.out.println(linearContains(List.of(1, 5, 15, 15, 15, 15, 20),
      5)); // true
```

```
        System.out.println(binaryContains(List.of("a", "d", "e", "f", "z"),
    "f")); // true
        System.out.println(binaryContains(List.of("john", "mark", "ronald",
    "sarah"), "sheila")); // false
    }

}
```

Now you can try doing searches on other types of data. These methods will work on any List of Comparables. That is the power of writing code generically.

2.2 *Maze solving*

Finding a path through a maze is analogous to many common search problems in computer science. Why not literally find a path through a maze, then, to illustrate the breadth-first search, depth-first search, and A* algorithms?

Our maze will be a two-dimensional grid of Cells. A Cell is an enum that knows how to turn itself into a String. For example, " " will represent an empty space, and "X" will represent a blocked space. There are also other cases for illustrative purposes when printing a maze.

Listing 2.9 Maze.java

```java
package chapter2;

import java.util.ArrayList;
import java.util.Arrays;
import java.util.List;

import chapter2.GenericSearch.Node;

public class Maze {

    public enum Cell {
        EMPTY(" "),
        BLOCKED("X"),
        START("S"),
        GOAL("G"),
        PATH("*");

        private final String code;

        private Cell(String c) {
            code = c;
        }

        @Override
        public String toString() {
            return code;
        }
    }
```

Once again, we are getting a few imports out of the way. Note that the last import (from `GenericSearch`) is of a class we have not yet defined. It is included here for convenience, but you may want to comment it out until you need it.

We will need a way to refer to an individual location in the maze. This will be a simple class, `MazeLocation`, with properties representing the row and column of the location in question. However, the class will also need a way for instances of it to compare themselves for equality to other instances of the same type. In Java, this is necessary to properly use several classes in the collections framework, like `HashSet` and `HashMap`. They use the methods `equals()` and `hashCode()` to avoid inserting duplicates, since they only allow unique instances.

Luckily, IDEs can do the hard work for us. The two methods following the constructor in the next listing were autogenerated by Eclipse. They will ensure two instances of `MazeLocation` with the same row and column are seen as equivalent to one another. In Eclipse, you can right-click and select Source > Generate hashCode() and equals() to have these methods created for you. You need to specify in a dialog which instance variables go into evaluating equality.

Listing 2.10   Maze.java continued

```java
public static class MazeLocation {
    public final int row;
    public final int column;

    public MazeLocation(int row, int column) {
        this.row = row;
        this.column = column;
    }

    // auto-generated by Eclipse
    @Override
    public int hashCode() {
        final int prime = 31;
        int result = 1;
        result = prime * result + column;
        result = prime * result + row;
        return result;
    }

    // auto-generated by Eclipse
    @Override
    public boolean equals(Object obj) {
        if (this == obj) {
            return true;
        }
        if (obj == null) {
            return false;
        }
        if (getClass() != obj.getClass()) {
            return false;
        }
```

```
        MazeLocation other = (MazeLocation) obj;
        if (column != other.column) {
            return false;
        }
        if (row != other.row) {
            return false;
        }
        return true;
    }
}
```

2.2.1 *Generating a random maze*

Our Maze class will internally keep track of a grid (a two-dimensional array) representing its state. It will also have instance variables for the number of rows, number of columns, start location, and goal location. Its grid will be randomly filled with blocked cells.

The maze that is generated should be fairly sparse so that there is almost always a path from a given starting location to a given goal location. (This is for testing our algorithms, after all.) We'll let the caller of a new maze decide on the exact sparseness, but we will provide a default value of 20% blocked. When a random number beats the threshold of the sparseness parameter in question, we will simply replace an empty space with a wall. If we do this for every possible place in the maze, statistically, the sparseness of the maze as a whole will approximate the sparseness parameter supplied.

Listing 2.11 Maze.java continued

```
private final int rows, columns;
private final MazeLocation start, goal;
private Cell[][] grid;

public Maze(int rows, int columns, MazeLocation start, MazeLocation goal,
        double sparseness) {
    // initialize basic instance variables
    this.rows = rows;
    this.columns = columns;
    this.start = start;
    this.goal = goal;
    // fill the grid with empty cells
    grid = new Cell[rows][columns];
    for (Cell[] row : grid) {
        Arrays.fill(row, Cell.EMPTY);
    }
    // populate the grid with blocked cells
    randomlyFill(sparseness);
    // fill the start and goal locations
    grid[start.row][start.column] = Cell.START;
    grid[goal.row][goal.column] = Cell.GOAL;
}

public Maze() {
    this(10, 10, new MazeLocation(0, 0), new MazeLocation(9, 9), 0.2);
}
```

```
private void randomlyFill(double sparseness) {
    for (int row = 0; row < rows; row++) {
        for (int column = 0; column < columns; column++) {
            if (Math.random() < sparseness) {
                grid[row][column] = Cell.BLOCKED;
            }
        }
    }
}
```

Now that we have a maze, we also want a way to print it succinctly to the console. We want its characters to be close together so it looks like a real maze.

Listing 2.12   Maze.java continued

```
// return a nicely formatted version of the maze for printing
@Override
public String toString() {
    StringBuilder sb = new StringBuilder();
    for (Cell[] row : grid) {
        for (Cell cell : row) {
            sb.append(cell.toString());
        }
        sb.append(System.lineSeparator());
    }
    return sb.toString();
}
```

Go ahead and test these maze functions in main() if you like.

Listing 2.13   Maze.java continued

```
    public static void main(String[] args) {
        Maze m = new Maze();
        System.out.println(m);
    }

}
```

2.2.2   *Miscellaneous maze minutiae*

It will be handy later to have a function that checks whether we have reached our goal during the search. In other words, we want to check whether a particular MazeLocation that the search has reached is the goal. We can add a method to Maze.

Listing 2.14   Maze.java continued

```
public boolean goalTest(MazeLocation ml) {
    return goal.equals(ml);
}
```

How can we move within our mazes? Let's say that we can move horizontally and vertically one space at a time from a given space in the maze. Using these criteria, a successors() function can find the possible next locations from a given MazeLocation. However, the successors() function will differ for every Maze because every Maze has a different size and set of walls. Therefore, we will define it as a method on Maze.

Listing 2.15   Maze.java continued

```java
public List<MazeLocation> successors(MazeLocation ml) {
    List<MazeLocation> locations = new ArrayList<>();
    if (ml.row + 1 < rows && grid[ml.row + 1][ml.column] != Cell.BLOCKED) {
        locations.add(new MazeLocation(ml.row + 1, ml.column));
    }
    if (ml.row - 1 >= 0 && grid[ml.row - 1][ml.column] != Cell.BLOCKED) {
        locations.add(new MazeLocation(ml.row - 1, ml.column));
    }
    if (ml.column + 1 < columns && grid[ml.row][ml.column + 1] != Cell.BLOCKED) {
        locations.add(new MazeLocation(ml.row, ml.column + 1));
    }
    if (ml.column - 1 >= 0 && grid[ml.row][ml.column - 1] != Cell.BLOCKED) {
        locations.add(new MazeLocation(ml.row, ml.column - 1));
    }
    return locations;
}
```

successors() simply checks above, below, to the right, and to the left of a MazeLocation in a Maze to see if it can find empty spaces that can be gone to from that location. It also avoids checking locations beyond the edges of the Maze. It puts every possible MazeLocation that it finds into a list that it ultimately returns to the caller. We will use the prior two methods in our search algorithms.

2.2.3   *Depth-first search*

A *depth-first search* (DFS) is what its name suggests: a search that goes as deeply as it can before backtracking to its last decision point if it reaches a dead end. We'll implement a generic depth-first search that can solve our maze problem. It will also be reusable for other problems. Figure 2.4 illustrates an in-progress depth-first search of a maze.

STACKS

The depth-first search algorithm relies on a data structure known as a *stack*. (We first saw stacks in chapter 1.) A stack is a data structure that operates under the Last-In-First-Out (LIFO) principle. Imagine a stack of papers. The last paper placed on top of the stack is the first paper pulled off the stack. It is common for a stack to be implemented on top of a more primitive data structure like a linked list by adding items on one end and removing them from the same end. We could easily implement a stack ourselves, but the Java standard library includes the convenient Stack class.

Stacks generally have at least two operations:

- push()—Places an item on top of the stack
- pop()—Removes the item from the top of the stack and returns it

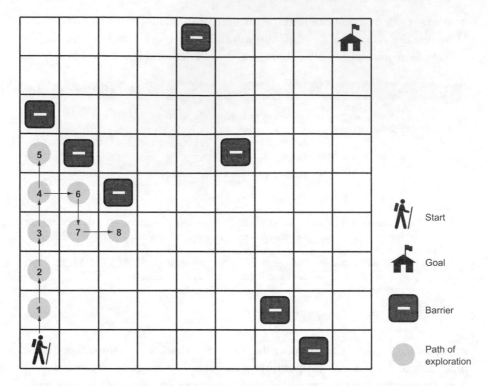

Figure 2.4   **In depth-first search, the search proceeds along a continuously deeper path until it hits a barrier and must backtrack to the last decision point.**

In other words, a stack is a meta-structure that enforces an ordering of removal on a list. The last item put into a stack must be the next item removed from a stack.

THE DFS ALGORITHM

We will need one more little tidbit before we can get to implementing DFS. We need a `Node` class that we will use to keep track of how we got from one state to another state (or from one place to another place) as we search. You can think of a `Node` as a wrapper around a state. In the case of our maze-solving problem, those states are of type `MazeLocation`. We'll call the `Node` that a state came from its `parent`. We will also define our `Node` class as having `cost` and `heuristic` properties, so we can reuse it later in the A* algorithm. Don't worry about them for now. A `Node` is `Comparable` by comparing the combination of its `cost` and `heuristic`.

Listing 2.16   GenericSearch.java continued

```java
public static class Node<T> implements Comparable<Node<T>> {
    final T state;
    Node<T> parent;
    double cost;
    double heuristic;
```

```
    // for dfs and bfs we won't use cost and heuristic
    Node(T state, Node<T> parent) {
        this.state = state;
        this.parent = parent;
    }

    // for astar we will use cost and heuristic
    Node(T state, Node<T> parent, double cost, double heuristic) {
        this.state = state;
        this.parent = parent;
        this.cost = cost;
        this.heuristic = heuristic;
    }

    @Override
    public int compareTo(Node<T> other) {
        Double mine = cost + heuristic;
        Double theirs = other.cost + other.heuristic;
        return mine.compareTo(theirs);
    }
}
```

TIP compareTo() here works by calling compareTo() on another type. This is a common pattern.

NOTE If a Node does not have a parent, we will use null as a sentinel to indicate such.

An in-progress depth-first search needs to keep track of two data structures: the stack of states (or "places") that we are considering searching, which we will call the frontier, and the set of states that we have already searched, which we will call explored. As long as there are more states to visit in the frontier, DFS will keep checking whether they are the goal (if a state is the goal, DFS will stop and return it) and adding their successors to the frontier. It will also mark each state that has already been searched as explored, so that the search does not get caught in a circle, reaching states that have prior visited states as successors. If the frontier is empty, it means there is nowhere left to search.

Listing 2.17 GenericSearch.java continued

```
public static <T> Node<T> dfs(T initial, Predicate<T> goalTest,
        Function<T, List<T>> successors) {
    // frontier is where we've yet to go
    Stack<Node<T>> frontier = new Stack<>();
    frontier.push(new Node<>(initial, null));
    // explored is where we've been
    Set<T> explored = new HashSet<>();
    explored.add(initial);

    // keep going while there is more to explore
    while (!frontier.isEmpty()) {
        Node<T> currentNode = frontier.pop();
```

```
        T currentState = currentNode.state;
        // if we found the goal, we're done
        if (goalTest.test(currentState)) {
            return currentNode;
        }
        // check where we can go next and haven't explored
        for (T child : successors.apply(currentState)) {
            if (explored.contains(child)) {
                continue; // skip children we already explored
            }
            explored.add(child);
            frontier.push(new Node<>(child, currentNode));
        }
    }
    return null; // went through everything and never found goal
}
```

Note the goalTest and successors function references. These allow different functions to be plugged into dfs() for different applications. This makes dfs() usable by more scenarios than just mazes. This is another example of solving a problem generically. A goalTest, being a Predicate<T>, is any function that takes a T (in our case, a MazeLocation) and returns a boolean. successors is any function that takes a T and returns a List of T.

If dfs() is successful, it returns the Node encapsulating the goal state. The path from the start to the goal can be reconstructed by working backward from this Node and its priors using the parent property.

Listing 2.18   GenericSearch.java continued

```
public static <T> List<T> nodeToPath(Node<T> node) {
    List<T> path = new ArrayList<>();
    path.add(node.state);
    // work backwards from end to front
    while (node.parent != null) {
        node = node.parent;
        path.add(0, node.state); // add to front
    }
    return path;
}
```

For display purposes, it will be useful to mark up the maze with the successful path, the start state, and the goal state. It will also be useful to be able to remove a path so that we can try different search algorithms on the same maze. The following two methods should be added to the Maze class in Maze.java.

Listing 2.19   Maze.java continued

```
public void mark(List<MazeLocation> path) {
    for (MazeLocation ml : path) {
        grid[ml.row][ml.column] = Cell.PATH;
    }
```

```
        grid[start.row][start.column] = Cell.START;
        grid[goal.row][goal.column] = Cell.GOAL;
}

public void clear(List<MazeLocation> path) {
    for (MazeLocation ml : path) {
        grid[ml.row][ml.column] = Cell.EMPTY;
    }
    grid[start.row][start.column] = Cell.START;
    grid[goal.row][goal.column] = Cell.GOAL;
}
```

It has been a long journey, but we are finally ready to solve the maze.

Listing 2.20   Maze.java continued

```
public static void main(String[] args) {
    Maze m = new Maze();
    System.out.println(m);

    Node<MazeLocation> solution1 = GenericSearch.dfs(m.start, m::goalTest,
     m::successors);
    if (solution1 == null) {
        System.out.println("No solution found using depth-first search!");
    } else {
        List<MazeLocation> path1 = GenericSearch.nodeToPath(solution1);
        m.mark(path1);
        System.out.println(m);
        m.clear(path1);
    }
}
}
```

A successful solution will look something like this:

```
S****X X
 X   *****
       X*
XX*******X
  X*
  X**X
 X   *****
        *
     X  *X
        *G
```

The asterisks represent the path that our depth-first search function found from the start to the goal. S is the start location and G is the goal location. Remember, because each maze is randomly generated, not every maze has a solution.

2.2.4   *Breadth-first search*

You may notice that the solution paths to the mazes found by depth-first traversal seem unnatural. They are usually not the shortest paths. *Breadth-first search* (BFS) always finds the shortest path by systematically looking one layer of nodes farther away from the start state in each iteration of the search. There are particular problems in which a depth-first search is likely to find a solution more quickly than a breadth-first search, and vice versa. Therefore, choosing between the two is sometimes a trade-off between the possibility of finding a solution quickly and the certainty of finding the shortest path to the goal (if one exists). Figure 2.5 illustrates an in-progress breadth-first search of a maze.

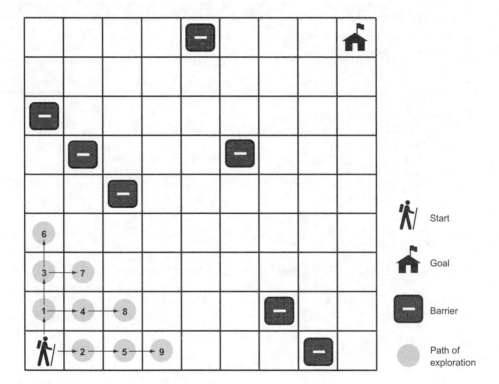

Figure 2.5   In a breadth-first search, the closest elements to the starting location are searched first.

To understand why a depth-first search sometimes returns a result faster than a breadth-first search, imagine looking for a marking on a particular layer of an onion. A searcher using a depth-first strategy may plunge a knife into the center of the onion and haphazardly examine the chunks cut out. If the marked layer happens to be near the chunk cut out, there is a chance that the searcher will find it more quickly than another searcher using a breadth-first strategy, who painstakingly peels the onion one layer at a time.

To get a better picture of why breadth-first search always finds the shortest solution path where one exists, consider trying to find the path with the fewest number of stops between Boston and New York by train. If you keep going in the same direction and backtracking when you hit a dead end (as in depth-first search), you may first find a route all the way to Seattle before it connects back to New York. However, in a breadth-first search, you will first check all of the stations one stop away from Boston. Then you will check all of the stations two stops away from Boston. Then you will check all of the stations three stops away from Boston. This will keep going until you find New York. Therefore, when you do find New York, you will know you have found the route with the fewest stops, because you already checked all of the stations that are fewer stops away from Boston, and none of them was New York.

QUEUES

To implement BFS, a data structure known as a *queue* is required. Whereas a stack is LIFO, a queue is FIFO (First-In-First-Out). A queue is like a line to use a restroom. The first person who got in line goes to the restroom first. At a minimum, a queue has the same push() and pop() methods as a stack. At an implementation level, the only thing that changes between a stack and a queue is that the queue removes items from the list at the opposite end from where it inserts them. This ensures that the oldest elements (the elements "waiting" the longest) are always removed first.

> **NOTE** Confusingly, the Java standard library does not have a Queue class, although it does have a Stack class. Instead it has a Queue interface that several Java standard library classes implement (including LinkedList). Even more confusingly, in the Java standard library's Queue interface, push() is called offer() and pop() is called poll().

THE BFS ALGORITHM

Amazingly, the algorithm for a breadth-first search is identical to the algorithm for a depth-first search, with the frontier changed from a stack to a queue. Changing the frontier from a stack to a queue changes the order in which states are searched and ensures that the states closest to the start state are searched first.

In the following implementation, we also have to change some calls from push() and pop() to offer() and poll(), respectively, because of the different naming schemes between the Java standard library's Stack class and Queue interface (see the previous note). But do take a moment to look back at dfs() (in listing 2.17) and admire how similar dfs() and bfs() are to one another, with just the frontier data structure changing.

Listing 2.21 GenericSearch.java continued

```java
public static <T> Node<T> bfs(T initial, Predicate<T> goalTest,
        Function<T, List<T>> successors) {
    // frontier is where we've yet to go
    Queue<Node<T>> frontier = new LinkedList<>();
```

```
    frontier.offer(new Node<>(initial, null));
    // explored is where we've been
    Set<T> explored = new HashSet<>();
    explored.add(initial);

    // keep going while there is more to explore
    while (!frontier.isEmpty()) {
        Node<T> currentNode = frontier.poll();
        T currentState = currentNode.state;
        // if we found the goal, we're done
        if (goalTest.test(currentState)) {
            return currentNode;
        }
        // check where we can go next and haven't explored
        for (T child : successors.apply(currentState)) {
            if (explored.contains(child)) {
                continue; // skip children we already explored
            }
            explored.add(child);
            frontier.offer(new Node<>(child, currentNode));
        }
    }
    return null; // went through everything and never found goal
}
```

If you try running bfs(), you will see that it always finds the shortest solution to the maze in question. The main() method in Maze.java can now be modified to try two different ways of solving the same maze, so results can be compared.

Listing 2.22   Maze.java continued

```
public static void main(String[] args) {
    Maze m = new Maze();
    System.out.println(m);

    Node<MazeLocation> solution1 = GenericSearch.dfs(m.start, m::goalTest,
     m::successors);
    if (solution1 == null) {
        System.out.println("No solution found using depth-first search!");
    } else {
        List<MazeLocation> path1 = GenericSearch.nodeToPath(solution1);
        m.mark(path1);
        System.out.println(m);
        m.clear(path1);
    }

    Node<MazeLocation> solution2 = GenericSearch.bfs(m.start, m::goalTest,
     m::successors);
    if (solution2 == null) {
        System.out.println("No solution found using breadth-first search!");
    } else {
        List<MazeLocation> path2 = GenericSearch.nodeToPath(solution2);
        m.mark(path2);
```

```
        System.out.println(m);
        m.clear(path2);
    }
}
```

It is amazing that you can keep an algorithm the same and just change the data structure that it accesses and get radically different results. The following is the result of calling `bfs()` on the same maze that we earlier called `dfs()` on. Notice how the path marked by the asterisks is more direct from start to goal than in the prior example.

```
S    X X
*X
*       X
*XX      X
* X
* X  X
*X
*
*    X  X
********G
```

2.2.5 A* search

It can be very time-consuming to peel back an onion, layer by layer, as a breadth-first search does. Like a BFS, an A* search aims to find the shortest path from start state to goal state. But unlike the preceding BFS implementation, an A* search uses a combination of a cost function and a heuristic function to focus its search on pathways most likely to get to the goal quickly.

The cost function, $g(n)$, examines the cost to get to a particular state. In the case of our maze, this would be how many previous cells we had to go through to get to the cell in question. The heuristic function, $h(n)$, gives an estimate of the cost to get from the state in question to the goal state. It can be proved that if $h(n)$ is an *admissible heuristic*, the final path found will be optimal. An admissible heuristic is one that never overestimates the cost to reach the goal. On a two-dimensional plane, one example is a straight-line distance heuristic, because a straight line is always the shortest path.[1]

The total cost for any state being considered is $f(n)$, which is simply the combination of $g(n)$ and $h(n)$. In fact, $f(n) = g(n) + h(n)$. When choosing the next state to explore from the frontier, an A* search picks the one with the lowest $f(n)$. This is how it distinguishes itself from BFS and DFS.

PRIORITY QUEUES

To pick the state on the frontier with the lowest $f(n)$, an A* search uses a *priority queue* as the data structure for its frontier. A priority queue keeps its elements in an internal order, such that the first element popped out is always the highest-priority

---

[1] For more information on heuristics, see Stuart Russell and Peter Norvig, *Artificial Intelligence: A Modern Approach*, 3rd edition (Pearson, 2010), p. 94.

element. (In our case, the highest-priority item is the one with the lowest f(n).) Usually this means the internal use of a binary heap, which results in O(lg n) pushes and O(lg n) pops.

Java's standard library contains the `PriorityQueue` class, which has the same `offer()` and `poll()` methods as the `Queue` interface. Anything put into a `PriorityQueue` must be `Comparable`. To determine the priority of a particular element versus another of its kind, `PriorityQueue` compares them by using the `compareTo()` method. This is why we needed to implement it earlier. One `Node` is compared to another by looking at its respective f(n), which is simply the sum of the properties `cost` and `heuristic`.

HEURISTICS

A *heuristic* is an intuition about the way to solve a problem.[2] In the case of maze solving, a heuristic aims to choose the best maze location to search next in the quest to get to the goal. In other words, it is an educated guess about which nodes on the frontier are closest to the goal. As was mentioned previously, if a heuristic used with an A* search produces an accurate relative result and is admissible (never overestimates the distance), then A* will deliver the shortest path. Heuristics that calculate smaller values end up leading to a search through more states, whereas heuristics closer to the exact real distance (but not over it, which would make them inadmissible) lead to a search through fewer states. Therefore, ideal heuristics come as close to the real distance as possible without ever going over it.

EUCLIDEAN DISTANCE

As we learn in geometry, the shortest path between two points is a straight line. It makes sense, then, that a straight-line heuristic will always be admissible for the maze-solving problem. The Euclidean distance, derived from the Pythagorean theorem, states that `distance` = $\sqrt{((\text{difference in x})^2 + (\text{difference in y})^2)}$. For our mazes, the difference in *x* is equivalent to the difference in columns between two maze locations, and the difference in *y* is equivalent to the difference in rows. Note that we are implementing this back in Maze.java.

Listing 2.23   Maze.java continued

```java
public double euclideanDistance(MazeLocation ml) {
    int xdist = ml.column - goal.column;
    int ydist = ml.row - goal.row;
    return Math.sqrt((xdist * xdist) + (ydist * ydist));
}
```

`euclideanDistance()` is a function that takes a maze location and returns its straight-line distance to the goal. This function "knows" the goal, because it is actually a method on `Maze`, and `Maze` has `goal` as an instance variable.

---

[2] For more about heuristics for A* pathfinding, check out the "Heuristics" chapter in Amit Patel's *Amit's Thoughts on Pathfinding*, http://mng.bz/z7O4.

Figure 2.6 illustrates Euclidean distance within the context of a grid, like the streets of Manhattan.

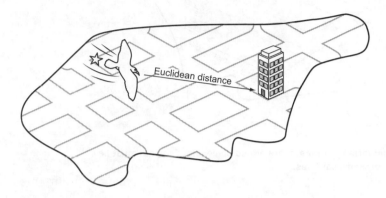

Figure 2.6   Euclidean distance is the length of a straight line from the starting point to the goal.

MANHATTAN DISTANCE

Euclidean distance is great, but for our particular problem (a maze in which you can move only in one of four directions) we can do even better. The *Manhattan distance* is derived from navigating the streets of Manhattan, the most famous of New York City's boroughs, which is laid out in a grid pattern. To get from anywhere to anywhere in Manhattan, one needs to walk a certain number of horizontal blocks and a certain number of vertical blocks. (There are almost no diagonal streets in Manhattan.) The Manhattan distance is derived by simply finding the difference in rows between two maze locations and summing it with the difference in columns. Figure 2.7 illustrates Manhattan distance.

Listing 2.24   Maze.java continued

```java
public double manhattanDistance(MazeLocation ml) {
    int xdist = Math.abs(ml.column - goal.column);
    int ydist = Math.abs(ml.row - goal.row);
    return (xdist + ydist);
}
```

Because this heuristic more accurately follows the actuality of navigating our mazes (moving vertically and horizontally instead of in diagonal straight lines), it comes closer to the actual distance between any maze location and the goal than Euclidean distance does. Therefore, when an A* search is coupled with Manhattan distance, it will result in searching through fewer states than when an A* search is coupled with Euclidean distance for our mazes. Solution paths will still be optimal, because Manhattan

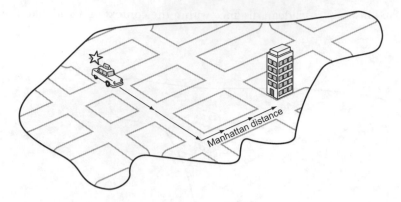

Figure 2.7   In Manhattan distance, there are no diagonals. The path must be along parallel or perpendicular lines.

distance is admissible (never overestimates distance) for mazes in which only four directions of movement are allowed.

THE A* ALGORITHM

To go from BFS to A* search, we need to make several small modifications. The first is changing the frontier from a queue to a priority queue. This way, the frontier will pop nodes with the lowest f(n). The second is changing the explored set to a `HashMap`. A `HashMap` will allow us to keep track of the lowest cost (g(n)) of each node we may visit. With the heuristic function now in play, it is possible some nodes may be visited twice if the heuristic is inconsistent. If the node found through the new direction has a lower cost to get to than the prior time we visited it, we will prefer the new route.

For the sake of simplicity, the method `astar()` does not take a cost-calculation function as a parameter. Instead, we just consider every hop in our maze to be a cost of 1. Each new `Node` gets assigned a cost based on this simple formula, as well as a heuristic score using a new function passed as a parameter to the search function, called `heuristic`. Other than these changes, `astar()` is remarkably similar to `bfs()`. Examine them side by side for comparison.

Listing 2.25   GenericSearch.java continued

```java
public static <T> Node<T> astar(T initial, Predicate<T> goalTest,
        Function<T, List<T>> successors, ToDoubleFunction<T> heuristic) {
    // frontier is where we've yet to go
    PriorityQueue<Node<T>> frontier = new PriorityQueue<>();
    frontier.offer(new Node<>(initial, null, 0.0,
     heuristic.applyAsDouble(initial)));
    // explored is where we've been
    Map<T, Double> explored = new HashMap<>();
    explored.put(initial, 0.0);
    // keep going while there is more to explore
```

```
    while (!frontier.isEmpty()) {
        Node<T> currentNode = frontier.poll();
        T currentState = currentNode.state;
        // if we found the goal, we're done
        if (goalTest.test(currentState)) {
            return currentNode;
        }
        // check where we can go next and haven't explored
        for (T child : successors.apply(currentState)) {
            // 1 here assumes a grid, need a cost function for more
sophisticated apps
            double newCost = currentNode.cost + 1;
            if (!explored.containsKey(child) || explored.get(child) > newCost) {
                explored.put(child, newCost);
                frontier.offer(new Node<>(child, currentNode, newCost,
heuristic.applyAsDouble(child)));
            }
        }
    }

    return null; // went through everything and never found goal
}
```

Congratulations. If you have followed along this far, you have learned not only how to solve a maze, but also some generic search functions that you can use in many different search applications. DFS and BFS are suitable for many smaller data sets and state spaces where performance is not critical. In some situations, DFS will outperform BFS, but BFS has the advantage of always delivering an optimal path. Interestingly, BFS and DFS have identical implementations, only differentiated by the use of a queue instead of a stack for the frontier. The slightly more complicated A* search, coupled with a good, consistent, admissible heuristic, not only delivers optimal paths, but also far outperforms BFS. And because all three of these functions were implemented generically, using them on nearly any search space is just an import away.

Go ahead and try out `astar()` with the same maze in Maze.java's testing section.

Listing 2.26 Maze.java continued

```
public static void main(String[] args) {
    Maze m = new Maze();
    System.out.println(m);

    Node<MazeLocation> solution1 = GenericSearch.dfs(m.start, m::goalTest,
     m::successors);
    if (solution1 == null) {
        System.out.println("No solution found using depth-first search!");
    } else {
        List<MazeLocation> path1 = GenericSearch.nodeToPath(solution1);
        m.mark(path1);
        System.out.println(m);
        m.clear(path1);
    }
```

```
    Node<MazeLocation> solution2 = GenericSearch.bfs(m.start, m::goalTest,
     m::successors);
    if (solution2 == null) {
        System.out.println("No solution found using breadth-first search!");
    } else {
        List<MazeLocation> path2 = GenericSearch.nodeToPath(solution2);
        m.mark(path2);
        System.out.println(m);
        m.clear(path2);
    }


    Node<MazeLocation> solution3 = GenericSearch.astar(m.start, m::goalTest,
     m::successors, m::manhattanDistance);
    if (solution3 == null) {
        System.out.println("No solution found using A*!");
    } else {
        List<MazeLocation> path3 = GenericSearch.nodeToPath(solution3);
        m.mark(path3);
        System.out.println(m);
        m.clear(path3);
    }
}
```

The output will interestingly be a little different from bfs(), even though both bfs()
and astar() are finding optimal paths (equivalent in length). If it uses a Manhattan
distance heuristic, astar() immediately drives through a diagonal toward the goal. It
will ultimately search fewer states than bfs(), resulting in better performance. Add a
state count to each if you want to prove this to yourself.

```
S**  X X
 X**
   *   X
 XX*    X
 X*
 X**X
X  ****
     *
   X * X
    **G
```

2.3   *Missionaries and cannibals*

Three missionaries and three cannibals are on the west bank of a river. They have a
canoe that can hold two people, and they all must cross to the east bank of the river.
There may never be more cannibals than missionaries on either side of the river, or
the cannibals will eat the missionaries. Further, the canoe must have at least one person on board to cross the river. What sequence of crossings will successfully take the
entire party across the river? Figure 2.8 illustrates the problem.

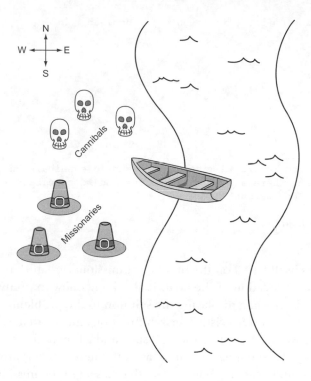

Figure 2.8 The missionaries and cannibals must use their single canoe to take everyone across the river from west to east. If the cannibals ever outnumber the missionaries, they will eat them.

2.3.1 Representing the problem

We will represent the problem by having a structure that keeps track of the west bank. How many missionaries and cannibals are on the west bank? Is the boat on the west bank? Once we have this knowledge, we can figure out what is on the east bank, because anything not on the west bank is on the east bank.

First, we will create a little convenience variable for keeping track of the maximum number of missionaries or cannibals. Then we will define the main class.

```
Listing 2.27   Missionaries.java
```

```java
package chapter2;

import java.util.ArrayList;
import java.util.List;
import java.util.function.Predicate;

import chapter2.GenericSearch.Node;

public class MCState {
    private static final int MAX_NUM = 3;
    private final int wm; // west bank missionaries
    private final int wc; // west bank cannibals
    private final int em; // east bank missionaries
    private final int ec; // east bank cannibals
    private final boolean boat; // is boat on west bank?
```

```java
public MCState(int missionaries, int cannibals, boolean boat) {
    wm = missionaries;
    wc = cannibals;
    em = MAX_NUM - wm;
    ec = MAX_NUM - wc;
    this.boat = boat;
}

@Override
public String toString() {
    return String.format(
    "On the west bank there are %d missionaries and %d cannibals.%n"
    + "On the east bank there are %d missionaries and %d cannibals.%n"
    + "The boat is on the %s bank.","
    wm, wc, em, ec,
    boat ? "west" : "east");
}
```

The class MCState initializes itself based on the number of missionaries and cannibals on the west bank as well as the location of the boat. It also knows how to pretty-print itself, which will be valuable later when displaying the solution to the problem.

Working within the confines of our existing search functions means that we must define a function for testing whether a state is the goal state and a function for finding the successors from any state. The goal test function, as in the maze-solving problem, is quite simple. The goal is simply reaching a legal state that has all of the missionaries and cannibals on the east bank. We add it as a method to MCState.

Listing 2.28   Missionaries.java continued

```java
public boolean goalTest() {
    return isLegal() && em == MAX_NUM && ec == MAX_NUM;
}
```

To create a successors function, it is necessary to go through all of the possible moves that can be made from one bank to another and then check if each of those moves will result in a legal state. Recall that a legal state is one in which cannibals do not outnumber missionaries on either bank. To determine this, we can define a convenience method on MCState that checks if a state is legal.

Listing 2.29   Missionaries.java continued

```java
public boolean isLegal() {
    if (wm < wc && wm > 0) {
        return false;
    }
    if (em < ec && em > 0) {
        return false;
    }
    return true;
}
```

The actual successors function is a bit verbose, for the sake of clarity. It tries adding every possible combination of one or two people moving across the river from the bank where the canoe currently resides. Once it has added all possible moves, it filters for the ones that are actually legal via removeIf() on a temporary List of potential states and a negated Predicate that checks isLegal(). Predicate.not() was added in Java 11. Once again, this is a method on MCState.

Listing 2.30 Missionaries.java continued

```java
public static List<MCState> successors(MCState mcs) {
    List<MCState> sucs = new ArrayList<>();
    if (mcs.boat) { // boat on west bank
        if (mcs.wm > 1) {
            sucs.add(new MCState(mcs.wm - 2, mcs.wc, !mcs.boat));
        }
        if (mcs.wm > 0) {
            sucs.add(new MCState(mcs.wm - 1, mcs.wc, !mcs.boat));
        }
        if (mcs.wc > 1) {
            sucs.add(new MCState(mcs.wm, mcs.wc - 2, !mcs.boat));
        }
        if (mcs.wc > 0) {
            sucs.add(new MCState(mcs.wm, mcs.wc - 1, !mcs.boat));
        }
        if (mcs.wc > 0 && mcs.wm > 0) {
            sucs.add(new MCState(mcs.wm - 1, mcs.wc - 1, !mcs.boat));
        }
    } else { // boat on east bank
        if (mcs.em > 1) {
            sucs.add(new MCState(mcs.wm + 2, mcs.wc, !mcs.boat));
        }
        if (mcs.em > 0) {
            sucs.add(new MCState(mcs.wm + 1, mcs.wc, !mcs.boat));
        }
        if (mcs.ec > 1) {
            sucs.add(new MCState(mcs.wm, mcs.wc + 2, !mcs.boat));
        }
        if (mcs.ec > 0) {
            sucs.add(new MCState(mcs.wm, mcs.wc + 1, !mcs.boat));
        }
        if (mcs.ec > 0 && mcs.em > 0) {
            sucs.add(new MCState(mcs.wm + 1, mcs.wc + 1, !mcs.boat));
        }
    }
    sucs.removeIf(Predicate.not(MCState::isLegal));
    return sucs;
}
```

2.3.2 Solving

We now have all of the ingredients in place to solve the problem. Recall that when we solve a problem using the search functions bfs(), dfs(), and astar(), we get back a Node that ultimately we convert using nodeToPath() into a list of states that leads to a solution. What we still need is a way to convert that list into a comprehensible printed sequence of steps to solve the missionaries and cannibals problem.

The function displaySolution() converts a solution path into printed output—a human-readable solution to the problem. It works by iterating through all of the states in the solution path while keeping track of the last state as well. It looks at the difference between the last state and the state it is currently iterating on to find out how many missionaries and cannibals moved across the river and in which direction.

Listing 2.31 Missionaries.java continued

```java
public static void displaySolution(List<MCState> path) {
    if (path.size() == 0) { // sanity check
        return;
    }
    MCState oldState = path.get(0);
    System.out.println(oldState);
    for (MCState currentState : path.subList(1, path.size())) {
        if (currentState.boat) {
            System.out.printf("%d missionaries and %d cannibals moved from the east bank to the west bank.%n",
                        oldState.em - currentState.em,
                        oldState.ec - currentState.ec);
        } else {
            System.out.printf("%d missionaries and %d cannibals moved from the west bank to the east bank.%n",
                        oldState.wm - currentState.wm,
                        oldState.wc - currentState.wc);
        }
        System.out.println(currentState);
        oldState = currentState;
    }
}
```

The displaySolution() method takes advantage of the fact that MCState knows how to pretty-print a nice summary of itself via toString().

The last thing we need to do is actually solve the missionaries and cannibals problem. To do so we can conveniently reuse a search function that we have already implemented, because we implemented them generically. This solution uses bfs(). To work properly with the search functions, recall that the explored data structure needs states to be easily compared for equality. So here again we let Eclipse autogenerate hashCode() and equals() before solving the problem in main().

Listing 2.32 Missionaries.java continued

```java
    // auto-generated by Eclipse
    @Override
    public int hashCode() {
        final int prime = 31;
        int result = 1;
        result = prime * result + (boat ? 1231 : 1237);
        result = prime * result + ec;
```

```java
        result = prime * result + em;
        result = prime * result + wc;
        result = prime * result + wm;
        return result;
    }

    // auto-generated by Eclipse
    @Override
    public boolean equals(Object obj) {
        if (this == obj) {
            return true;
        }
        if (obj == null) {
            return false;
        }
        if (getClass() != obj.getClass()) {
            return false;
        }
        MCState other = (MCState) obj;
        if (boat != other.boat) {
            return false;
        }
        if (ec != other.ec) {
            return false;
        }
        if (em != other.em) {
            return false;
        }
        if (wc != other.wc) {
            return false;
        }
        if (wm != other.wm) {
            return false;
        }
        return true;
    }

    public static void main(String[] args) {
        MCState start = new MCState(MAX_NUM, MAX_NUM, true);
        Node<MCState> solution = GenericSearch.bfs(start, MCState::goalTest,
    MCState::successors);
        if (solution == null) {
            System.out.println("No solution found!");
        } else {
            List<MCState> path = GenericSearch.nodeToPath(solution);
            displaySolution(path);
        }
    }

}
```

It is great to see how flexible our generic search functions can be. They can easily be adapted for solving a diverse set of problems. You should see output that looks similar to the following (abridged):

```
On the west bank there are 3 missionaries and 3 cannibals.
On the east bank there are 0 missionaries and 0 cannibals.
The boast is on the west bank.
0 missionaries and 2 cannibals moved from the west bank to the east bank.
On the west bank there are 3 missionaries and 1 cannibals.
On the east bank there are 0 missionaries and 2 cannibals.
The boast is on the east bank.
0 missionaries and 1 cannibals moved from the east bank to the west bank.
...

On the west bank there are 0 missionaries and 0 cannibals.
On the east bank there are 3 missionaries and 3 cannibals.
The boast is on the east bank.
```

2.4   *Real-world applications*

Search plays some role in all useful software. In some cases, it is the central element (Google Search, Spotlight, Lucene); in others, it is the basis for using the structures that underlie data storage. Knowing the correct search algorithm to apply to a data structure is essential for performance. For example, it would be very costly to use linear search, instead of binary search, on a sorted data structure.

A* is one of the most widely deployed pathfinding algorithms. It is only beaten by algorithms that do precalculation in the search space. For a blind search, A* is yet to be reliably beaten in all scenarios, and this has made it an essential component of everything from route planning to figuring out the shortest way to parse a programming language. Most directions-providing map software (think Google Maps) uses Dijkstra's algorithm (which A* is a variant of) to navigate. (There is more about Dijkstra's algorithm in chapter 4.) Whenever an AI character in a game is finding the shortest path from one end of the world to the other without human intervention, it is probably using A*.

Breadth-first search and depth-first search are often the basis for more complex search algorithms like uniform-cost search and backtracking search (which you will see in the next chapter). Breadth-first search is often a sufficient technique for finding the shortest path in a fairly small graph. But due to its similarity to A*, it is easy to swap out for A* if a good heuristic exists for a larger graph.

2.5   *Exercises*

1 Show the performance advantage of binary search over linear search by creating a list of one million numbers and timing how long it takes the generic `linearContains()` and `binaryContains()` defined in this chapter to find various numbers in the list.

2 Add a counter to `dfs()`, `bfs()`, and `astar()` to see how many states each searches through for the same maze. Find the counts for 100 different mazes to get statistically significant results.

3 Find a solution to the missionaries and cannibals problem for a different number of starting missionaries and cannibals.

Constraint-satisfaction problems

A large number of problems that computational tools are used to solve can be broadly categorized as *constraint-satisfaction problems* (CSPs). CSPs are composed of *variables* with possible values that fall into ranges known as *domains. Constraints* between the variables must be satisfied in order for constraint-satisfaction problems to be solved. Those three core concepts—variables, domains, and constraints— are simple to understand, and their generality underlies the wide applicability of constraint-satisfaction problem solving.

Let's consider an example problem. Suppose you are trying to schedule a Friday meeting for Joe, Mary, and Sue. Sue has to be at the meeting with at least one other person. For this scheduling problem, the three people—Joe, Mary, and Sue—may be the variables. The domain for each variable may be their respective hours of availability. For instance, the variable Mary has the domain 2 p.m., 3 p.m., and 4 p.m. This problem also has two constraints. One is that Sue has to be at the meeting. The other is that at least two people must attend the meeting. A constraint-satisfaction problem solver will be provided with the three variables, three domains, and two constraints, and it will then solve the problem without having the user explain exactly *how*. Figure 3.1 illustrates this example.

Programming languages like Prolog and Picat have facilities for solving constraint-satisfaction problems built in. The usual technique in other languages is to build a framework that incorporates a backtracking search and several heuristics to improve the performance of that search. In this chapter, we will first build a framework for CSPs that solves them using a simple recursive backtracking search. Then we will use the framework to solve several different example problems.

Friday meeting

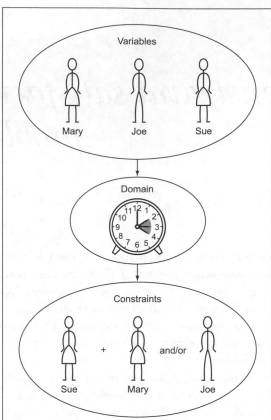

Figure 3.1   Scheduling problems are a classic application of constraint-satisfaction frameworks.

3.1   *Building a constraint-satisfaction problem framework*

Constraints will be defined as subclasses of a `Constraint` class. Each `Constraint` consists of the `variables` it constrains and a method that checks whether it is `satisfied()`. The determination of whether a constraint is satisfied is the main logic that goes into defining a specific constraint-satisfaction problem.

The default implementation should be overridden. In fact, it must be, because we are defining our `Constraint` class as an abstract base class. Abstract base classes are not meant to be instantiated. Instead, only their subclasses that override and implement their `abstract` methods are for actual use.

Listing 3.1   **Constraint.java**

```
package chapter3;

import java.util.List;
import java.util.Map;
```

```
// V is the variable type, and D is the domain type
public abstract class Constraint<V, D> {

    // the variables that the constraint is between
    protected List<V> variables;

    public Constraint(List<V> variables) {
        this.variables = variables;
    }

    // must be overridden by subclasses
    public abstract boolean satisfied(Map<V, D> assignment);
}
```

TIP It can be difficult to choose between an abstract class and an interface in Java. Only abstract classes can have instance variables. Since we have the variables instance variable, we opted for an abstract class here.

The centerpiece of our constraint-satisfaction framework will be a class called CSP. CSP is the gathering point for variables, domains, and constraints. It uses generics to make itself flexible enough to work with any kind of variables and domain values (V keys and D domain values). Within CSP, the variables, domains, and constraints collections are of types that you would expect. The variables collection is a List of variables, domains is a Map mapping variables to lists of possible values (the domains of those variables), and constraints is a Map that maps each variable to a List of the constraints imposed on it.

Listing 3.2   CSP.java

```
package chapter3;

import java.util.ArrayList;
import java.util.HashMap;
import java.util.List;
import java.util.Map;

public class CSP<V, D> {
    private List<V> variables;
    private Map<V, List<D>> domains;
    private Map<V, List<Constraint<V, D>>> constraints = new HashMap<>();

    public CSP(List<V> variables, Map<V, List<D>> domains) {
        this.variables = variables;
        this.domains = domains;
        for (V variable : variables) {
            constraints.put(variable, new ArrayList<>());
            if (!domains.containsKey(variable)) {
                throw new IllegalArgumentException("Every variable should
    have a domain assigned to it.");
            }
        }
    }
```

```java
public void addConstraint(Constraint<V, D> constraint) {
    for (V variable : constraint.variables) {
        if (!variables.contains(variable)) {
            throw new IllegalArgumentException("Variable in constraint
not in CSP");
        }
        constraints.get(variable).add(constraint);
    }
}
```

The constructor creates the `constraints` Map. The `addConstraint()` method goes through all of the variables touched by a given constraint and adds itself to the `constraints` mapping for each of them. Both methods have basic error-checking in place and will raise an exception when a `variable` is missing a domain or a `constraint` is on a nonexistent variable.

How do we know if a given configuration of variables and selected domain values satisfies the constraints? We will call such a given configuration an *assignment*. In other words, an assignment is a specific domain value selected for each variable. We need a function that checks every constraint for a given variable against an assignment to see if the variable's value in the assignment is consistent with the constraints. Here, we implement a `consistent()` function as a method on CSP.

Listing 3.3   CSP.java continued

```java
// Check if the value assignment is consistent by checking all
// constraints for the given variable against it
public boolean consistent(V variable, Map<V, D> assignment) {
    for (Constraint<V, D> constraint : constraints.get(variable)) {
        if (!constraint.satisfied(assignment)) {
            return false;
        }
    }
    return true;
}
```

`consistent()` goes through every constraint for a given variable (it will always be the variable that was just added to the assignment) and checks if the constraint is satisfied, given the new assignment. If the assignment satisfies every constraint, `true` is returned. If any constraint imposed on the variable is not satisfied, `false` is returned.

This constraint-satisfaction framework will use a simple backtracking search to find solutions to problems. *Backtracking* is the idea that once you hit a wall in your search, you go back to the last known point where you made a decision before the wall, and you choose a different path. If you think that sounds like depth-first search from chapter 2, you are perceptive. The backtracking search implemented in the following `backtrackingSearch()` method is a kind of recursive depth-first search, combining ideas you saw in chapters 1 and 2. We also implement a helper method that just calls `backtrackingSearch()` with an empty initial Map. The helper method will be useful for starting a search.

Listing 3.4   CSP.java continued

```java
public Map<V, D> backtrackingSearch(Map<V, D> assignment) {
    // assignment is complete if every variable is assigned (base case)
    if (assignment.size() == variables.size()) {
        return assignment;
    }
    // get the first variable in the CSP but not in the assignment
    V unassigned = variables.stream().filter(v ->
 !assignment.containsKey(v)).findFirst().get();
    // look through every domain value of the first unassigned variable
    for (D value : domains.get(unassigned)) {
        // shallow copy of assignment that we can change
        Map<V, D> localAssignment = new HashMap<>(assignment);
        localAssignment.put(unassigned, value);
        // if we're still consistent, we recurse (continue)
        if (consistent(unassigned, localAssignment)) {
            Map<V, D> result = backtrackingSearch(localAssignment);
            // if we didn't find the result, we end up backtracking
            if (result != null) {
                return result;
            }
        }
    }
    return null;
}

// helper for backtrackingSearch when nothing known yet
public Map<V, D> backtrackingSearch() {
    return backtrackingSearch(new HashMap<>());
}
}
```

Let's walk through backtrackingSearch(), line by line:

```java
if (assignment.size() == variables.size()) {
    return assignment;
}
```

The base case for the recursive search is having found a valid assignment for every variable. Once we have, we return the first instance of a solution that was valid. (We do not keep searching.)

```java
V unassigned = variables.stream().filter(v ->
    !assignment.containsKey(v)).findFirst().get();
```

To select a new variable whose domain we will explore, we simply go through all of the variables and find the first that does not have an assignment. To do this, we create a Stream of variables filtered by whether they are yet in assignment, and we pull the first one that is not assigned using findFirst(). filter() takes a Predicate. A Predicate is a functional interface that describes a function that takes one argument and returns a boolean. Our predicate is a lambda expression (v -> !assignment.containsKey(v)) that returns `true` if assignment does not contain the argument, which in this case will be a variable for our CSP.

```
for (D value : domains.get(unassigned)) {
    Map<V, D> localAssignment = new HashMap<>(assignment);
    localAssignment.put(unassigned, value);
```

We try assigning all possible domain values for that variable, one at a time. The new assignment for each is stored in a local map called `localAssignment`.

```
if (consistent(unassigned, localAssignment)) {
    Map<V, D> result = backtrackingSearch(localAssignment);
    if (result != null) {
        return result;
    }
}
```

If the new assignment in `localAssignment` is consistent with all of the constraints (this is what `consistent()` checks for), we continue recursively searching with the new assignment in place. If the new assignment turns out to be complete (the base case), we return the new assignment up the recursion chain.

```
return null;
```

Finally, if we have gone through every possible domain value for a particular variable, and there is no solution utilizing the existing set of assignments, we return `null`, indicating no solution. This will lead to backtracking up the recursion chain to the point where a different prior assignment could have been made.

3.2   *The Australian map-coloring problem*

Imagine you have a map of Australia that you want to color by state/territory (which we will collectively call *regions*). No two adjacent regions should share a color. Can you color the regions with just three different colors?

The answer is yes. Try it out on your own. (The easiest way is to print out a map of Australia with a white background.) As human beings, we can quickly figure out the solution by inspection and a little trial and error. It is a trivial problem, really, and a great first problem for our backtracking constraint-satisfaction solver. A solution to the problem is illustrated in figure 3.2.

To model the problem as a CSP, we need to define the variables, domains, and constraints. The variables are the seven regions of Australia (at least the seven that we will restrict ourselves to): Western Australia, Northern Territory, South Australia, Queensland, New South Wales, Victoria, and Tasmania. In our CSP, they can be modeled with strings. The domain of each variable is the three different colors that can possibly be assigned. (We will use red, green, and blue.) The constraints are the tricky part. No two adjacent regions can be colored with the same color, so our constraints will be dependent on which regions border one another. We can use what are called

Figure 3.2 In a solution to the Australian map-coloring problem, no two adjacent parts of Australia can be colored with the same color.

binary constraints (constraints between two variables). Every two regions that share a border will also share a binary constraint indicating that they cannot be assigned the same color.

To implement these binary constraints in code, we need to subclass the `Constraint` class. The `MapColoringConstraint` subclass will take two variables in its constructor: the two regions that share a border. Its overridden `satisfied()` method will check first whether the two regions have domain values (colors) assigned to them; if either does not, the constraint is trivially satisfied until they do. (There cannot be a conflict when one does not yet have a color.) Then it will check whether the two regions are assigned the same color. Obviously, there is a conflict, meaning that the constraint is not satisfied, when they are the same.

The class is presented here in its entirety except for its `main()` driver. `MapColoring-Constraint` itself is not generic, but it subclasses a parameterized version of the generic class `Constraint` that indicates both variables and domains are of type `String`.

Listing 3.5   MapColoringConstraint.java

```java
package chapter3;

import java.util.HashMap;
import java.util.List;
import java.util.Map;

public final class MapColoringConstraint extends Constraint<String, String> {
    private String place1, place2;

    public MapColoringConstraint(String place1, String place2) {
        super(List.of(place1, place2));
        this.place1 = place1;
        this.place2 = place2;
    }

    @Override
    public boolean satisfied(Map<String, String> assignment) {
        // if either place is not in the assignment, then it is not
        // yet possible for their colors to be conflicting
        if (!assignment.containsKey(place1) ||
            !assignment.containsKey(place2)) {
          return true;
        }
        // check the color assigned to place1 is not the same as the
        // color assigned to place2
        return !assignment.get(place1).equals(assignment.get(place2));
    }
}
```

Now that we have a way of implementing the constraints between regions, fleshing out the Australian map-coloring problem with our CSP solver is simply a matter of filling in domains and variables, and then adding constraints.

Listing 3.6   MapColoringConstraint.java continued

```java
public static void main(String[] args) {
    List<String> variables = List.of("Western Australia", "Northern
    Territory", "South Australia", "Queensland", "New South Wales",
    "Victoria", "Tasmania");
    Map<String, List<String>> domains = new HashMap<>();
    for (String variable : variables) {
        domains.put(variable, List.of("red", "green", "blue"));
    }
    CSP<String, String> csp = new CSP<>(variables, domains);
    csp.addConstraint(new MapColoringConstraint("Western Australia",
    "Northern Territory"));
    csp.addConstraint(new MapColoringConstraint("Western Australia",
    "South Australia"));
    csp.addConstraint(new MapColoringConstraint("South Australia",
    "Northern Territory"));
    csp.addConstraint(new MapColoringConstraint("Queensland", "Northern
    Territory"));
```

```
        csp.addConstraint(new MapColoringConstraint("Queensland", "South
    Australia"));
        csp.addConstraint(new MapColoringConstraint("Queensland", "New South
    Wales"));
        csp.addConstraint(new MapColoringConstraint("New South Wales", "South
    Australia"));
        csp.addConstraint(new MapColoringConstraint("Victoria", "South
    Australia"));
        csp.addConstraint(new MapColoringConstraint("Victoria", "New South
    Wales"));
        csp.addConstraint(new MapColoringConstraint("Victoria", "Tasmania"));
```

Finally, backtrackingSearch() is called to find a solution.

Listing 3.7   MapColoringConstraint.java continued

```
        Map<String, String> solution = csp.backtrackingSearch();
        if (solution == null) {
            System.out.println("No solution found!");
        } else {
            System.out.println(solution);
        }
    }

}
```

A correct solution will include an assigned color for every region:

```
{Western Australia=red, New South Wales=green, Victoria=red, Tasmania=green,
    Northern Territory=green, South Australia=blue, Queensland=red}
```

3.3   *The eight queens problem*

A chessboard is an eight-by-eight grid of squares. A queen is a chess piece that can move on the chessboard any number of squares along any row, column, or diagonal. A queen is attacking another piece if, in a single move, it can move to the square the piece is on without jumping over any other piece. (In other words, if the other piece is in the line of sight of the queen, then it is attacked by it.) The eight queens problem poses the question of how eight queens can be placed on a chessboard without any queen attacking another queen. One of many potential solutions to the problem is illustrated in figure 3.3.

To represent squares on the chessboard, we will assign each an integer row and an integer column. We can ensure each of the eight queens is not in the same column by simply assigning them sequentially the columns 1 through 8. The variables in our constraint-satisfaction problem can just be the column of the queen in question. The domains can be the possible rows (again, 1 through 8). Listing 3.8 shows the end of our file, where we define these variables and domains.

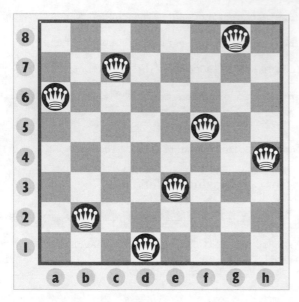

Figure 3.3   In a solution to the eight queens problem (there are many solutions), no two queens can be threatening each other.

Listing 3.8   QueensConstraint.java

```java
public static void main(String[] args) {
    List<Integer> columns = List.of(1, 2, 3, 4, 5, 6, 7, 8);
    Map<Integer, List<Integer>> rows = new HashMap<>();
    for (int column : columns) {
        rows.put(column, List.of(1, 2, 3, 4, 5, 6, 7, 8));
    }
    CSP<Integer, Integer> csp = new CSP<>(columns, rows);
```

To solve the problem, we will need a constraint that checks whether any two queens are on the same row or diagonal. (They were all assigned different sequential columns to begin with.) Checking for the same row is trivial, but checking for the same diagonal requires a little bit of math. If any two queens are on the same diagonal, the difference between their rows will be the same as the difference between their columns. Can you see where these checks take place in QueensConstraint? Note that the following code is at the top of our source file.

Listing 3.9   QueensConstraint.java continued

```java
package chapter3;

import java.util.HashMap;
import java.util.List;
import java.util.Map;
import java.util.Map.Entry;

public class QueensConstraint extends Constraint<Integer, Integer> {
    private List<Integer> columns;
```

```java
    public QueensConstraint(List<Integer> columns) {
        super(columns);
        this.columns = columns;
    }

    @Override
    public boolean satisfied(Map<Integer, Integer> assignment) {
        for (Entry<Integer, Integer> item : assignment.entrySet()) {
            // q1c = queen 1 column, q1r = queen 1 row
            int q1c = item.getKey();
            int q1r = item.getValue();
            // q2c = queen 2 column
            for (int q2c = q1c + 1; q2c <= columns.size(); q2c++) {
                if (assignment.containsKey(q2c)) {
                    // q2r = queen 2 row
                    int q2r = assignment.get(q2c);
                    // same row?
                    if (q1r == q2r) {
                        return false;
                    }
                    // same diagonal?
                    if (Math.abs(q1r - q2r) == Math.abs(q1c - q2c)) {
                        return false;
                    }
                }
            }
        }
        return true; // no conflict
    }
```

All that is left is to add the constraint and run the search. We're now back at the bottom of the file within the end of main().

Listing 3.10   QueensConstraint.java continued

```java
        csp.addConstraint(new QueensConstraint(columns));
        Map<Integer, Integer> solution = csp.backtrackingSearch();
        if (solution == null) {
            System.out.println("No solution found!");
        } else {
            System.out.println(solution);
        }
    }
}
```

Notice that we were able to reuse the constraint-satisfaction problem-solving framework that we built for map coloring fairly easily for a completely different type of problem. This is the power of writing code generically! Algorithms should be implemented in as broadly applicable a manner as possible unless a performance optimization for a particular application requires specialization.

A correct solution will assign a column and row to every queen:

```
{1=1, 2=5, 3=8, 4=6, 5=3, 6=7, 7=2, 8=4}
```

3.4   *Word search*

A word search is a grid of letters with hidden words placed along rows, columns, and diagonals. A player of a word-search puzzle attempts to find the hidden words by carefully scanning through the grid. Finding places to put the words so that they all fit on the grid is a kind of constraint-satisfaction problem. The variables are the words, and the domains are the possible locations of those words. The problem is illustrated in figure 3.4. Our goal in this section is to generate a word-search puzzle, not to solve one.

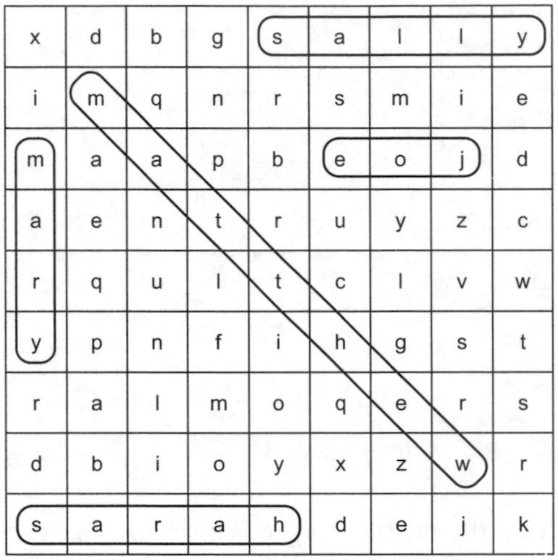

x	d	b	g	s	a	l	l	y
i	m	q	n	r	s	m	i	e
m	a	a	p	b	e	o	j	d
a	e	n	t	r	u	y	z	c
r	q	u	l	t	c	l	v	w
y	p	n	f	i	h	g	s	t
r	a	l	m	o	q	e	r	s
d	b	i	o	y	x	z	w	r
s	a	r	a	h	d	e	j	k

Figure 3.4   A classic word search, such as you might find in a children's puzzle book

For the purposes of expediency, our word search will not include words that overlap. You can improve it to allow for overlapping words as an exercise.

The grid of this word-search problem is not entirely dissimilar from the mazes of chapter 2. Some of the following data types should look familiar. WordGrid is analogous to Maze, and GridLocation is analogous to MazeLocation.

Listing 3.11   WordGrid.java

```java
package chapter3;

import java.util.ArrayList;
import java.util.List;
import java.util.Random;

public class WordGrid {

    public static class GridLocation {
        public final int row, column;
```

```java
    public GridLocation(int row, int column) {
        this.row = row;
        this.column = column;
    }

    // auto-generated by Eclipse
    @Override
    public int hashCode() {
        final int prime = 31;
        int result = 1;
        result = prime * result + column;
        result = prime * result + row;
        return result;
    }

    // auto-generated by Eclipse
    @Override
    public boolean equals(Object obj) {
        if (this == obj) {
            return true;
        }
        if (obj == null) {
            return false;
        }
        if (getClass() != obj.getClass()) {
            return false;
        }
        GridLocation other = (GridLocation) obj;
        if (column != other.column) {
            return false;
        }
        if (row != other.row) {
            return false;
        }
        return true;
    }
}
```

Initially, we will fill the grid with random letters of the English alphabet (A-Z). We do this by generating random char codes (integers, effectively) equivalent to where the letters land in ASCII. We will also need a method to mark a word on the grid given a list of locations, and a method for displaying the grid.

Listing 3.12 WordGrid.java continued

```java
    private final char ALPHABET_LENGTH = 26;
    private final char FIRST_LETTER = 'A';
    private final int rows, columns;
    private char[][] grid;

    public WordGrid(int rows, int columns) {
        this.rows = rows;
        this.columns = columns;
        grid = new char[rows][columns];
```

```
        // initialize grid with random letters
        Random random = new Random();
        for (int row = 0; row < rows; row++) {
            for (int column = 0; column < columns; column++) {
                char randomLetter = (char) (random.nextInt(ALPHABET_LENGTH) +
    FIRST_LETTER);
                grid[row][column] = randomLetter;
            }
        }
    }

    public void mark(String word, List<GridLocation> locations) {
        for (int i = 0; i < word.length(); i++) {
            GridLocation location = locations.get(i);
            grid[location.row][location.column] = word.charAt(i);
        }
    }

    // get a pretty printed version of the grid
    @Override
    public String toString() {
        StringBuilder sb = new StringBuilder();
        for (char[] rowArray : grid) {
            sb.append(rowArray);
            sb.append(System.lineSeparator());
        }
        return sb.toString();
    }
```

To figure out where words can fit in the grid, we will generate their domains. The domain of a word is a list of lists of the possible locations of all of its letters (List<List<GridLocation>>). Words cannot go just anywhere, though. They must stay within a row, column, or diagonal that is within the bounds of the grid. In other words, they should not go off the end of the grid. The purpose of generateDomain() and its helper "fill" methods is to build these lists for every word.

Listing 3.13 WordGrid.java continued

```
    public List<List<GridLocation>> generateDomain(String word) {
        List<List<GridLocation>> domain = new ArrayList<>();
        int length = word.length();

        for (int row = 0; row < rows; row++) {
            for (int column = 0; column < columns; column++) {
                if (column + length <= columns) {
                    // left to right
                    fillRight(domain, row, column, length);
                    // diagonal towards bottom right
                    if (row + length <= rows) {
                        fillDiagonalRight(domain, row, column, length);
                    }
                }
```

```java
            if (row + length <= rows) {
                // top to bottom
                fillDown(domain, row, column, length);
                // diagonal towards bottom left
                if (column - length >= 0) {
                    fillDiagonalLeft(domain, row, column, length);
                }
            }
        }
    }
    return domain;
}

private void fillRight(List<List<GridLocation>> domain, int row, int
  column, int length) {
    List<GridLocation> locations = new ArrayList<>();
    for (int c = column; c < (column + length); c++) {
        locations.add(new GridLocation(row, c));
    }
    domain.add(locations);
}

private void fillDiagonalRight(List<List<GridLocation>> domain, int row,
  int column, int length) {
    List<GridLocation> locations = new ArrayList<>();
    int r = row;
    for (int c = column; c < (column + length); c++) {
        locations.add(new GridLocation(r, c));
        r++;
    }
    domain.add(locations);
}

private void fillDown(List<List<GridLocation>> domain, int row, int
  column, int length) {
    List<GridLocation> locations = new ArrayList<>();
    for (int r = row; r < (row + length); r++) {
        locations.add(new GridLocation(r, column));
    }
    domain.add(locations);
}

private void fillDiagonalLeft(List<List<GridLocation>> domain, int row,
  int column, int length) {
    List<GridLocation> locations = new ArrayList<>();
    int c = column;
    for (int r = row; r < (row + length); r++) {
        locations.add(new GridLocation(r, c));
        c--;
    }
    domain.add(locations);
}

}
```

For the range of potential locations of a word (along a row, column, or diagonal), for loops translate the range into a list of GridLocations. Because generateDomain() loops through every grid location from the top left through to the bottom right for every word, it involves a lot of computation. Can you think of a way to do it more efficiently? What if we looked through all of the words of the same length at once, inside the loop?

To check if a potential solution is valid, we must implement a custom constraint for the word search. The satisfied() method of WordSearchConstraint simply checks whether any of the locations proposed for one word are the same as a location proposed for another word. It does this using a Set. Converting a List into a Set will remove all duplicates. If there are fewer items in a Set converted from a List than there were in the original List, that means the original List contained some duplicates. To prepare the data for this check, we will use a flatMap() to combine multiple sublists of locations for each word in the assignment into a single larger list of locations.

Listing 3.14   WordSearchConstraint.java

```java
package chapter3;

import java.util.Collection;
import java.util.Collections;
import java.util.HashMap;
import java.util.HashSet;
import java.util.List;
import java.util.Map;
import java.util.Map.Entry;
import java.util.Random;
import java.util.Set;
import java.util.stream.Collectors;

import chapter3.WordGrid.GridLocation;

public class WordSearchConstraint extends Constraint<String,
    List<GridLocation>> {

    public WordSearchConstraint(List<String> words) {
        super(words);
    }

    @Override
    public boolean satisfied(Map<String, List<GridLocation>> assignment) {
        // combine all GridLocations into one giant List
        List<GridLocation> allLocations = assignment.values().stream()
          .flatMap(Collection::stream).collect(Collectors.toList());
        // a set will eliminate duplicates using equals()
        Set<GridLocation> allLocationsSet = new HashSet<>(allLocations);
        // if there are any duplicate grid locations then there is an overlap
        return allLocations.size() == allLocationsSet.size();
    }
```

Finally, we are ready to run it. For this example, we have five words (names, in this example) in a nine-by-nine grid. The solution we get back should contain mappings between each word and the locations where its letters can fit in the grid.

Listing 3.15 WordSearchConstraint.java continued

```java
public static void main(String[] args) {
    WordGrid grid = new WordGrid(9, 9);
    List<String> words = List.of("MATTHEW", "JOE", "MARY", "SARAH",
"SALLY");
    // generate domains for all words
    Map<String, List<List<GridLocation>>> domains = new HashMap<>();
    for (String word : words) {
        domains.put(word, grid.generateDomain(word));
    }
    CSP<String, List<GridLocation>> csp = new CSP<>(words, domains);
    csp.addConstraint(new WordSearchConstraint(words));
    Map<String, List<GridLocation>> solution = csp.backtrackingSearch();
    if (solution == null) {
        System.out.println("No solution found!");
    } else {
        Random random = new Random();
        for (Entry<String, List<GridLocation>> item :
solution.entrySet()) {
            String word = item.getKey();
            List<GridLocation> locations = item.getValue();
            // random reverse half the time
            if (random.nextBoolean()) {
                Collections.reverse(locations);
            }
            grid.mark(word, locations);
        }
        System.out.println(grid);
    }
}
```

There is a finishing touch in the code that fills the grid with words. Some words are randomly chosen to be reversed. This is valid, because this example does not allow overlapping words. Your ultimate output should look something like the following. Can you find Matthew, Joe, Mary, Sarah, and Sally?

```
LWEHTTAMJ
MARYLISGO
DKOJYHAYE
IAJYHALAG
GYZJWRLGM
LLOTCAYIX
PEUTUSLKO
AJZYGIKDU
HSLZOFNNR
```

3.5   *SEND+MORE=MONEY*

SEND+MORE=MONEY is a cryptarithmetic puzzle, meaning that it is about finding digits that replace letters to make a mathematical statement true. Each letter in the problem represents one digit (0–9). No two letters can represent the same digit. When a letter repeats, it means a digit repeats in the solution.

To solve this puzzle by hand, it helps to line up the words.

```
 SEND
+MORE
=MONEY
```

It is absolutely solvable by hand, with a bit of algebra and intuition. But a fairly simple computer program can solve it faster by brute-forcing many possible solutions. Let's represent SEND+MORE=MONEY as a constraint-satisfaction problem.

Listing 3.16   SendMoreMoneyConstraint.java

```java
package chapter3;

import java.util.HashMap;
import java.util.HashSet;
import java.util.List;
import java.util.Map;

public class SendMoreMoneyConstraint extends Constraint<Character, Integer> {
    private List<Character> letters;

    public SendMoreMoneyConstraint(List<Character> letters) {
        super(letters);
        this.letters = letters;
    }

    @Override
    public boolean satisfied(Map<Character, Integer> assignment) {
        // if there are duplicate values then it's not a solution
        if ((new HashSet<>(assignment.values())).size() < assignment.size())
        {
            return false;
        }

        // if all variables have been assigned, check if it adds correctly
        if (assignment.size() == letters.size()) {
            int s = assignment.get('S');
            int e = assignment.get('E');
            int n = assignment.get('N');
            int d = assignment.get('D');
            int m = assignment.get('M');
            int o = assignment.get('O');
            int r = assignment.get('R');
            int y = assignment.get('Y');
            int send = s * 1000 + e * 100 + n * 10 + d;
            int more = m * 1000 + o * 100 + r * 10 + e;
```

```
            int money = m * 10000 + o * 1000 + n * 100 + e * 10 + y;
            return send + more == money;
        }
        return true; // no conflicts
    }
```

`SendMoreMoneyConstraint`'s `satisfied()` method does a few things. First, it checks if multiple letters represent the same digits. If they do, that's an invalid solution, and it returns `false`. Next, it checks if all letters have been assigned. If they have, it checks to see if the formula (SEND+MORE=MONEY) is correct with the given assignment. If it is, a solution has been found, and it returns `true`. Otherwise, it returns `false`. Finally, if all letters have not yet been assigned, it returns `true`. This is to ensure that a partial solution continues to be worked on.

Let's try running it.

Listing 3.17   SendMoreMoneyConstraint.java continued

```
    public static void main(String[] args) {
        List<Character> letters = List.of('S', 'E', 'N', 'D', 'M', 'O', 'R',
    'Y');
        Map<Character, List<Integer>> possibleDigits = new HashMap<>();
        for (Character letter : letters) {
            possibleDigits.put(letter, List.of(0, 1, 2, 3, 4, 5, 6, 7, 8, 9));
        }
        // so we don't get answers starting with a 0
        possibleDigits.replace('M', List.of(1));
        CSP<Character, Integer> csp = new CSP<>(letters, possibleDigits);
        csp.addConstraint(new SendMoreMoneyConstraint(letters));
        Map<Character, Integer> solution = csp.backtrackingSearch();
        if (solution == null) {
            System.out.println("No solution found!");
        } else {
            System.out.println(solution);
        }
    }
}
```

You will notice that we preassigned the answer for the letter M. This was to ensure that the answer doesn't include a 0 for M, because if you think about it, our constraint has no notion of the concept that a number can't start with zero. Feel free to try it out without that preassigned answer.

The solution should look something like this:

`{R=8, S=9, D=7, E=5, Y=2, M=1, N=6, O=0}`

3.6   *Circuit board layout*

A manufacturer needs to fit certain rectangular chips onto a rectangular circuit board. Essentially, this problem asks, "How can several different-sized rectangles all fit snugly inside of another rectangle?" A constraint-satisfaction problem solver can find the solution. The problem is illustrated in figure 3.5.

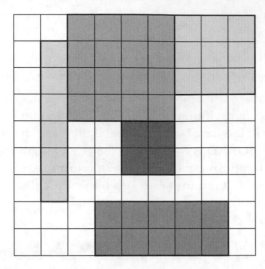

Figure 3.5   The circuit board layout problem is very similar to the word-search problem, but the rectangles are of variable width.

The circuit board layout problem is similar to the word-search problem. Instead of $1 \times N$ rectangles (words), the problem presents $M \times N$ rectangles. Like in the word-search problem, the rectangles cannot overlap. The rectangles cannot be put on diagonals, so in that sense the problem is actually simpler than the word search.

On your own, try rewriting the word-search solution to accommodate circuit board layout. You can reuse much of the code, including the code for the grid.

3.7   *Real-world applications*

As was mentioned in the introduction to this chapter, constraint-satisfaction problem solvers are commonly used in scheduling. Several people need to be at a meeting, and they are the variables. The domains consist of the open times on their calendars. The constraints may involve what combinations of people are required at the meeting.

Constraint-satisfaction problem solvers are also used in motion planning. Imagine a robot arm that needs to fit inside of a tube. It has constraints (the walls of the tube), variables (the joints), and domains (possible movements of the joints).

There are also applications in computational biology. You can imagine constraints between molecules required for a chemical reaction. And, of course, as is common with AI, there are applications in games. Writing a Sudoku solver is one of the following exercises, but many logic puzzles can be solved using constraint-satisfaction problem solving.

In this chapter, we built a simple backtracking, depth-first search, problem-solving framework. But it can be greatly improved by adding heuristics (remember A*?)—intuitions that can aid the search process. A newer technique than backtracking, known as *constraint propagation*, is also an efficient avenue for real-world applications. For more information, check out chapter 6 of Stuart Russell and Peter Norvig's *Artificial Intelligence: A Modern Approach*, third edition (Pearson, 2010).

The simple example frameworks we build in this book are not appropriate for production environments. If you need to solve a more sophisticated constraint problem in Java, you may consider the Choco framework, available at https://choco-solver.org.

3.8 *Exercises*

1 Revise `WordSearchConstraint` so that overlapping letters are allowed.

2 Build the circuit board layout problem solver described in section 3.6, if you have not already.

3 Build a program that can solve Sudoku problems using this chapter's constraint-satisfaction problem-solving framework.

Graph problems

A *graph* is an abstract mathematical construct that is used for modeling a real-world problem by dividing the problem into a set of connected nodes. We call each of the nodes a *vertex* and each of the connections an *edge*. For instance, a subway map can be thought of as a graph representing a transportation network. Each of the dots represents a station, and each of the lines represents a route between two stations. In graph terminology, we would call the stations "vertices" and the routes "edges."

Why is this useful? Not only do graphs help us think abstractly about a problem, but they also let us apply several well-understood and performant search and optimization techniques. For instance, in the subway example, suppose we want to know the shortest route from one station to another. Or suppose we want to know the minimum amount of track needed to connect all of the stations. Graph algorithms that you will learn in this chapter can solve both of those problems. Further, graph algorithms can be applied to any kind of network problem—not just transportation networks. Think of computer networks, distribution networks, and utility networks. Search and optimization problems across all of these spaces can be solved using graph algorithms.

4.1 A map as a graph

In this chapter, we'll work with a graph of, not subway stations, but cities of the United States and potential routes between them. Figure 4.1 is a map of the continental United States and the 15 largest metropolitan statistical areas (MSAs) in the country, as estimated by the US Census Bureau.[1]

---

[1] Data is from the United States Census Bureau, https://www.census.gov/.

Figure 4.1   A map of the 15 largest MSAs in the United States

Famous entrepreneur Elon Musk has suggested building a new high-speed transportation network composed of capsules traveling in pressurized tubes. According to Musk, the capsules would travel at 700 miles per hour and be suitable for cost-effective transportation between cities less than 900 miles apart.[2] He calls this new transportation system the "Hyperloop." In this chapter we will explore classic graph problems in the context of building out this transportation network.

Musk initially proposed the Hyperloop idea for connecting Los Angeles and San Francisco. If one were to build a national Hyperloop network, it would make sense to do so between America's largest metropolitan areas. In figure 4.2, the state outlines from figure 4.1 are removed. In addition, each of the MSAs is connected with some of its neighbors. To make the graph a little more interesting, those neighbors are not always the MSA's closest neighbors.

Figure 4.2 is a graph with vertices representing the 15 largest MSAs in the United States and edges representing potential Hyperloop routes between cities. The routes were chosen for illustrative purposes. Certainly, other potential routes could be part of a new Hyperloop network.

This abstract representation of a real-world problem highlights the power of graphs. With this abstraction, we can ignore the geography of the United States and concentrate on thinking about the potential Hyperloop network simply in the context of connecting cities. In fact, as long as we keep the edges the same, we can think about

---

[2] Elon Musk, "Hyperloop Alpha," https://www.tesla.com/sites/default/files/blog_images/hyperloop-alpha.pdf.

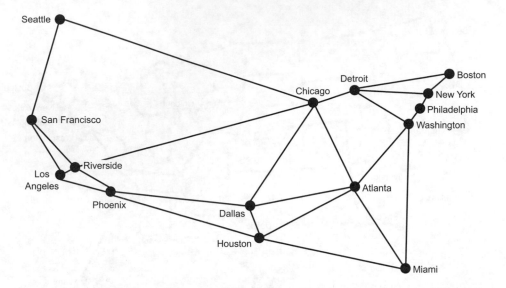

Figure 4.2   A graph with vertices representing the 15 largest MSAs in the United States and edges representing potential Hyperloop routes between them

the problem with a different-looking graph. In figure 4.3, for example, the location of Miami has moved. The graph in figure 4.3, being an abstract representation, can address the same fundamental computational problems as the graph in figure 4.2, even if Miami is not where we would expect it. But for our sanity, we will stick with the representation in figure 4.2.

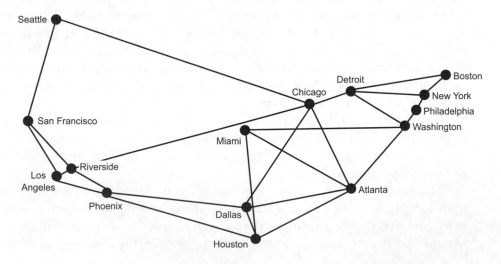

Figure 4.3   A graph equivalent to that in figure 4.2, with the location of Miami moved

4.2 Building a graph framework

In this section, we will define two different types of graphs: *unweighted* and *weighted*. Weighted graphs, which we will discuss later in the chapter, associate a weight (read *number*, such as a length in the case of our example) with each edge.

At its heart, Java is an object-oriented programming language. We will make use of the inheritance model, fundamental to Java's object-oriented class hierarchies, so we do not duplicate our effort. The classes for both unweighted and weighted graphs will be derived from an abstract base class known as Graph. This will allow them to inherit much of their functionality, with small tweaks for what makes a weighted graph distinct from an unweighted graph.

We want this graph framework to be as flexible as possible so that it can represent as many different problems as possible. To achieve this goal, we will use generics to abstract away the type of the vertices. Every vertex will ultimately be assigned an integer index, but it will be stored as the user-defined generic type.

Let's start work on the framework by defining the Edge class, which is the simplest machinery in our graph framework.

Listing 4.1 Edge.java

```
package chapter4;

public class Edge {
    public final int u; // the "from" vertex
    public final int v; // the "to" vertex

    public Edge(int u, int v) {
        this.u = u;
        this.v = v;
    }

    public Edge reversed() {
        return new Edge(v, u);
    }

    @Override
    public String toString() {
        return u + " -> " + v;
    }

}
```

An Edge is defined as a connection between two vertices, each of which is represented by an integer index. By convention, u is used to refer to the first vertex, and v is used to represent the second vertex. You can also think of u as "from" and v as "to." In this chapter, we are only working with undirected graphs (graphs with edges that allow travel in both directions), but in *directed graphs*, also known as *digraphs*, edges can also be one-way. The reversed() method is meant to return an Edge that travels in the opposite direction of the edge it is applied to.

The `Graph` abstract class focuses on the essential role of a graph: associating vertices with edges. Again, we want to let the actual types of the vertices be whatever the user of the framework desires. We do this by making the vertex type generic (`V`). This lets the framework be used for a wide range of problems without needing to make intermediate data structures that glue everything together. For example, in a graph like the one for Hyperloop routes, we might define the type of the vertices to be `String`, because we would use strings like "New York" and "Los Angeles" as the vertices. The type of the edges in the graph (`E`) is also generic, so that it can be set by the subclasses to be an unweighted or weighted edge type. Let's begin the `Graph` class.

Listing 4.2   Graph.java

```java
package chapter4;

import java.util.ArrayList;
import java.util.Arrays;
import java.util.List;
import java.util.stream.Collectors;

// V is the type of the vertices in the Graph
// E is the type of the edges
public abstract class Graph<V, E extends Edge> {

    private ArrayList<V> vertices = new ArrayList<>();
    protected ArrayList<ArrayList<E>> edges = new ArrayList<>();

    public Graph() {
    }

    public Graph(List<V> vertices) {
        this.vertices.addAll(vertices);
        for (V vertex : vertices) {
            edges.add(new ArrayList<>());
        }
    }
}
```

The `vertices` list is the heart of a `Graph`. Each vertex will be stored in the list, but we will later refer to them by their integer index in the list. The vertex itself may be a complex data type, but its index will always be an `int`, which is easy to work with. On another level, by putting this index between graph algorithms and the `vertices` list, it allows us to have two vertices that are equal in the same graph. (Imagine a graph with a country's cities as vertices, where the country has more than one city named "Springfield.") Even though they are the same, they will have different integer indices.

There are many ways to implement a graph data structure, but the two most common are to use a *vertex matrix* or *adjacency lists*. In a vertex matrix, each cell of the matrix represents the intersection of two vertices in the graph, and the value of that cell indicates the connection (or lack thereof) between them. Our graph data structure uses adjacency lists. In this graph representation, every vertex has a list of vertices that it is connected to. Our specific representation uses a list of lists of edges, so for every vertex there is a list of edges via which the vertex is connected to other vertices. edges is this list of lists.

The rest of the Graph class is now presented in its entirety. You will notice the use of short, mostly one-line methods, with verbose and clear method names. This should make the rest of the class largely self-explanatory, but short comments are included so that there is no room for misinterpretation.

Listing 4.3 Graph.java continued

```java
// Number of vertices
public int getVertexCount() {
    return vertices.size();
}

// Number of edges
public int getEdgeCount() {
    return edges.stream().mapToInt(ArrayList::size).sum();
}

// Add a vertex to the graph and return its index
public int addVertex(V vertex) {
    vertices.add(vertex);
    edges.add(new ArrayList<>());
    return getVertexCount() - 1;
}

// Find the vertex at a specific index
public V vertexAt(int index) {
    return vertices.get(index);
}

// Find the index of a vertex in the graph
public int indexOf(V vertex) {
    return vertices.indexOf(vertex);
}

// Find the vertices that a vertex at some index is connected to
public List<V> neighborsOf(int index) {
    return edges.get(index).stream()
            .map(edge -> vertexAt(edge.v))
            .collect(Collectors.toList());
}

// Look up a vertex's index and find its neighbors (convenience method)
public List<V> neighborsOf(V vertex) {
    return neighborsOf(indexOf(vertex));
}

// Return all of the edges associated with a vertex at some index
public List<E> edgesOf(int index) {
    return edges.get(index);
}
```

```
    // Look up the index of a vertex and return its edges (convenience method)
    public List<E> edgesOf(V vertex) {
        return edgesOf(indexOf(vertex));
    }

    // Make it easy to pretty-print a Graph
    @Override
    public String toString() {
        StringBuilder sb = new StringBuilder();
        for (int i = 0; i < getVertexCount(); i++) {
            sb.append(vertexAt(i));
            sb.append(" -> ");
            sb.append(Arrays.toString(neighborsOf(i).toArray()));
            sb.append(System.lineSeparator());
        }
        return sb.toString();
    }
}
```

Let's step back for a moment and consider why this class has two versions of most of its methods. We know from the class definition that the list vertices is a list of elements of type V, which can be any Java class. So we have vertices of type V that are stored in the vertices list. But if we want to retrieve or manipulate them later, we need to know where they are stored in that list. Hence, every vertex has an index in the list (an integer) associated with it. If we don't know a vertex's index, we need to look it up by searching through vertices. That is why there are two versions of every method. One operates on int indices, and one operates on V itself. The methods that operate on V look up the relevant indices and call the index-based function. Therefore, they can be considered convenience methods.

Most of the functions are fairly self-explanatory, but neighborsOf() deserves a little unpacking. It returns the *neighbors* of a vertex. A vertex's neighbors are all of the other vertices that are directly connected to it by an edge. For example, in figure 4.2, New York and Washington are the only neighbors of Philadelphia. We find the neighbors for a vertex by looking at the ends (the vs) of all of the edges going out from it:

```
public List<V> neighborsOf(int index) {
    return edges.get(index).stream()
            .map(edge -> vertexAt(edge.v))
            .collect(Collectors.toList());
}
```

edges.get(index) returns the adjacency list, the list of edges through which the vertex in question is connected to other vertices. In the stream passed to the map() call, edge represents one particular edge, and edge.v represents the index of the neighbor that the edge is connected to. map() will return all of the vertices (as opposed to just their indices), because map() applies the vertexAt() method on every edge.v.

Now that we have the basic functionality of a graph implemented in the Graph abstract class, we can define a concrete subclass. Beyond being undirected or directed, graphs can also be *unweighted* or *weighted*. A weighted graph is one that has some comparable value, usually numeric, associated with each of its edges. We could think of the weights in our potential Hyperloop network as being the distances between the stations. For now, though, we will deal with an unweighted version of the graph. An unweighted edge is simply a connection between two vertices; hence, the Edge class is unweighted. Another way of putting it is that in an unweighted graph we know which vertices are connected, whereas in a weighted graph we know which vertices are connected and also know something about those connections. UnweightedGraph represents a graph that has no values associated with its edges. In other words, it's the combination of Graph with the other class we've defined, Edge.

Listing 4.4 UnweightedGraph.java

```java
package chapter4;

import java.util.List;

import chapter2.GenericSearch;
import chapter2.GenericSearch.Node;

public class UnweightedGraph<V> extends Graph<V, Edge> {

    public UnweightedGraph(List<V> vertices) {
        super(vertices);
    }

    // This is an undirected graph, so we always add
    // edges in both directions
    public void addEdge(Edge edge) {
        edges.get(edge.u).add(edge);
        edges.get(edge.v).add(edge.reversed());
    }

    // Add an edge using vertex indices (convenience method)
    public void addEdge(int u, int v) {
        addEdge(new Edge(u, v));
    }

    // Add an edge by looking up vertex indices (convenience method)
    public void addEdge(V first, V second) {
        addEdge(new Edge(indexOf(first), indexOf(second)));
    }
```

One detail worth pointing out is the way addEdge() works. addEdge() first adds an edge to the adjacency list of the "from" vertex (u) and then adds a reversed version of the edge to the adjacency list of the "to" vertex (v). The second step is necessary because this graph is undirected. We want every edge to be added in both directions; this means that u will be a neighbor of v in the same way that v is a neighbor of u. You can think of an undirected graph as being *bidirectional* if it helps you remember that it means any edge can be traversed in either direction.

```
public void addEdge(Edge edge) {
    edges.get(edge.u).add(edge);
    edges.get(edge.v).add(edge.reversed());
}
```

As was mentioned earlier, we are only dealing with undirected graphs in this chapter.

4.2.1 *Working with Edge and UnweightedGraph*

Now that we have concrete implementations of Edge and Graph, we can create a representation of the potential Hyperloop network. The vertices and edges in cityGraph correspond to the vertices and edges represented in figure 4.2. Using generics, we can specify that vertices will be of type String (UnweightedGraph<String>). In other words, the String type fills in for the type variable V.

Listing 4.5   UnweightedGraph.java continued

```
public static void main(String[] args) {
    // Represents the 15 largest MSAs in the United States
    UnweightedGraph<String> cityGraph = new UnweightedGraph<>(
            List.of("Seattle", "San Francisco", "Los Angeles",
    "Riverside", "Phoenix", "Chicago", "Boston", "New York", "Atlanta",
    "Miami", "Dallas", "Houston", "Detroit", "Philadelphia", "Washington"));

    cityGraph.addEdge("Seattle", "Chicago");
    cityGraph.addEdge("Seattle", "San Francisco");
    cityGraph.addEdge("San Francisco", "Riverside");
    cityGraph.addEdge("San Francisco", "Los Angeles");
    cityGraph.addEdge("Los Angeles", "Riverside");
    cityGraph.addEdge("Los Angeles", "Phoenix");
    cityGraph.addEdge("Riverside", "Phoenix");
    cityGraph.addEdge("Riverside", "Chicago");
    cityGraph.addEdge("Phoenix", "Dallas");
    cityGraph.addEdge("Phoenix", "Houston");
    cityGraph.addEdge("Dallas", "Chicago");
    cityGraph.addEdge("Dallas", "Atlanta");
    cityGraph.addEdge("Dallas", "Houston");
    cityGraph.addEdge("Houston", "Atlanta");
    cityGraph.addEdge("Houston", "Miami");
    cityGraph.addEdge("Atlanta", "Chicago");
    cityGraph.addEdge("Atlanta", "Washington");
    cityGraph.addEdge("Atlanta", "Miami");
    cityGraph.addEdge("Miami", "Washington");
    cityGraph.addEdge("Chicago", "Detroit");
    cityGraph.addEdge("Detroit", "Boston");
    cityGraph.addEdge("Detroit", "Washington");
    cityGraph.addEdge("Detroit", "New York");
    cityGraph.addEdge("Boston", "New York");
    cityGraph.addEdge("New York", "Philadelphia");
    cityGraph.addEdge("Philadelphia", "Washington");
    System.out.println(cityGraph.toString());
  }
}
```

cityGraph has vertices of type String, and we indicate each vertex with the name of the MSA that it represents. It is irrelevant in what order we add the edges to city-Graph. Because we implemented toString() with a nicely printed description of the graph, we can now pretty-print (that's a real term!) the graph. You should get output similar to the following:

```
Seattle -> [Chicago, San Francisco]
San Francisco -> [Seattle, Riverside, Los Angeles]
Los Angeles -> [San Francisco, Riverside, Phoenix]
Riverside -> [San Francisco, Los Angeles, Phoenix, Chicago]
Phoenix -> [Los Angeles, Riverside, Dallas, Houston]
Chicago -> [Seattle, Riverside, Dallas, Atlanta, Detroit]
Boston -> [Detroit, New York]
New York -> [Detroit, Boston, Philadelphia]
Atlanta -> [Dallas, Houston, Chicago, Washington, Miami]
Miami -> [Houston, Atlanta, Washington]
Dallas -> [Phoenix, Chicago, Atlanta, Houston]
Houston -> [Phoenix, Dallas, Atlanta, Miami]
Detroit -> [Chicago, Boston, Washington, New York]
Philadelphia -> [New York, Washington]
Washington -> [Atlanta, Miami, Detroit, Philadelphia]
```

4.3 Finding the shortest path

The Hyperloop is so fast that for optimizing travel time from one station to another, it probably matters less how long the distances are between the stations and more how many hops it takes (how many stations need to be visited) to get from one station to another. Each station may involve a layover, so just like with flights, the fewer stops, the better.

In graph theory, a set of edges that connects two vertices is known as a *path*. In other words, a path is a way of getting from one vertex to another vertex. In the context of the Hyperloop network, a set of tubes (edges) represents the path from one city (vertex) to another (vertex). Finding optimal paths between vertices is one of the most common problems that graphs are used for.

Informally, we can also think of a list of vertices sequentially connected to one another by edges as a path. This description is really just another side of the same coin. It is like taking a list of edges, figuring out which vertices they connect, keeping that list of vertices, and throwing away the edges. In this brief example, we will find such a list of vertices that connects two cities on our Hyperloop.

4.3.1 Revisiting breadth-first search (BFS)

In an unweighted graph, finding the shortest path means finding the path that has the fewest edges between the starting vertex and the destination vertex. To build out the Hyperloop network, it might make sense to first connect the furthest cities on the highly populated seaboards. That raises the question, "What is the shortest path between Boston and Miami?"

TIP   This section assumes that you have read chapter 2. Before continuing, ensure that you are comfortable with the material on breadth-first search in chapter 2.

Luckily, we already have an algorithm for finding shortest paths, and we can reuse it to answer this question. Breadth-first search, introduced in chapter 2, is just as viable for graphs as it is for mazes. In fact, the mazes we worked with in chapter 2 really are graphs. The vertices are the locations in the maze, and the edges are the moves that can be made from one location to another. In an unweighted graph, a breadth-first search will find the shortest path between any two vertices.

We can reuse the breadth-first search implementation from chapter 2 to work with Graph. In fact, we can reuse it completely unchanged. This is the power of writing code generically!

Recall that bfs() in chapter 2 requires three parameters: an initial state, a Predicate (read *function that returns a boolean*) for testing for a goal, and a Function that finds the successor states for a given state. The initial state will be the vertex represented by the string "Boston." The goal test will be a lambda that checks if a vertex is equivalent to "Miami." Finally, successor vertices can be generated by the Graph method neighborsOf().

With this plan in mind, we can add code to the end of the main() method of UnweightedGraph.java to find the shortest route between Boston and Miami on cityGraph.

NOTE   Listing 4.4 (earlier in the chapter where UnweightedGraph was first defined) included imports that support this section (i.e., chapter2.Generic-Search, chapter2.genericSearch.Node). These imports will only work if the chapter2 package is accessible from the chapter4 package. If you did not configure your development environment in this way, you should be able to copy the GenericSearch class directly into the chapter4 package and eliminate the imports.

Listing 4.6   UnweightedGraph.java continued

```java
        Node<String> bfsResult = GenericSearch.bfs("Boston",
                v -> v.equals("Miami"),
                cityGraph::neighborsOf);
if (bfsResult == null) {
    System.out.println("No solution found using breadth-first search!");
} else {
    List<String> path = GenericSearch.nodeToPath(bfsResult);
    System.out.println("Path from Boston to Miami:");
    System.out.println(path);
}
```

The output should look something like this:

```
Path from Boston to Miami:
[Boston, Detroit, Washington, Miami]
```

Boston to Detroit to Washington to Miami, composed of three edges, is the shortest route between Boston and Miami in terms of the number of edges. Figure 4.4 highlights this route.

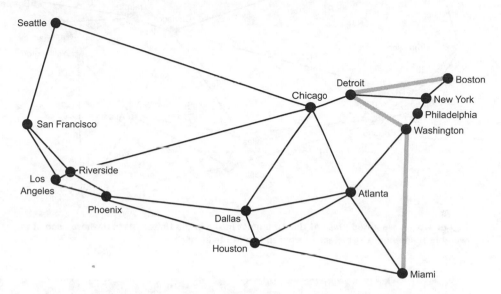

Figure 4.4 **The shortest route between Boston and Miami, in terms of the number of edges, is highlighted.**

4.4   *Minimizing the cost of building the network*

Imagine that we want to connect all 15 of the largest MSAs to the Hyperloop network. Our goal is to minimize the cost of rolling out the network, so that means using a minimum amount of track. Then the question is, "How can we connect all of the MSAs using the minimum amount of track?"

4.4.1   *Working with weights*

To understand the amount of track that a particular edge may require, we need to know the distance that the edge represents. This is an opportunity to reintroduce the concept of weights. In the Hyperloop network, the weight of an edge is the distance between the two MSAs that it connects. Figure 4.5 is the same as figure 4.2 except that it has a weight added to each edge, representing the distance in miles between the two vertices that the edge connects.

To handle weights, we will need a subclass of Edge (WeightedEdge) and a subclass of Graph (WeightedGraph). Every WeightedEdge will have a double associated with it, representing its weight. Jarník's algorithm, which we will cover later in the chapter, requires the ability to compare one edge with another to determine the edge with the lowest weight. This is easy to do with numeric weights.

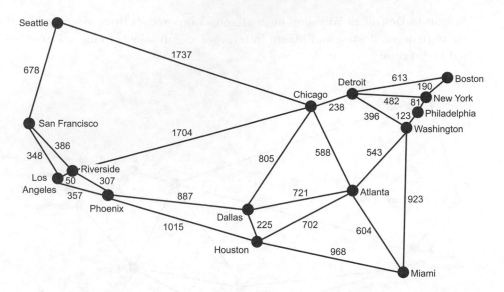

Figure 4.5   A weighted graph of the 15 largest MSAs in the United States, where each of the weights represents the distance between two MSAs in miles

Listing 4.7   WeightedEdge.java

```java
package chapter4;

public class WeightedEdge extends Edge implements Comparable<WeightedEdge> {
    public final double weight;

    public WeightedEdge(int u, int v, double weight) {
        super(u, v);
        this.weight = weight;
    }

    @Override
    public WeightedEdge reversed() {
        return new WeightedEdge(v, u, weight);
    }

    // so that we can order edges by weight to find the minimum weight edge
    @Override
    public int compareTo(WeightedEdge other) {
        Double mine = weight;
        Double theirs = other.weight;
        return mine.compareTo(theirs);
    }

    @Override
    public String toString() {
        return u + " " + weight + "> " + v;
    }
}
```

The implementation of `WeightedEdge` is not immensely different from that of `Edge`. It only differs in the addition of a `weight` property and the implementation of the `Comparable` interface via `compareTo()`, so that two `WeightedEdges` are comparable. The `compareTo()` method is only interested in looking at weights (as opposed to including the inherited properties u and v), because Jarník's algorithm needs to find the smallest edge by weight.

A `WeightedGraph` inherits much of its functionality from `Graph`. Other than that, it has a constructor, it has convenience methods for adding `WeightedEdges`, and it implements its own version of `toString()`.

Listing 4.8 WeightedGraph.java

```java
package chapter4;

import java.util.Arrays;
import java.util.Collections;
import java.util.HashMap;
import java.util.LinkedList;
import java.util.List;
import java.util.Map;
import java.util.PriorityQueue;
import java.util.function.IntConsumer;

public class WeightedGraph<V> extends Graph<V, WeightedEdge> {

    public WeightedGraph(List<V> vertices) {
        super(vertices);
    }

    // This is an undirected graph, so we always add
    // edges in both directions
    public void addEdge(WeightedEdge edge) {
        edges.get(edge.u).add(edge);
        edges.get(edge.v).add(edge.reversed());
    }

    public void addEdge(int u, int v, float weight) {
        addEdge(new WeightedEdge(u, v, weight));
    }

    public void addEdge(V first, V second, float weight) {
        addEdge(indexOf(first), indexOf(second), weight);
    }

    // Make it easy to pretty-print a Graph
    @Override
    public String toString() {
        StringBuilder sb = new StringBuilder();
        for (int i = 0; i < getVertexCount(); i++) {
            sb.append(vertexAt(i));
            sb.append(" -> ");
```

```
        sb.append(Arrays.toString(edgesOf(i).stream()
                .map(we -> "(" + vertexAt(we.v) + ", " + we.weight +
    ")")").toArray()));
        sb.append(System.lineSeparator());
    }
    return sb.toString();
}
```

It is now possible to actually define a weighted graph. The weighted graph we will work with is a representation of figure 4.5 called `cityGraph2`.

Listing 4.9 WeightedGraph.java continued

```
public static void main(String[] args) {
    // Represents the 15 largest MSAs in the United States
    WeightedGraph<String> cityGraph2 = new WeightedGraph<>(
            List.of("Seattle", "San Francisco", "Los Angeles",
    "Riverside", "Phoenix", "Chicago", "Boston",
                    "New York", "Atlanta", "Miami", "Dallas", "Houston",
    "Detroit", "Philadelphia", "Washington"));

    cityGraph2.addEdge("Seattle", "Chicago", 1737);
    cityGraph2.addEdge("Seattle", "San Francisco", 678);
    cityGraph2.addEdge("San Francisco", "Riverside", 386);
    cityGraph2.addEdge("San Francisco", "Los Angeles", 348);
    cityGraph2.addEdge("Los Angeles", "Riverside", 50);
    cityGraph2.addEdge("Los Angeles", "Phoenix", 357);
    cityGraph2.addEdge("Riverside", "Phoenix", 307);
    cityGraph2.addEdge("Riverside", "Chicago", 1704);
    cityGraph2.addEdge("Phoenix", "Dallas", 887);
    cityGraph2.addEdge("Phoenix", "Houston", 1015);
    cityGraph2.addEdge("Dallas", "Chicago", 805);
    cityGraph2.addEdge("Dallas", "Atlanta", 721);
    cityGraph2.addEdge("Dallas", "Houston", 225);
    cityGraph2.addEdge("Houston", "Atlanta", 702);
    cityGraph2.addEdge("Houston", "Miami", 968);
    cityGraph2.addEdge("Atlanta", "Chicago", 588);
    cityGraph2.addEdge("Atlanta", "Washington", 543);
    cityGraph2.addEdge("Atlanta", "Miami", 604);
    cityGraph2.addEdge("Miami", "Washington", 923);
    cityGraph2.addEdge("Chicago", "Detroit", 238);
    cityGraph2.addEdge("Detroit", "Boston", 613);
    cityGraph2.addEdge("Detroit", "Washington", 396);
    cityGraph2.addEdge("Detroit", "New York", 482);
    cityGraph2.addEdge("Boston", "New York", 190);
    cityGraph2.addEdge("New York", "Philadelphia", 81);
    cityGraph2.addEdge("Philadelphia", "Washington", 123);

    System.out.println(cityGraph2);
    }
}
```

Because `WeightedGraph` implements `toString()`, we can pretty-print `cityGraph2`. In the output, you will see both the vertices that each vertex is connected to and the weights of those connections:

```
Seattle -> [(Chicago, 1737.0), (San Francisco, 678.0)]
San Francisco -> [(Seattle, 678.0), (Riverside, 386.0), (Los Angeles, 348.0)]
Los Angeles -> [(San Francisco, 348.0), (Riverside, 50.0), (Phoenix, 357.0)]
Riverside -> [(San Francisco, 386.0), (Los Angeles, 50.0), (Phoenix, 307.0),
     (Chicago, 1704.0)]
Phoenix -> [(Los Angeles, 357.0), (Riverside, 307.0), (Dallas, 887.0), (Houston,
     1015.0)]
Chicago -> [(Seattle, 1737.0), (Riverside, 1704.0), (Dallas, 805.0), (Atlanta,
     588.0), (Detroit, 238.0)]
Boston -> [(Detroit, 613.0), (New York, 190.0)]
New York -> [(Detroit, 482.0), (Boston, 190.0), (Philadelphia, 81.0)]
Atlanta -> [(Dallas, 721.0), (Houston, 702.0), (Chicago, 588.0), (Washington,
     543.0), (Miami, 604.0)]
Miami -> [(Houston, 968.0), (Atlanta, 604.0), (Washington, 923.0)]
Dallas -> [(Phoenix, 887.0), (Chicago, 805.0), (Atlanta, 721.0), (Houston,
     225.0)]
Houston -> [(Phoenix, 1015.0), (Dallas, 225.0), (Atlanta, 702.0), (Miami,
     968.0)]
Detroit -> [(Chicago, 238.0), (Boston, 613.0), (Washington, 396.0), (New York,
     482.0)]
Philadelphia -> [(New York, 81.0), (Washington, 123.0)]
Washington -> [(Atlanta, 543.0), (Miami, 923.0), (Detroit, 396.0),
     (Philadelphia, 123.0)]
```

4.4.2 Finding the minimum spanning tree

A *tree* is a special kind of graph that has one, and only one, path between any two verti-ces. This implies that there are no *cycles* in a tree (which is sometimes called *acyclic*). A cycle can be thought of as a loop: if it is possible to traverse a graph from a starting ver-tex, never repeat any edges, and get back to the same starting vertex, then it has a cycle. Any connected graph that is not a tree can become a tree by pruning edges. Fig-ure 4.6 illustrates pruning an edge to turn a graph into a tree.

Figure 4.6 In the left graph, a cycle exists between vertices B, C, and D, so it is not a tree. In the right graph, the edge connecting C and D has been pruned, so the graph is a tree.

A *connected* graph is a graph that has some way of getting from any vertex to any other vertex. (All of the graphs we are looking at in this chapter are connected.) A *spanning tree* is a tree that connects every vertex in a graph. A *minimum spanning tree* is a tree that connects every vertex in a weighted graph with the minimum total weight (compared to other spanning trees). For every connected weighted graph, it is possible to efficiently find its minimum spanning tree.

Whew—that was a lot of terminology! The point is that finding a minimum spanning tree is the same as finding a way to connect every vertex in a weighted graph with the minimum weight. This is an important and practical problem for anyone designing a network (transportation network, computer network, and so on): how can every node in the network be connected for the minimum cost? That cost may be in terms of wire, track, road, or anything else. For instance, for a telephone network, another way of posing the problem is, "What is the minimum length of cable one needs to connect every phone?"

CALCULATING THE TOTAL WEIGHT OF A WEIGHTED PATH

Before we develop a method for finding a minimum spanning tree, we will develop a function we can use to test the total weight of a solution. The solution to the minimum spanning tree problem will consist of a list of weighted edges that compose the tree. For our purposes, we will think about a weighted path as a list of `WeightedEdges`. We will define a `totalWeight()` method that takes a list of `WeightedEdges` and finds the total weight that results from adding all of its edges' weights together. Note that this method, and the rest in this chapter, will be added to the existing `WeightedGraph` class.

> **Listing 4.10   WeightedGraph.java continued**

```
public static double totalWeight(List<WeightedEdge> path) {
    return path.stream().mapToDouble(we -> we.weight).sum();
}
```

JARNÍK'S ALGORITHM

Jarník's algorithm for finding a minimum spanning tree works by dividing a graph into two parts: the vertices in the still-being-assembled minimum spanning tree and the vertices not yet in the minimum spanning tree. It takes the following steps:

1 Pick an arbitrary vertex to include in the minimum spanning tree.
2 Find the lowest-weight edge connecting the minimum spanning tree to the vertices not yet in the minimum spanning tree.
3 Add the vertex at the end of that minimum edge to the minimum spanning tree.
4 Repeat steps 2 and 3 until every vertex in the graph is in the minimum spanning tree.

NOTE Jarník's algorithm is commonly referred to as Prim's algorithm. Two Czech mathematicians, Otakar Borůvka and Vojtěch Jarník, interested in minimizing the cost of laying electric lines in the late 1920s, came up with algorithms to solve the problem of finding a minimum spanning tree. Their algorithms were "rediscovered" decades later by others.[3]

---

[3] Helena Durnová, "Otakar Borůvka (1899-1995) and the Minimum Spanning Tree" (Institute of Mathematics of the Czech Academy of Sciences, 2006), http://mng.bz/O2vj.

To run Jarník's algorithm efficiently, a priority queue is used (see chapter 2 for more on priority queues). Every time a new vertex is added to the minimum spanning tree, all of its outgoing edges that link to vertices outside the tree are added to the priority queue. The lowest-weight edge is always popped off the priority queue, and the algorithm keeps executing until the priority queue is empty. This ensures that the lowest-weight edges are always added to the tree first. Edges that connect to vertices already in the tree are ignored when they are popped.

The following code for mst() is the full implementation of Jarník's algorithm,[4] along with a utility function for printing a weighted path.

WARNING Jarník's algorithm will not necessarily work correctly in a graph with directed edges. It also will not work in a graph that is not connected.

Listing 4.11 WeightedGraph.java continued

```java
public List<WeightedEdge> mst(int start) {
    LinkedList<WeightedEdge> result = new LinkedList<>(); // mst
    if (start < 0 || start > (getVertexCount() - 1)) {
        return result;
    }
    PriorityQueue<WeightedEdge> pq = new PriorityQueue<>();
    boolean[] visited = new boolean[getVertexCount()]; // seen it

    // this is like a "visit" inner function
    IntConsumer visit = index -> {
        visited[index] = true; // mark as visited
        for (WeightedEdge edge : edgesOf(index)) {
            // add all edges coming from here to pq
            if (!visited[edge.v]) {
                pq.offer(edge);
            }
        }
    };

    visit.accept(start); // the start vertex is where we begin
    while (!pq.isEmpty()) { // keep going while there are edges
        WeightedEdge edge = pq.poll();
        if (visited[edge.v]) {
            continue; // don't ever revisit
        }
        // this is the current smallest, so add it to solution
        result.add(edge);
        visit.accept(edge.v); // visit where this connects
    }

    return result;
}
```

---

[4] Inspired by a solution by Robert Sedgewick and Kevin Wayne, *Algorithms*, 4th ed. (Addison-Wesley Professional, 2011), p. 619.

```
public void printWeightedPath(List<WeightedEdge> wp) {
    for (WeightedEdge edge : wp) {
        System.out.println(vertexAt(edge.u) + " "
        + edge.weight + "> " + vertexAt(edge.v));
    }
    System.out.println("Total Weight: " + totalWeight(wp));
}
```

Let's walk through mst(), line by line:

```
public List<WeightedEdge> mst(int start) {
    LinkedList<WeightedEdge> result = new LinkedList<>(); // mst
    if (start < 0 || start > (getVertexCount() - 1)) {
        return result;
    }
```

The algorithm returns a weighted path (List<WeightedEdge>) representing the minimum spanning tree. If it so happens that the start is invalid, mst() returns an empty list as its result. result will ultimately hold the weighted path containing the minimum spanning tree. This is where we will add WeightedEdges, as the lowest-weight edge is popped off and takes us to a new part of the graph.

```
PriorityQueue<WeightedEdge> pq = new PriorityQueue<>();
boolean[] visited = new boolean[getVertexCount()]; // seen it
```

Jarník's algorithm is considered a *greedy algorithm* because it always selects the lowest-weight edge. pq is where newly discovered edges are stored and the next-lowest-weight edge is popped. visited keeps track of vertex indices that we have already been to. This could also have been accomplished with a Set, similar to explored in bfs().

```
IntConsumer visit = index -> {
    visited[index] = true; // mark as visited
    for (WeightedEdge edge : edgesOf(index)) {
        // add all edges coming from here to pq
        if (!visited[edge.v]) {
            pq.offer(edge);
        }
    }
};
```

visit is an inner convenience function that marks a vertex as visited and adds all of its edges that connect to vertices not yet visited to pq. visit is implemented as an IntConsumer, which is just a Function that takes an int as its only parameter. In this case, that int will be the index of the vertex to be visited. Note how easy the adjacency-list model makes finding edges belonging to a particular vertex.

```
visit.accept(start); // the start vertex is where we begin
```

accept() is the IntConsumer method that causes its associated function to be run with the int parameter provided. It does not matter which vertex is visited first unless the graph is not connected. If the graph is not connected, but is instead made up of disconnected *components*, mst() will return a tree that spans the particular component that the starting vertex belongs to.

```java
while (!pq.isEmpty()) { // keep going while there are edges
    WeightedEdge edge = pq.poll();
    if (visited[edge.v]) {
        continue; // don't ever revisit
    }
    // this is the current smallest, so add it to solution
    result.add(edge);
    visit.accept(edge.v); // visit where this connects
}

return result;
```

While there are still edges on the priority queue, we pop them off and check if they lead to vertices not yet in the tree. Because the priority queue is ascending, it pops the lowest-weight edges first. This ensures that the result is indeed of minimum total weight. Any edge popped that does not lead to an unexplored vertex is ignored. Otherwise, because the edge is the lowest seen so far, it is added to the result set, and the new vertex it leads to is explored. When there are no edges left to explore, the result is returned.

As promised, let's return to the problem of connecting all 15 of the largest MSAs in the United States by Hyperloop, using a minimum amount of track. The route that accomplishes this is simply the minimum spanning tree of cityGraph2. Let's try running mst() on cityGraph2 by adding code to main().

Listing 4.12   WeightedGraph.java continued

```java
List<WeightedEdge> mst = cityGraph2.mst(0);
cityGraph2.printWeightedPath(mst);
```

Thanks to the pretty-printing printWeightedPath() method, the minimum spanning tree is easy to read:

```
Seattle 678.0> San Francisco
San Francisco 348.0> Los Angeles
Los Angeles 50.0> Riverside
Riverside 307.0> Phoenix
Phoenix 887.0> Dallas
Dallas 225.0> Houston
Houston 702.0> Atlanta
Atlanta 543.0> Washington
Washington 123.0> Philadelphia
Philadelphia 81.0> New York
New York 190.0> Boston
Washington 396.0> Detroit
Detroit 238.0> Chicago
Atlanta 604.0> Miami
Total Weight: 5372.0
```

In other words, this is the cumulatively shortest collection of edges that connects all of the MSAs in the weighted graph. The minimum length of track needed to connect all of them is 5,372 miles. Figure 4.7 illustrates the minimum spanning tree.

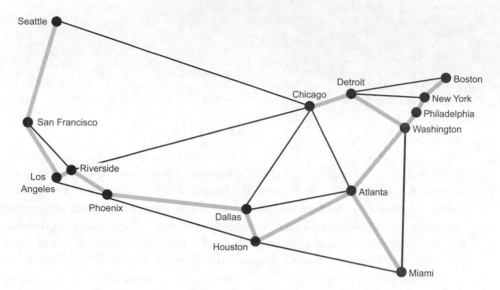

Figure 4.7   The highlighted edges represent a minimum spanning tree that connects all 15 MSAs.

4.5   *Finding shortest paths in a weighted graph*

As the Hyperloop network gets built, it is unlikely the builders will have the ambition to connect the whole country at once. Instead, it is likely the builders will want to minimize the cost to lay track between key cities. The cost to extend the network to particular cities will obviously depend on where the builders start.

Finding the cost to any city from some starting city is a version of the "single-source shortest path" problem. That problem asks, "What is the shortest path (in terms of total edge weight) from some vertex to every other vertex in a weighted graph?"

4.5.1   *Dijkstra's algorithm*

Dijkstra's algorithm solves the single-source shortest path problem. It is provided a starting vertex, and it returns the lowest-weight path to any other vertex on a weighted graph. It also returns the minimum total weight to every other vertex from the starting vertex. Dijkstra's algorithm starts at the single-source vertex and then continually explores the closest vertices to the starting vertex. For this reason, like Jarník's algorithm, Dijkstra's algorithm is greedy. When Dijkstra's algorithm encounters a new vertex, it keeps track of how far it is from the starting vertex and updates this value if it ever finds a shorter path. It also keeps track of which edge got it to each vertex.

Here are all of the algorithm's steps:

1 Add the starting vertex to a priority queue.
2 Pop the closest vertex from the priority queue (at the beginning, this is just the starting vertex); we'll call it the current vertex.
3 Look at all of the neighbors connected to the current vertex. If they have not previously been recorded, or if the edge offers a new shortest path to them, then for each of them record its distance from the start, record the edge that produced this distance, and add the new vertex to the priority queue.
4 Repeat steps 2 and 3 until the priority queue is empty.
5 Return the shortest distance to every vertex from the starting vertex and the path to get to each of them.

Our code for Dijkstra's algorithm includes `DijkstraNode`, a simple data structure for keeping track of costs associated with each vertex explored so far and for comparing them. This is similar to the `Node` class in chapter 2. It also includes `DijkstraResult`, a class for pairing the distances calculated by the algorithm and the paths calculated by the algorithm. And, finally, it includes utility functions for converting the returned array of distances to something easier to use for looking up by vertex and for calculating a shortest path to a particular destination vertex from the path dictionary returned by `dijkstra()`.

Without further ado, here is the code for Dijkstra's algorithm. We will go over it line by line after. All of this code is again going within `WeightedGraph`.

Listing 4.13   WeightedGraph.java continued

```java
public static final class DijkstraNode implements
 Comparable<DijkstraNode> {
    public final int vertex;
    public final double distance;

    public DijkstraNode(int vertex, double distance) {
        this.vertex = vertex;
        this.distance = distance;
    }

    @Override
    public int compareTo(DijkstraNode other) {
        Double mine = distance;
        Double theirs = other.distance;
        return mine.compareTo(theirs);
    }
}

public static final class DijkstraResult {
    public final double[] distances;
    public final Map<Integer, WeightedEdge> pathMap;
```

```java
        public DijkstraResult(double[] distances, Map<Integer, WeightedEdge>
    pathMap) {
            this.distances = distances;
            this.pathMap = pathMap;
        }
    }

    public DijkstraResult dijkstra(V root) {
        int first = indexOf(root); // find starting index
        // distances are unknown at first
        double[] distances = new double[getVertexCount()];
        distances[first] = 0; // root's distance to root is 0
        boolean[] visited = new boolean[getVertexCount()];
        visited[first] = true;
        // how we got to each vertex
        HashMap<Integer, WeightedEdge> pathMap = new HashMap<>();
        PriorityQueue<DijkstraNode> pq = new PriorityQueue<>();
        pq.offer(new DijkstraNode(first, 0));

        while (!pq.isEmpty()) {
            int u = pq.poll().vertex; // explore next closest vertex
            double distU = distances[u]; // should already have seen
            // look at every edge/vertex from the vertex in question
            for (WeightedEdge we : edgesOf(u)) {
                // the old distance to this vertex
                double distV = distances[we.v];
                // the new distance to this vertex
                double pathWeight = we.weight + distU;
                // new vertex or found shorter path?
                if (!visited[we.v] || (distV > pathWeight)) {
                    visited[we.v] = true;
                    // update the distance to this vertex
                    distances[we.v] = pathWeight;
                    // update the edge on the shortest path
                    pathMap.put(we.v, we);
                    // explore it in the future
                    pq.offer(new DijkstraNode(we.v, pathWeight));
                }
            }
        }

        return new DijkstraResult(distances, pathMap);
    }

    // Helper function to get easier access to dijkstra results
    public Map<V, Double> distanceArrayToDistanceMap(double[] distances) {
        HashMap<V, Double> distanceMap = new HashMap<>();
        for (int i = 0; i < distances.length; i++) {
            distanceMap.put(vertexAt(i), distances[i]);
        }
        return distanceMap;
    }

    // Takes a map of edges to reach each node and returns a list of
    // edges that goes from *start* to *end*
```

```java
public static List<WeightedEdge> pathMapToPath(int start, int end,
 Map<Integer, WeightedEdge> pathMap) {
    if (pathMap.size() == 0) {
        return List.of();
    }
    LinkedList<WeightedEdge> path = new LinkedList<>();
    WeightedEdge edge = pathMap.get(end);
    path.add(edge);
    while (edge.u != start) {
        edge = pathMap.get(edge.u);
        path.add(edge);
    }
    Collections.reverse(path);
    return path;
}
```

The first few lines of `dijkstra()` use data structures you have become familiar with, except for `distances`, which is a placeholder for the distances to every vertex in the graph from the root. Initially all of these distances are `0`, because we do not yet know how far each of them is; that is what we are using Dijkstra's algorithm to figure out!

```java
public DijkstraResult dijkstra(V root) {
    int first = indexOf(root); // find starting index
    // distances are unknown at first
    double[] distances = new double[getVertexCount()];
    distances[first] = 0; // root's distance to root is 0
    boolean[] visited = new boolean[getVertexCount()];
    visited[first] = true;
    // how we got to each vertex
    HashMap<Integer, WeightedEdge> pathMap = new HashMap<>();
    PriorityQueue<DijkstraNode> pq = new PriorityQueue<>();
    pq.offer(new DijkstraNode(first, 0));
```

The first node pushed on to the priority queue contains the root vertex.

```java
    while (!pq.isEmpty()) {
        int u = pq.poll().vertex; // explore next closest vertex
        double distU = distances[u]; // should already have seen
```

We keep running Dijkstra's algorithm until the priority queue is empty. `u` is the current vertex we are searching from, and `distU` is the stored distance for getting to `u` along known routes. Every vertex explored at this stage has already been found, so it must have a known distance.

```java
        // look at every edge/vertex from the vertex in question
        for (WeightedEdge we : edgesOf(u)) {
            // the old distance to this vertex
            double distV = distances[we.v];
            // the new distance to this vertex
            double pathWeight = we.weight + distU;
```

Next, every edge connected to u is explored. distV is the distance to any known vertex attached by an edge from u. pathWeight is the distance using the new route being explored.

```
// new vertex or found shorter path?
if (!visited[we.v] || (distV > pathWeight)) {
    visited[we.v] = true;
    // update the distance to this vertex
    distances[we.v] = pathWeight;
    // update the edge on the shortest path to this vertex
    pathMap.put(we.v, we);
    // explore it in the future
    pq.offer(new DijkstraNode(we.v, pathWeight));
}
```

If we have found a vertex that has not yet been explored (!visited[we.v]), or we have found a new, shorter path to it (distV > pathWeight), we record that new shortest distance to v and the edge that got us there. Finally, we push any vertices that have new paths to them to the priority queue.

```
return new DijkstraResult(distances, pathMap);
```

dijkstra() returns both the distances to every vertex in the weighted graph from the root vertex and the pathMap that can unlock the shortest paths to them.

It is safe to run Dijkstra's algorithm now. We will start by finding the distance from Los Angeles to every other MSA in the graph. Then we will find the shortest path between Los Angeles and Boston. Finally, we will use printWeightedPath() to pretty-print the result. The following can go into main().

Listing 4.14   WeightedGraph.java continued

```
System.out.println(); // spacing

DijkstraResult dijkstraResult = cityGraph2.dijkstra("Los Angeles");
Map<String, Double> nameDistance =
    cityGraph2.distanceArrayToDistanceMap(dijkstraResult.distances);
System.out.println("Distances from Los Angeles:");
nameDistance.forEach((name, distance) -> System.out.println(name + " : " +
    distance));

System.out.println(); // spacing

System.out.println("Shortest path from Los Angeles to Boston:");
List<WeightedEdge> path = pathMapToPath(cityGraph2.indexOf("Los Angeles"),
    cityGraph2.indexOf("Boston"), dijkstraResult.pathMap);
cityGraph2.printWeightedPath(path);
```

Your output should look something like this:

```
Distances from Los Angeles:
New York : 2474.0
```

```
Detroit : 1992.0
Seattle : 1026.0
Chicago : 1754.0
Washington : 2388.0
Miami : 2340.0
San Francisco : 348.0
Atlanta : 1965.0
Phoenix : 357.0
Los Angeles : 0.0
Dallas : 1244.0
Philadelphia : 2511.0
Riverside : 50.0
Boston : 2605.0
Houston : 1372.0


Shortest path from Los Angeles to Boston:
Los Angeles 50.0> Riverside
Riverside 1704.0> Chicago
Chicago 238.0> Detroit
Detroit 613.0> Boston
Total Weight: 2605.0
```

You may have noticed that Dijkstra's algorithm has some resemblance to Jarník's algorithm. They are both greedy, and it is possible to implement them using quite similar code if one is sufficiently motivated. Another algorithm that Dijkstra's algorithm resembles is A* from chapter 2. A* can be thought of as a modification of Dijkstra's algorithm. Add a heuristic and restrict Dijkstra's algorithm to finding a single destination, and the two algorithms are the same.

> **NOTE** Dijkstra's algorithm is designed for graphs with positive weights. Graphs with negatively weighted edges can pose a challenge for Dijkstra's algorithm and will require modification or an alternative algorithm.

4.6   *Real-world applications*

A huge amount of our world can be represented using graphs. You have seen in this chapter how effective they are for working with transportation networks, but many other kinds of networks have the same essential optimization problems: telephone networks, computer networks, utility networks (electricity, plumbing, and so on). As a result, graph algorithms are essential for efficiency in the telecommunications, shipping, transportation, and utility industries.

Retailers must handle complex distribution problems. Stores and warehouses can be thought of as vertices and the distances between them as edges. The algorithms are the same. The internet itself is a giant graph, with each connected device a vertex and each wired or wireless connection being an edge. Whether a business is saving fuel or wire, minimum spanning tree and shortest path problem-solving are useful for more than just games. Some of the world's most famous brands became successful by optimizing graph problems: think of Walmart building out an efficient distribution network,

Google indexing the web (a giant graph), and FedEx finding the right set of hubs to connect the world's addresses.

Some obvious applications of graph algorithms are social networks and map applications. In a social network, people are vertices, and connections (friendships on Facebook, for instance) are edges. In fact, one of Facebook's most prominent developer tools is known as the Graph API (https://developers.facebook.com/docs/graph-api). In map applications like Apple Maps and Google Maps, graph algorithms are used to provide directions and calculate trip times.

Several popular video games also make explicit use of graph algorithms. Mini-Metro and Ticket to Ride are two examples of games that closely mimic the problems solved in this chapter.

4.7   *Exercises*

1   Add support to the graph framework for removing edges and vertices.
2   Add support to the graph framework for directed graphs (digraphs).
3   Use this chapter's graph framework to prove or disprove the classic Seven Bridges of Königsberg problem, as described on Wikipedia: https://en.wikipedia.org/wiki/Seven_Bridges_of_Königsberg.

Genetic algorithms 5

Genetic algorithms are not used for everyday programmatic problems. They are called upon when traditional algorithmic approaches are insufficient for arriving at a solution to a problem in a reasonable amount of time. In other words, genetic algorithms are usually reserved for complex problems without easy solutions. If you need a sense of what some of these complex problems might be, feel free to read ahead in section 5.7 before proceeding. One interesting example, though, is protein-ligand docking and drug design. Computational biologists need to design molecules that will bind to receptors to deliver drugs. There may be no obvious algorithm for designing a particular molecule, but as you will see, sometimes genetic algorithms can provide an answer without much direction beyond a definition of the goal of a problem.

5.1 *Biological background*

In biology, the theory of evolution is an explanation of how genetic mutation, coupled with the constraints of an environment, leads to changes in organisms over time (including speciation—the creation of new species). The mechanism by which the well-adapted organisms succeed and the less well-adapted organisms fail is known as *natural selection*. Each generation of a species will include individuals with different (and sometimes new) traits that come about through genetic mutation. All individuals compete for limited resources to survive, and because there are more individuals than there are resources, some individuals must die.

An individual with a mutation that makes it better adapted for survival in its environment will have a higher probability of living and reproducing. Over time, the better-adapted individuals in an environment will have more children and through inheritance will pass on their mutations to those children. Therefore, a mutation that benefits survival is likely to eventually proliferate among a population.

For example, if bacteria are being killed by a specific antibiotic, and one individual bacterium in the population has a mutation in a gene that makes it more resistant to the antibiotic, it is more likely to survive and reproduce. If the antibiotic is continually applied over time, the children who have inherited the gene for antibiotic resistance will also be more likely to reproduce and have children of their own. Eventually the whole population may gain the mutation, as continued assault by the antibiotic kills off the individuals without the mutation. The antibiotic does not cause the mutation to develop, but it does lead to the proliferation of individuals with the mutation.

Natural selection has been applied in spheres beyond biology. Social Darwinism is natural selection applied to the sphere of social theory. In computer science, genetic algorithms are a simulation of natural selection to solve computational challenges.

A genetic algorithm includes a *population* (group) of individuals known as *chromosomes*. The chromosomes, each composed of *genes* that specify their traits, compete to solve some problem. How well a chromosome solves a problem is defined by a *fitness function*.

The genetic algorithm goes through *generations*. In each generation, the chromosomes that are more fit are more likely to be *selected* to reproduce. There is also a probability in each generation that two chromosomes will have their genes merged. This is known as *crossover*. And finally, there is the important possibility in each generation that a gene in a chromosome may *mutate* (randomly change).

After the fitness function of some individual in the population crosses some specified threshold, or the algorithm runs through some specified maximum number of generations, the best individual (the one that scored highest in the fitness function) is returned.

Genetic algorithms are not a good solution for all problems. They depend on three partially or fully *stochastic* (randomly determined) operations: selection, crossover, and mutation. Therefore, they may not find an optimal solution in a reasonable amount of time. For most problems, more deterministic algorithms exist with better guarantees. But there are problems for which no fast deterministic algorithm is known to exist. In these cases, genetic algorithms are a good choice.

5.2   *A generic genetic algorithm*

Genetic algorithms are often highly specialized and tuned for a particular application. In this chapter, we will define a generic genetic algorithm that can be used with multiple problems while not being particularly well tuned for any of them. It will include some configurable options, but the goal is to show the algorithm's fundamentals instead of its tunability.

We will start by defining an interface for the individuals that the generic algorithm can operate on. The abstract class `Chromosome` defines five essential features. A chromosome must be able to do the following:

- Determine its own fitness
- Implement crossover (combine itself with another of the same type to create children)—in other words, mix itself with another chromosome
- Mutate—make a small, fairly random change in itself
- Copy itself
- Compare itself to other chromosomes of the same type

Here is the code for Chromosome, codifying these five needs.

Listing 5.1 Chromosome.java

```java
package chapter5;

import java.util.List;

public abstract class Chromosome<T extends Chromosome<T>> implements
    Comparable<T> {
    public abstract double fitness();

    public abstract List<T> crossover(T other);

    public abstract void mutate();

    public abstract T copy();

    @Override
    public int compareTo(T other) {
        Double mine = this.fitness();
        Double theirs = other.fitness();
        return mine.compareTo(theirs);
    }
}
```

NOTE You'll notice that Chromosome's generic type T is bound to Chromosome itself (Chromosome<T extends Chromosome<T>>). This means that anything that fills in for type T must be a subclass of Chromosome. This is helpful for the methods crossover(), copy(), and compareTo() since we want the implementations of these methods to be operating with relation to other chromosomes of the same type.

We will implement the algorithm itself (the code that will manipulate chromosomes) as a generic class that is open to subclassing for future specialized applications. Before we do so, though, let's revisit the description of a genetic algorithm from the beginning of the chapter and clearly define the steps that a genetic algorithm takes:

1 Create an initial population of random chromosomes for the first generation of the algorithm.
2 Measure the fitness of each chromosome in this generation of the population. If any exceeds the threshold, return it, and the algorithm ends.

3　Select some individuals to reproduce, with a higher probability of selecting those with the highest fitness.

4　Crossover (combine), with some probability, some of the selected chromosomes to create children that represent the population of the next generation.

5　Mutate, usually with a low probability, some of those chromosomes. The population of the new generation is now complete, and it replaces the population of the last generation.

6　Return to step 2 unless the maximum number of generations has been reached. If that is the case, return the best chromosome found so far.

This general outline of a genetic algorithm (illustrated in figure 5.1) is missing a lot of important details. How many chromosomes should be in the population? What is the threshold that stops the algorithm? How should the chromosomes be selected for reproduction? How should they be combined (crossover) and at what probability? At what probability should mutations occur? How many generations should be run?

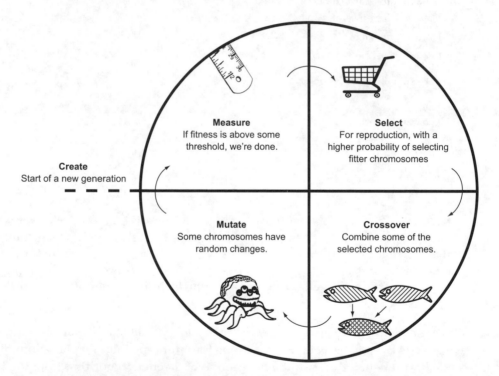

Figure 5.1　The general outline of a genetic algorithm

All of these points will be configurable in our `GeneticAlgorithm` class. We will define it piece by piece so we can talk about each piece separately.

Listing 5.2 GeneticAlgorithm.java

```java
package chapter5;

import java.util.ArrayList;
import java.util.Collections;
import java.util.List;
import java.util.Random;

public class GeneticAlgorithm<C extends Chromosome<C>> {

    public enum SelectionType {
        ROULETTE, TOURNAMENT;
    }
```

GeneticAlgorithm takes a generic type that conforms to Chromosome, and its name is C. The enum SelectionType is an internal type used for specifying the selection method used by the algorithm. The two most common genetic algorithm selection methods are known as *roulette-wheel selection* (sometimes called *fitness proportionate selection*) and *tournament selection*. The former gives every chromosome a chance of being picked, proportionate to its fitness. In tournament selection, a certain number of random chromosomes are challenged against one another, and the one with the best fitness is selected.

Listing 5.3 GeneticAlgorithm.java continued

```java
    private ArrayList<C> population;
    private double mutationChance;
    private double crossoverChance;
    private SelectionType selectionType;
    private Random random;

    public GeneticAlgorithm(List<C> initialPopulation, double mutationChance,
      double crossoverChance, SelectionType selectionType) {
        this.population = new ArrayList<>(initialPopulation);
        this.mutationChance = mutationChance;
        this.crossoverChance = crossoverChance;
        this.selectionType = selectionType;
        this.random = new Random();
    }
```

The preceding constructor defines several properties of the genetic algorithm that will be configured at the time of creation. initialPopulation is the chromosomes in the first generation of the algorithm. mutationChance is the probability of each chromosome in each generation mutating. crossoverChance is the probability that two parents selected to reproduce have children that are a mixture of their genes; otherwise, the children are just duplicates of the parents. Finally, selectionType is the type of selection method to use, as delineated by the enum SelectionType.

In our example problems later in the chapter, population is initialized with a random set of chromosomes. In other words, the first generation of chromosomes is just composed of random individuals. This is a point of potential optimization for a more sophisticated genetic algorithm. Instead of starting with purely random individuals, the first generation could contain individuals that are closer to the solution, through some knowledge of the problem. This is referred to as *seeding*.

Now we will examine the two selection methods that our class supports.

Listing 5.4   GeneticAlgorithm.java continued

```java
// Use the probability distribution wheel to pick numPicks individuals
private List<C> pickRoulette(double[] wheel, int numPicks) {
    List<C> picks = new ArrayList<>();
    for (int i = 0; i < numPicks; i++) {
        double pick = random.nextDouble();
        for (int j = 0; j < wheel.length; j++) {
            pick -= wheel[j];
            if (pick <= 0) { // went "over", leads to a pick
                picks.add(population.get(j));
                break;
            }
        }
    }
    return picks;
}
```

Roulette-wheel selection is based on each chromosome's proportion of fitness to the sum of all fitness values in a generation. The chromosomes with the highest fitness have a better chance of being picked. The values that represent each chromosome's percentage of total fitness are provided in the parameter wheel. These percentages are represented by floating-point values between 0 and 1. A random number (pick) between 0 and 1 is used to figure out which chromosome to select. The algorithm works by decreasing pick by each chromosome's proportional fitness value sequentially. When it crosses 0, that's the chromosome to select.

Does it make sense to you why this process results in each chromosome being pickable by its proportion? If not, think about it with pencil and paper. Consider drawing a proportional roulette wheel, as in figure 5.2.

The most basic form of tournament selection is simpler than roulette-wheel selection. Instead of figuring out proportions, we simply pick numParticipants chromosomes from the whole population at random. The numPicks chromosomes with the best fitness out of the randomly selected bunch win.

Listing 5.5   GeneticAlgorithm.java continued

```java
// Pick a certain number of individuals via a tournament
private List<C> pickTournament(int numParticipants, int numPicks) {
    // Find numParticipants random participants to be in the tournament
    Collections.shuffle(population);
    List<C> tournament = population.subList(0, numParticipants);
    // Find the numPicks highest fitnesses in the tournament
    Collections.sort(tournament, Collections.reverseOrder());
    return tournament.subList(0, numPicks);
}
```

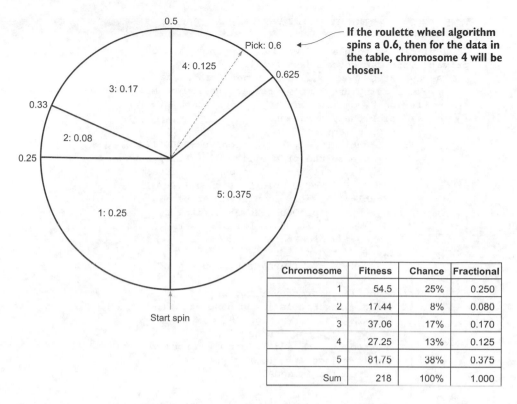

Figure 5.2   An example of roulette-wheel selection in action

Chromosome	Fitness	Chance	Fractional
1	54.5	25%	0.250
2	17.44	8%	0.080
3	37.06	17%	0.170
4	27.25	13%	0.125
5	81.75	38%	0.375
Sum	218	100%	1.000

The code for `pickTournament()` first uses `shuffle()` to randomize the order of the population, and then takes the first `numParticipants` from the population. This is just a simple way of getting `numParticipants` random chromosomes. Next, it sorts the participating chromosomes by their fitness and returns the `numPicks` most fit participants.

What is the right number for `numParticipants`? As with many parameters in a genetic algorithm, trial and error may be the best way to determine it. One thing to keep in mind is that a higher number of participants in the tournament leads to less diversity in the population, because chromosomes with poor fitness are more likely to be eliminated in matchups.[1] More sophisticated forms of tournament selection may pick individuals that are not the best, but are second or third best, based on some kind of decreasing probability model.

These two methods, `pickRoulette()` and `pickTournament()`, are used for selection, which occurs during reproduction. Reproduction is implemented in `reproduce-AndReplace()`, and it also takes care of ensuring that a new population of an equal number of chromosomes replaces the chromosomes in the last generation.

---

[1]   Artem Sokolov and Darrell Whitley, "Unbiased Tournament Selection," GECCO '05 (June 25–29, 2005, Washington, D.C., U.S.A.), http://mng.bz/S716.

Listing 5.6   GeneticAlgorithm.java continued

```java
// Replace the population with a new generation of individuals
private void reproduceAndReplace() {
    ArrayList<C> nextPopulation = new ArrayList<>();
    // keep going until we've filled the new generation
    while (nextPopulation.size() < population.size()) {
        // pick the two parents
        List<C> parents;
        if (selectionType == SelectionType.ROULETTE) {
            // create the probability distribution wheel
            double totalFitness = population.stream()
                    .mapToDouble(C::fitness).sum();
            double[] wheel = population.stream()
                    .mapToDouble(C -> C.fitness()
                        / totalFitness).toArray();
            parents = pickRoulette(wheel, 2);
        } else { // tournament
            parents = pickTournament(population.size() / 2, 2);
        }
        // potentially crossover the 2 parents
        if (random.nextDouble() < crossoverChance) {
            C parent1 = parents.get(0);
            C parent2 = parents.get(1);
            nextPopulation.addAll(parent1.crossover(parent2));
        } else { // just add the two parents
            nextPopulation.addAll(parents);
        }
    }
    // if we have an odd number, we'll have 1 extra, so we remove it
    if (nextPopulation.size() > population.size()) {
        nextPopulation.remove(0);
    }
    // replace the reference/generation
    population = nextPopulation;
}
```

In reproduceAndReplace(), the following steps occur in broad strokes:

1 Two chromosomes, called parents, are selected for reproduction using one of the two selection methods. For tournament selection, we always run the tournament among half of the total population, but this too could be a configuration option.

2 There is crossoverChance that the two parents will be combined to produce two new chromosomes, in which case they are added to nextPopulation. If there are no children, the two parents are just added to nextPopulation.

3 If nextPopulation has as many chromosomes as population, it replaces it. Otherwise, we return to step 1.

The method that implements mutation, mutate(), is very simple, with the details of how to perform a mutation being left to individual chromosomes. Each of our chromosome implementations will know how to mutate itself.

Listing 5.7 GeneticAlgorithm.java continued

```java
    // With mutationChance probability, mutate each individual
    private void mutate() {
        for (C individual : population) {
            if (random.nextDouble() < mutationChance) {
                individual.mutate();
            }
        }
    }
```

We now have all of the building blocks needed to run the genetic algorithm. `run()` coordinates the measurement, reproduction (which includes selection), and mutation steps that bring the population from one generation to the next. It also keeps track of the best (fittest) chromosome found at any point in the search.

Listing 5.8 GeneticAlgorithm.java continued

```java
    // Run the genetic algorithm for maxGenerations iterations
    // and return the best individual found
    public C run(int maxGenerations, double threshold) {
        C best = Collections.max(population).copy();
        for (int generation = 0; generation < maxGenerations; generation++) {
            // early exit if we beat threshold
            if (best.fitness() >= threshold) {
                return best;
            }
            // Debug printout
            System.out.println("Generation " + generation +
                    " Best " + best.fitness() +
                    " Avg " + population.stream()
                .mapToDouble(C::fitness).average().orElse(0.0));
            reproduceAndReplace();
            mutate();
            C highest = Collections.max(population);
            if (highest.fitness() > best.fitness()) {
                best = highest.copy();
            }
        }
        return best;
    }
}
```

`best` keeps track of the best chromosome found so far. The main loop executes `max-Generations` times. If any chromosome meets or exceeds `threshold` in fitness, it is returned, and the loop ends early. Otherwise, it calls `reproduceAndReplace()` as well as `mutate()` to create the next generation and run the loop again. If `maxGenerations` is reached, the best chromosome found so far is returned.

5.3   *A naive test*

The generic genetic algorithm, `GeneticAlgorithm`, will work with any type that implements `Chromosome`. As a test, we will start by implementing a simple problem that can be easily solved using traditional methods. We will try to maximize the equation $6x - x^2 + 4y - y^2$. In other words, what values for x and y in that equation will yield the largest number?

The maximizing values can be found, using calculus, by taking partial derivatives and setting each equal to zero. The result is $x = 3$ and $y = 2$. Can our genetic algorithm reach the same result without using calculus? Let's dig in.

Listing 5.9   SimpleEquation.java

```java
package chapter5;

import java.util.ArrayList;
import java.util.List;
import java.util.Random;

public class SimpleEquation extends Chromosome<SimpleEquation> {
    private int x, y;

    private static final int MAX_START = 100;

    public SimpleEquation(int x, int y) {
        this.x = x;
        this.y = y;
    }

    public static SimpleEquation randomInstance() {
        Random random = new Random();
        return new SimpleEquation(random.nextInt(MAX_START),
     random.nextInt(MAX_START));
    }

    // 6x - x^2 + 4y - y^2
    @Override
    public double fitness() {
        return 6 * x - x * x + 4 * y - y * y;
    }

    @Override
    public List<SimpleEquation> crossover(SimpleEquation other) {
        SimpleEquation child1 = new SimpleEquation(x, other.y);
        SimpleEquation child2 = new SimpleEquation(other.x, y);
        return List.of(child1, child2);
    }

    @Override
    public void mutate() {
        Random random = new Random();
        if (random.nextDouble() > 0.5) { // mutate x
```

```
            if (random.nextDouble() > 0.5) {
                x += 1;
            } else {
                x -= 1;
            }
        } else { // otherwise mutate y
            if (random.nextDouble() > 0.5) {
                y += 1;
            } else {
                y -= 1;
            }
        }

    }

    @Override
    public SimpleEquation copy() {
        return new SimpleEquation(x, y);
    }

    @Override
    public String toString() {
        return "X: " + x + " Y: " + y + " Fitness: " + fitness();
    }
```

`SimpleEquation` conforms to `Chromosome`, and true to its name, it does so as simply as possible. The genes of a `SimpleEquation` chromosome can be thought of as x and y. The method `fitness()` evaluates x and y using the equation $6x - x^2 + 4y - y^2$. The higher the value, the more fit the individual chromosome is, according to `Genetic-Algorithm`. In the case of a random instance, x and y are initially set to be random integers between 0 and 100, so `randomInstance()` does not need to do anything other than instantiate a new `SimpleEquation` with these values. To combine one `Simple-Equation` with another in `crossover()`, the y values of the two instances are simply swapped to create the two children. `mutate()` randomly increments or decrements x or y. And that is pretty much it.

Because `SimpleEquation` conforms to `Chromosome`, we can already plug it into `GeneticAlgorithm`.

Listing 5.10 SimpleEquation.java continued

```
public static void main(String[] args) {
    ArrayList<SimpleEquation> initialPopulation = new ArrayList<>();
    final int POPULATION_SIZE = 20;
    final int GENERATIONS = 100;
    final double THRESHOLD = 13.0;
    for (int i = 0; i < POPULATION_SIZE; i++) {
        initialPopulation.add(SimpleEquation.randomInstance());
    }
    GeneticAlgorithm<SimpleEquation> ga = new GeneticAlgorithm<>(
            initialPopulation,
            0.1, 0.7, GeneticAlgorithm.SelectionType.TOURNAMENT);
```

```
        SimpleEquation result = ga.run(100, 13.0);
        System.out.println(GENERATIONS, THRESHOLD);
    }

}
```

The parameters used here were derived through guess-and-check. You can try others. threshold is set to 13.0 because we already know the correct answer. When *x* = 3 and *y* = 2, the equation evaluates to 13.

If you did not previously know the answer, you might want to see the best result that could be found in a certain number of generations. In that case, you would set threshold to some arbitrarily large number. Remember, because genetic algorithms are stochastic, every run will be different.

Here is some sample output from a run in which the genetic algorithm solved the equation in seven generations:

```
Generation 0 Best -72.0 Avg -4436.95
Generation 1 Best 9.0 Avg -579.0
Generation 2 Best 9.0 Avg -38.15
Generation 3 Best 12.0 Avg 9.0
Generation 4 Best 12.0 Avg 9.2
Generation 5 Best 12.0 Avg 11.25
Generation 6 Best 12.0 Avg 11.95
X: 3 Y: 2 Fitness: 13.0
```

As you can see, it came to the proper solution derived earlier with calculus, *x* = 3 and *y* = 2. You may also note that each successive generation got closer to the right answer.

Take into consideration that the genetic algorithm took more computational power than other methods would have to find the solution. In the real world, such a simple maximization problem would not be a good use of a genetic algorithm. But its simple implementation at least suffices to prove that our genetic algorithm works.

5.4   *SEND+MORE=MONEY revisited*

In chapter 3, we solved the classic cryptarithmetic problem SEND+MORE=MONEY using a constraint-satisfaction framework. (For a refresher on what the problem is all about, look back to the description in chapter 3.) The problem can also be solved in a reasonable amount of time using a genetic algorithm.

One of the largest difficulties in formulating a problem for a genetic algorithm solution is determining how to represent it. A convenient representation for cryptarithmetic problems is to use list indices as digits.[2] Hence, to represent the 10 possible digits (0, 1, 2, 3, 4, 5, 6, 7, 8, 9), a 10-element list is required. The characters to be searched within the problem can then be shifted around from place to place. For example, if it is suspected that the solution to a problem includes the character "E" representing the

---

[2]   Reza Abbasian and Masoud Mazloom, "Solving Cryptarithmetic Problems Using Parallel Genetic Algorithm,"
    2009 Second International Conference on Computer and Electrical Engineering, http://mng.bz/RQ7V.

digit 4, then position 4 in the list will hold an "E." SEND+MORE=MONEY has eight distinct letters (S, E, N, D, M, O, R, Y), leaving two slots in the array empty. They can be filled with spaces indicating no letter.

A chromosome that represents the SEND+MORE=MONEY problem is represented in SendMoreMoney2. Note how the fitness() method is strikingly similar to satisfied() from SendMoreMoneyConstraint in chapter 3.

Listing 5.11 SendMoreMoney2.java

```java
package chapter5;

import java.util.ArrayList;
import java.util.Collections;
import java.util.List;
import java.util.Random;

public class SendMoreMoney2 extends Chromosome<SendMoreMoney2> {

    private List<Character> letters;
    private Random random;

    public SendMoreMoney2(List<Character> letters) {
        this.letters = letters;
        random = new Random();
    }

    public static SendMoreMoney2 randomInstance() {
        List<Character> letters = new ArrayList<>(
                List.of('S', 'E', 'N', 'D', 'M', 'O', 'R', 'Y', ' ', ' '));
        Collections.shuffle(letters);
        return new SendMoreMoney2(letters);
    }

    @Override
    public double fitness() {
        int s = letters.indexOf('S');
        int e = letters.indexOf('E');
        int n = letters.indexOf('N');
        int d = letters.indexOf('D');
        int m = letters.indexOf('M');
        int o = letters.indexOf('O');
        int r = letters.indexOf('R');
        int y = letters.indexOf('Y');
        int send = s * 1000 + e * 100 + n * 10 + d;
        int more = m * 1000 + o * 100 + r * 10 + e;
        int money = m * 10000 + o * 1000 + n * 100 + e * 10 + y;
        int difference = Math.abs(money - (send + more));
        return 1.0 / (difference + 1.0);
    }

    @Override
    public List<SendMoreMoney2> crossover(SendMoreMoney2 other) {
        SendMoreMoney2 child1 = new SendMoreMoney2(new ArrayList<>(letters));
```

```
        SendMoreMoney2 child2 = new SendMoreMoney2(new
    ArrayList<>(other.letters));
        int idx1 = random.nextInt(letters.size());
        int idx2 = random.nextInt(other.letters.size());
        Character l1 = letters.get(idx1);
        Character l2 = other.letters.get(idx2);
        int idx3 = letters.indexOf(l2);
        int idx4 = other.letters.indexOf(l1);
        Collections.swap(child1.letters, idx1, idx3);
        Collections.swap(child2.letters, idx2, idx4);
        return List.of(child1, child2);
    }

    @Override
    public void mutate() {
        int idx1 = random.nextInt(letters.size());
        int idx2 = random.nextInt(letters.size());
        Collections.swap(letters, idx1, idx2);
    }

    @Override
    public SendMoreMoney2 copy() {
        return new SendMoreMoney2(new ArrayList<>(letters));
    }

    @Override
    public String toString() {
        int s = letters.indexOf('S');
        int e = letters.indexOf('E');
        int n = letters.indexOf('N');
        int d = letters.indexOf('D');
        int m = letters.indexOf('M');
        int o = letters.indexOf('O');
        int r = letters.indexOf('R');
        int y = letters.indexOf('Y');
        int send = s * 1000 + e * 100 + n * 10 + d;
        int more = m * 1000 + o * 100 + r * 10 + e;
        int money = m * 10000 + o * 1000 + n * 100 + e * 10 + y;
        int difference = Math.abs(money - (send + more));
        return (send + " + " + more + " = " + money + " Difference: " +
    difference);
    }
```

There is, however, a major difference between satisfied() in chapter 3 and fitness().
Here, we return 1 / (difference + 1). difference is the absolute value of the difference between MONEY and SEND+MORE. This represents how far off the chromosome is from solving the problem. If we were trying to minimize fitness(), returning difference on its own would be fine. But because GeneticAlgorithm tries to maximize the value of fitness(), it needs to be flipped (so smaller values look like larger values), and that is why 1 is divided by difference. First, 1 is added to difference, so that a difference of 0 does not yield a fitness() of 0 but instead of 1. Table 5.1 illustrates how this works.

Table 5.1 How the equation `1 / (difference + 1)` yields fitness values for maximization

difference	difference + 1	fitness (1/(difference + 1))
0	1	1
1	2	0.5
2	3	0.33
3	4	0.25

Remember, lower differences are better, and higher fitness values are better. Because this formula causes those two facts to line up, it works well. Dividing 1 by a fitness value is a simple way to convert a minimization problem into a maximization problem. It does introduce some biases, though, so it is not foolproof.[3]

`randomInstance()` makes use of the `shuffle()` function in the `Collections` class. `crossover()` selects two random indices in the `letters` lists of both chromosomes and swaps letters so that we end up with one letter from the first chromosome in the same place in the second chromosome, and vice versa. It performs these swaps in children so that the placement of letters in the two children ends up being a combination of the parents. `mutate()` swaps two random locations in the `letters` list.

We can plug `SendMoreMoney2` into `GeneticAlgorithm` just as easily as we plugged in `SimpleEquation`. But be forewarned: This is a fairly tough problem, and it will take a long time to execute if the parameters are not well tweaked. And there's still some randomness even if one gets them right! The problem may be solved in a few seconds or a few minutes. Unfortunately, that is the nature of genetic algorithms.

Listing 5.12 SendMoreMoney2.java continued

```
public static void main(String[] args) {
    ArrayList<SendMoreMoney2> initialPopulation = new ArrayList<>();
    final int POPULATION_SIZE = 1000;
    final int GENERATIONS = 1000;
    final double THRESHOLD = 1.0;
    for (int i = 0; i < POPULATION_SIZE; i++) {
        initialPopulation.add(SendMoreMoney2.randomInstance());
    }
    GeneticAlgorithm<SendMoreMoney2> ga = new GeneticAlgorithm<>(
            initialPopulation,
            0.2, 0.7, GeneticAlgorithm.SelectionType.ROULETTE);
```

---

[3] For example, we might end up with more numbers closer to 0 than we would closer to 1 if we were to simply divide 1 by a uniform distribution of integers, which—with the subtleties of how typical microprocessors interpret floating-point numbers—could lead to some unexpected results. An alternative way to convert a minimization problem into a maximization problem is to simply flip the sign (make it negative instead of positive). However, this will only work if the values are all positive to begin with.

```
        SendMoreMoney2 result = ga.run(GENERATIONS, THRESHOLD);
        System.out.println(result);
    }

}
```

The following output is from a run that solved the problem in three generations using 1,000 individuals in each generation (as created above). See if you can mess around with the configurable parameters of GeneticAlgorithm and get a similar result with fewer individuals. Does it seem to work better with roulette selection than it does with tournament selection?

```
Generation 0 Best 0.07142857142857142 Avg 2.588160841027962E-4
Generation 1 Best 0.16666666666666666 Avg 0.005418719421172926
Generation 2 Best 0.5 Avg 0.022271971406414452
8324 + 913 = 9237 Difference: 0
```

This solution indicates that SEND = 8324, MORE = 913, and MONEY = 9237. How is that possible? It looks like letters are missing from the solution. In fact, if M = 0, there are several solutions to the problem not possible in the version from chapter 3. MORE is actually 0913 here, and MONEY is 09237. The 0 is just ignored.

5.5   *Optimizing list compression*

Suppose that we have some information we want to compress. Suppose that it is a list of items, and we do not care about the order of the items, as long as all of them are intact. What order of the items will maximize the compression ratio? Did you even know that the order of the items will affect the compression ratio for most compression algorithms?

The answer will depend on the compression algorithm used. For this example, we will use the GZIPOutputStream class from the java.util.zip package. The solution is shown here in its entirety for a list of 12 first names. If we do not run the genetic algorithm and we just run compress() on the 12 names in the order they were originally presented, the resulting compressed data will be 164 bytes.

> **Listing 5.13 ListCompression.java**

```java
package chapter5;

import java.io.ByteArrayOutputStream;
import java.io.IOException;
import java.io.ObjectOutputStream;
import java.util.ArrayList;
import java.util.Collections;
import java.util.List;
import java.util.Random;
import java.util.zip.GZIPOutputStream;

public class ListCompression extends Chromosome<ListCompression> {
```

```java
private static final List<String> ORIGINAL_LIST = List.of("Michael",
 "Sarah", "Joshua", "Narine", "David", "Sajid", "Melanie", "Daniel",
 "Wei", "Dean", "Brian", "Murat", "Lisa");
private List<String> myList;
private Random random;

public ListCompression(List<String> list) {
    myList = new ArrayList<>(list);
    random = new Random();
}

public static ListCompression randomInstance() {
    ArrayList<String> tempList = new ArrayList<>(ORIGINAL_LIST);
    Collections.shuffle(tempList);
    return new ListCompression(tempList);
}

private int bytesCompressed() {
    try {
        ByteArrayOutputStream baos = new ByteArrayOutputStream();
        GZIPOutputStream gos = new GZIPOutputStream(baos);
        ObjectOutputStream oos = new ObjectOutputStream(gos);
        oos.writeObject(myList);
        oos.close();
        return baos.size();
    } catch (IOException ioe) {
        System.out.println("Could not compress list!");
        ioe.printStackTrace();
        return 0;
    }

}

@Override
public double fitness() {
    return 1.0 / bytesCompressed();
}

@Override
public List<ListCompression> crossover(ListCompression other) {
    ListCompression child1 = new ListCompression(new
 ArrayList<>(myList));
    ListCompression child2 = new ListCompression(new
 ArrayList<>(myList));
    int idx1 = random.nextInt(myList.size());
    int idx2 = random.nextInt(other.myList.size());
    String s1 = myList.get(idx1);
    String s2 = other.myList.get(idx2);
    int idx3 = myList.indexOf(s2);
    int idx4 = other.myList.indexOf(s1);
    Collections.swap(child1.myList, idx1, idx3);
    Collections.swap(child2.myList, idx2, idx4);
    return List.of(child1, child2);
}
```

```java
@Override
public void mutate() {
    int idx1 = random.nextInt(myList.size());
    int idx2 = random.nextInt(myList.size());
    Collections.swap(myList, idx1, idx2);
}

@Override
public ListCompression copy() {
    return new ListCompression(new ArrayList<>(myList));
}

@Override
public String toString() {
    return "Order: " + myList + " Bytes: " + bytesCompressed();
}

public static void main(String[] args) {
    ListCompression originalOrder = new ListCompression(ORIGINAL_LIST);
    System.out.println(originalOrder);
    ArrayList<ListCompression> initialPopulation = new ArrayList<>();
    final int POPULATION_SIZE = 100;
    final int GENERATIONS = 100;
    final double THRESHOLD = 1.0;
    for (int i = 0; i < POPULATION_SIZE; i++) {
        initialPopulation.add(ListCompression.randomInstance());
    }
    GeneticAlgorithm<ListCompression> ga = new GeneticAlgorithm<>(
            initialPopulation,
            0.2, 0.7, GeneticAlgorithm.SelectionType.TOURNAMENT);
    ListCompression result = ga.run(GENERATIONS, THRESHOLD);
    System.out.println(result);
}
}
```

Note how similar this implementation is to the implementation from SEND+MORE= MONEY in section 5.4. The crossover() and mutate() functions are essentially the same. In both problems' solutions, we take a list of items and continually rearrange them and test those rearrangements. One could write a generic superclass for both problems' solutions that would work with a wide variety of problems. Any problem that can be represented as a list of items that needs to find its optimal order could be solved the same way. The only real point of customization for the subclasses would be their respective fitness functions.

If we run ListCompression.java, it may take a very long time to complete. This is because we don't know what constitutes the "right" answer ahead of time, unlike the prior two problems, so we have no real threshold that we are working toward. Instead, we set the number of generations and the number of individuals in each generation to an arbitrarily high number and hope for the best. What is the minimum number of bytes that rearranging the 12 names will yield in compression? Frankly, we don't know the answer to that. In my best run, using the configuration in the preceding solution, after 100 generations the genetic algorithm found an order of the 12 names that yielded 158 bytes compressed.

That's only a savings of 6 bytes over the original order—a savings of ~4%. One might say that 4% is irrelevant, but if this were a far larger list that would be transferred many times over the network, that could add up. Imagine if this were a 1 MB list that would eventually be transferred across the internet 10,000,000 times. If the genetic algorithm could optimize the order of the list for compression to save 4%, it would save ~40 kilobytes per transfer and ultimately 400 GB in bandwidth across all transfers. That's not a huge amount, but perhaps it could be significant enough that it's worth running the algorithm once to find a near optimal order for compression.

Consider this, though—we don't really know if we found the optimal order for the 12 names, let alone for the hypothetical 1 MB list. How would we know if we did? Unless we have a deep understanding of the compression algorithm, we would have to try compressing every possible order of the list. Just for a list of 12 items, that's a fairly unfeasible 479,001,600 possible orders (12!, where ! means factorial). Using a genetic algorithm that attempts to find optimality is perhaps more feasible, even if we don't know whether its ultimate solution is truly optimal.

5.6 *Challenges for genetic algorithms*

Genetic algorithms are not a panacea. In fact, they are not suitable for most problems. For any problem for which a fast deterministic algorithm exists, a genetic algorithm approach does not make sense. Their inherently stochastic nature makes their runtimes unpredictable. To solve this problem, they can be cut off after a certain number of generations. But then it is not clear if a truly optimal solution has been found.

Steven Skiena, author of one of the most popular texts on algorithms, even went so far as to write this:

> *I have never encountered any problem where genetic algorithms seemed to me the right way to attack it. Further, I have never seen any computational results reported using genetic algorithms that have favorably impressed me.*[4]

Skiena's view is a little extreme, but it is indicative of the fact that genetic algorithms should only be chosen when you are reasonably confident that a better solution does not exist, or you are exploring an unknown problem space. Another issue with genetic algorithms is determining how to represent a potential solution to a problem as a chromosome. The traditional practice is to represent most problems as binary strings (sequences of 1s and 0s, raw bits). This is often optimal in terms of space usage, and it lends itself to easy crossover functions. But most complex problems are not easily represented as divisible bit strings.

Another, more specific issue worth mentioning is challenges related to the roulette-wheel selection method described in this chapter. Roulette-wheel selection, sometimes

---

[4] Steven Skiena, *The Algorithm Design Manual*, 2nd ed. (Springer, 2009), p. 267.

referred to as *fitness proportional selection*, can lead to a lack of diversity in a population due to the dominance of relatively fit individuals each time selection is run. On the other hand, if fitness values are close together, roulette-wheel selection can lead to a lack of selection pressure.[5] Further, roulette-wheel selection, as constructed in this chapter, does not work for problems in which fitness can be measured with negative values, as in our simple equation example in section 5.3.

In short, for most problems large enough to warrant using them, genetic algorithms cannot guarantee the discovery of an optimal solution in a predictable amount of time. For this reason, they are best utilized in situations that do not call for an optimal solution, but instead for a "good enough" solution. They are fairly easy to implement, but tweaking their configurable parameters can take a lot of trial and error.

5.7   *Real-world applications*

Despite what Skiena wrote, genetic algorithms are frequently and effectively applied in a myriad of problem spaces. They are often used on hard problems that do not require perfectly optimal solutions, such as constraint-satisfaction problems too large to be solved using traditional methods. One example is complex scheduling problems.

Genetic algorithms have found many applications in computational biology. They have been used successfully for protein-ligand docking, which is a search for the configuration of a small molecule when it is bound to a receptor. This is used in pharmaceutical research and to better understand mechanisms in nature.

The Traveling Salesman Problem, which we will revisit in chapter 9, is one of the most famous problems in computer science. A traveling salesman wants to find the shortest route on a map that visits every city exactly once and brings him back to his starting location. It may sound like minimum spanning trees in chapter 4, but it is different. In the Traveling Salesman, the solution is a giant cycle that minimizes the cost to traverse it, whereas a minimum spanning tree minimizes the cost to connect every city. A person traveling a minimum spanning tree of cities may have to visit the same city twice to reach every city. Even though they sound similar, there is no reasonably timed known algorithm for finding a solution to the Traveling Salesman Problem for an arbitrary number of cities. Genetic algorithms have been shown to find suboptimal, but pretty good, solutions in short periods of time. The problem is widely applicable to the efficient distribution of goods. For example, dispatchers of FedEx and UPS trucks use software to solve the Traveling Salesman Problem every day. Algorithms that help solve the problem can cut costs in a large variety of industries.

In computer-generated art, genetic algorithms are sometimes used to mimic photographs using stochastic methods. Imagine 50 polygons placed randomly on a screen and gradually twisted, turned, moved, resized, and changed in color until they match a photograph as closely as possible. The result looks like the work of an abstract artist or, if more angular shapes are used, a stained-glass window.

---

[5] A. E. Eiben and J. E. Smith, *Introduction to Evolutionary Computation*, 2nd edition (Springer, 2015), p. 80.

Genetic algorithms are part of a larger field called *evolutionary computation.* One area of evolutionary computation closely related to genetic algorithms is *genetic programming*, in which programs use the selection, crossover, and mutation operations to modify themselves to find nonobvious solutions to programming problems. Genetic programming is not a widely used technique, but imagine a future where programs write themselves.

A benefit of genetic algorithms is that they lend themselves to easy parallelization. In the most obvious form, each population can be simulated on a separate processor. In the most granular form, each individual can be mutated and crossed, and have its fitness calculated in a separate thread. There are also many possibilities in between.

5.8   *Exercises*

1 Add support to `GeneticAlgorithm` for an advanced form of tournament selection that may sometimes choose the second- or third-best chromosome, based on a diminishing probability.

2 Add a new function to the constraint-satisfaction framework from chapter 3 that solves any arbitrary CSP using a genetic algorithm. A possible measure of fitness is the number of constraints that are resolved by a chromosome.

3 Create a class, `BitString`, that implements `Chromosome`. Recall what a bit string is from chapter 1. Then use your new class to solve the simple equation problem from section 5.3. How can the problem be encoded as a bit string?

K-means clustering

Humanity has never had more data about more facets of society than it does today. Computers are great for storing data sets, but those data sets have little value to society until they are analyzed by human beings. Computational techniques can guide humans on the road to deriving meaning from a data set.

Clustering is a computational technique that divides the points in a data set into groups. A successful clustering results in groups that contain points that are related to one another. Whether those relationships are meaningful generally requires human verification.

In clustering, the group (a.k.a. *cluster*) that a data point belongs to is not predetermined, but instead is decided during the run of the clustering algorithm. In fact, the algorithm is not guided to place any particular data point in any particular cluster by presupposed information. For this reason, clustering is considered an *unsupervised* method within the realm of machine learning. You can think of *unsupervised* as meaning *not guided by foreknowledge*.

Clustering is a useful technique when you want to learn about the structure of a data set but you do not know ahead of time its constituent parts. For example, imagine you own a grocery store, and you collect data about customers and their transactions. You want to run mobile advertisements of specials at relevant times of the week to bring customers into your store. You could try clustering your data by day of the week and demographic information. Perhaps you will find a cluster that indicates younger shoppers prefer to shop on Tuesdays, and you could use that information to run an ad specifically targeting them on that day.

6.1 Preliminaries

Our clustering algorithm will require some statistical primitives (mean, standard deviation, and so on). Since Java version 8, the Java standard library provides several useful statistical primitives via the class `DoubleSummaryStatistics` in the `util` package. We will use these primitives to develop some more sophisticated statistics. It should be noted that while we keep to the standard library in this book, there are many useful third-party statistics libraries for Java that should be utilized in performance-critical applications—notably, those dealing with big data. A veteran, battle-tested library will almost always be a better choice in terms of performance and capability than rolling your own. However, in this book we're in the business of learning by rolling our own.

For simplicity's sake, the data sets we will work with in this chapter are all expressible with the `double` type, or its object equivalent, `Double`. In the `Statistics` class that follows, the statistical primitives `sum()`, `mean()`, `max()`, and `min()` are implemented via `DoubleSummaryStatistics`. `variance()`, `std()` (standard deviation), and `zscored()` are built on top of these primitives. Their definitions follow directly from the formulas you would find in a statistics textbook.

Listing 6.1 Statistics.java

```java
package chapter6;

import java.util.DoubleSummaryStatistics;
import java.util.List;
import java.util.stream.Collectors;

public final class Statistics {
    private List<Double> list;
    private DoubleSummaryStatistics dss;

    public Statistics(List<Double> list) {
        this.list = list;
        dss = list.stream().collect(Collectors.summarizingDouble(d -> d));
    }

    public double sum() {
        return dss.getSum();
    }

    // Find the average (mean)
    public double mean() {
        return dss.getAverage();
    }

    // Find the variance sum((Xi - mean)^2) / N
    public double variance() {
        double mean = mean();
        return list.stream().mapToDouble(x -> Math.pow((x - mean), 2))
                .average().getAsDouble();
    }
```

```
    // Find the standard deviation sqrt(variance)
    public double std() {
        return Math.sqrt(variance());
    }

    // Convert elements to respective z-scores (formula z-score =
    // (x - mean) / std)
    public List<Double> zscored() {
        double mean = mean();
        double std = std();
        return list.stream()
               .map(x -> std != 0 ? ((x - mean) / std) : 0.0)
               .collect(Collectors.toList());
    }

    public double max() {
        return dss.getMax();
    }

    public double min() {
        return dss.getMin();
    }
}
```

TIP variance() finds the variance of a population. A slightly different formula, which we are not using, finds the variance of a sample. We will always be evaluating the entire population of data points at one time.

zscored() transforms each item in the list into its z-score, which is the number of standard deviations the original value is from the data set's mean. There will be more about z-scores later in the chapter.

NOTE It is beyond the purview of this book to teach elementary statistics, but you do not need more than a rudimentary understanding of mean and standard deviation to follow the rest of the chapter. If it has been a while and you need a refresher, or you never previously learned these terms, it may be worthwhile to quickly peruse a statistics resource that explains these two fundamental concepts.

All clustering algorithms work with points of data, and our implementation of k-means will be no exception. We will define a common base class called DataPoint.

Listing 6.2   DataPoint.java

```
package chapter6;

import java.util.ArrayList;
import java.util.List;

public class DataPoint {
    public final int numDimensions;
    private List<Double> originals;
    public List<Double> dimensions;
```

```java
    public DataPoint(List<Double> initials) {
        originals = initials;
        dimensions = new ArrayList<>(initials);
        numDimensions = dimensions.size();
    }

    public double distance(DataPoint other) {
        double differences = 0.0;
        for (int i = 0; i < numDimensions; i++) {
            double difference = dimensions.get(i) - other.dimensions.get(i);
            differences += Math.pow(difference, 2);
        }
        return Math.sqrt(differences);
    }

    @Override
    public String toString() {
        return originals.toString();
    }
}
```

Every data point must be human-readable for debug printing (`toString()`). Every data point type has a certain number of dimensions (`numDimensions`). The list `dimensions` stores the actual values for each of those dimensions as `doubles`. The constructor takes a list of initial values. These dimensions may later be replaced with z-scores by k-means, so we also keep a copy of the initial data in `originals` for later printing.

One final preliminary we need before we can dig into k-means is a way of calculating the distance between any two data points of the same type. There are many ways to calculate distance, but the form most commonly used with k-means is Euclidean distance. This is the distance formula familiar to most from a grade-school course in geometry, derivable from the Pythagorean theorem. In fact, we already discussed the formula and derived a version of it for two-dimensional spaces in chapter 2, where we used it to find the distance between any two locations within a maze. Our version for `DataPoint` needs to be slightly more sophisticated, because a `DataPoint` can involve any number of dimensions. The squares of each of the differences are summed, and the final value returned by `distance()` is the square root of this sum.

6.2   *The k-means clustering algorithm*

K-means is a clustering algorithm that attempts to group data points into a certain predefined number of clusters. In every round of k-means, the distance between every data point and every center of a cluster (a point known as a *centroid*) is calculated. Points are assigned to the cluster whose centroid they are closest to. Then the algorithm recalculates all of the centroids, finding the mean of each cluster's assigned points and replacing the old centroid with the new mean. The process of assigning points and recalculating centroids continues until the centroids stop moving or a certain number of iterations occurs.

Each dimension of the initial points provided to k-means needs to be comparable in magnitude. If not, k-means will skew toward clustering based on dimensions with the largest differences. The process of making different types of data (in our case, different dimensions) comparable is known as *normalization*. One common way of normalizing data is to evaluate each value based on its *z-score* (also known as *standard score*) relative to the other values of the same type. A z-score is calculated by taking a value, subtracting the mean of all of the values from it, and dividing that result by the standard deviation of all of the values. The `zscored()` function devised near the beginning of the previous section does exactly this for every value in a list of `doubles`.

The main difficulty with k-means is choosing how to assign the initial centroids. In the most basic form of the algorithm, which is what we will be implementing, the initial centroids are placed randomly within the range of the data. Another difficulty is deciding how many clusters to divide the data into (the "k" in k-means). In the classical algorithm, that number is determined by the user, but the user may not know the right number, and this will require some experimentation. We will let the user define "k."

Putting all of these steps and considerations together, here is our k-means clustering algorithm:

1 Initialize all of the data points and "k" empty clusters.
2 Normalize all of the data points.
3 Create random centroids associated with each cluster.
4 Assign each data point to the cluster of the centroid it is closest to.
5 Recalculate each centroid so it is the center (mean) of the cluster it is associated with.
6 Repeat steps 4 and 5 until a maximum number of iterations is reached or the centroids stop moving (convergence).

Conceptually, k-means is actually quite simple: In each iteration, every data point is associated with the cluster that it is closest to in terms of the cluster's center. That center moves as new points are associated with the cluster. This is illustrated in figure 6.1.

We will implement a class for maintaining state and running the algorithm, similar to `GeneticAlgorithm` in chapter 5. We will start with an internal class to represent a cluster.

Listing 6.3   KMeans.java

```
import java.util.ArrayList;
import java.util.List;
import java.util.Random;
import java.util.stream.Collectors;

public class KMeans<Point extends DataPoint> {

    public class Cluster {
        public List<Point> points;
        public DataPoint centroid;
```

```java
    public Cluster(List<Point> points, DataPoint randPoint) {
        this.points = points;
        this.centroid = randPoint;
    }
}
```

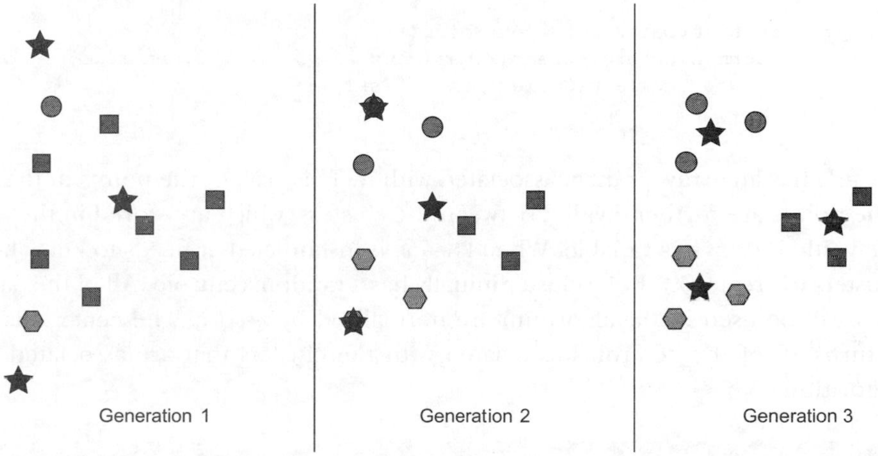

Figure 6.1 An example of k-means running through three generations on an arbitrary data set. Stars indicate centroids. Colors and shapes represent current cluster membership (which changes).

KMeans is a generic class. It works with DataPoint or any subclass of DataPoint, as defined by the Point type's bound (Point extends DataPoint). It has an internal class, Cluster, that keeps track of the individual clusters in the operation. Each Cluster has data points and a centroid associated with it.

> **NOTE** In this chapter, to condense the code size and make it more readable, we are letting some instance variables be public that would normally be accessed through getters/setters.

Now we will continue with the outer class's constructor.

Listing 6.4 KMeans.java continued

```java
private List<Point> points;
private List<Cluster> clusters;

public KMeans(int k, List<Point> points) {
    if (k < 1) { // can't have negative or zero clusters
        throw new IllegalArgumentException("k must be >= 1");
    }
    this.points = points;
    zScoreNormalize();
    // initialize empty clusters with random centroids
```

```
        clusters = new ArrayList<>();
        for (int i = 0; i < k; i++) {
            DataPoint randPoint = randomPoint();
            Cluster cluster = new Cluster(new ArrayList<Point>(), randPoint);
            clusters.add(cluster);
        }
    }

    private List<DataPoint> centroids() {
        return clusters.stream().map(cluster -> cluster.centroid)
                .collect(Collectors.toList());
    }
```

KMeans has an array, `points`, associated with it. This is all of the points in the data set. The points are further divided between the clusters, which are stored in the appropriately titled `clusters` variable. When KMeans is instantiated, it needs to know how many clusters to create (k). Every cluster initially has a random centroid. All of the data points that will be used in the algorithm are normalized by z-score. The `centroids` method returns all of the centroids associated with the clusters that are associated with the algorithm.

Listing 6.5   KMeans.java continued

```
    private List<Double> dimensionSlice(int dimension) {
        return points.stream().map(x -> x.dimensions.get(dimension))
                .collect(Collectors.toList());
    }
```

`dimensionSlice()` is a convenience method that can be thought of as returning a column of data. It will return a list composed of every value at a particular index in every data point. For instance, if the data points were of type `DataPoint`, then `dimensionSlice(0)` would return a list of the value of the first dimension of every data point. This is helpful in the following normalization method.

Listing 6.6   KMeans.java continued

```
    private void zScoreNormalize() {
        List<List<Double>> zscored = new ArrayList<>();
        for (Point point : points) {
            zscored.add(new ArrayList<Double>());
        }
        for (int dimension = 0; dimension <
        points.get(0).numDimensions; dimension++) {
            List<Double> dimensionSlice = dimensionSlice(dimension);
            Statistics stats = new Statistics(dimensionSlice);
            List<Double> zscores = stats.zscored();
            for (int index = 0; index < zscores.size(); index++) {
                zscored.get(index).add(zscores.get(index));
            }
        }
```

```
        for (int i = 0; i < points.size(); i++) {
            points.get(i).dimensions = zscored.get(i);
        }
    }
```

zScoreNormalize() replaces the values in the dimensions list of every data point with its z-scored equivalent. This uses the zscored() function that we defined for lists of double earlier. Although the values in the dimensions list are replaced, the originals list in the DataPoint are not. This is useful; the user of the algorithm can still retrieve the original values of the dimensions before normalization after the algorithm runs if they are stored in both places.

Listing 6.7   KMeans.java continued

```
    private DataPoint randomPoint() {
        List<Double> randDimensions = new ArrayList<>();
        Random random = new Random();
        for (int dimension = 0; dimension < points.get(0).numDimensions;
    dimension++) {
            List<Double> values = dimensionSlice(dimension);
            Statistics stats = new Statistics(values);
            Double randValue = random.doubles(stats.min(),
    stats.max()).findFirst().getAsDouble();
            randDimensions.add(randValue);
        }
        return new DataPoint(randDimensions);
    }
```

The preceding randomPoint() method is used in the constructor to create the initial random centroids for each cluster. It constrains the random values of each point to be within the range of the existing data points' values. It uses the constructor we specified earlier on DataPoint to create a new point from a list of values.

Now we will look at our method that finds the appropriate cluster for a data point to belong to.

Listing 6.8   KMeans.java continued

```
    // Find the closest cluster centroid to each point and assign the point
    // to that cluster
    private void assignClusters() {
        for (Point point : points) {
            double lowestDistance = Double.MAX_VALUE;
            Cluster closestCluster = clusters.get(0);
            for (Cluster cluster : clusters) {
                double centroidDistance =
                    point.distance(cluster.centroid);
                if (centroidDistance < lowestDistance) {
                    lowestDistance = centroidDistance;
                    closestCluster = cluster;
                }
            }
```

```
            closestCluster.points.add(point);
        }
    }
```

Throughout the book, we have created several functions that find the minimum or find the maximum in a list. This one is not dissimilar. In this case we are looking for the cluster centroid that has the minimum distance to each individual point. The point is then assigned to that cluster.

Listing 6.9   KMeans.java continued

```
    // Find the center of each cluster and move the centroid to there
    private void generateCentroids() {
        for (Cluster cluster : clusters) {
            // Ignore if the cluster is empty
            if (cluster.points.isEmpty()) {
                continue;
            }
            List<Double> means = new ArrayList<>();
            for (int i = 0; i < cluster.points.get(0).numDimensions; i++) {
                // needed to use in scope of closure
                int dimension = i;
                Double dimensionMean = cluster.points.stream()
                        .mapToDouble(x ->
                x.dimensions.get(dimension)).average().getAsDouble();
                means.add(dimensionMean);
            }
            cluster.centroid = new DataPoint(means);
        }
    }
```

After every point is assigned to a cluster, the new centroids are calculated. This involves calculating the mean of each dimension of every point in the cluster. The means of these dimensions are then combined to find the "mean point" in the cluster, which becomes the new centroid. Note that we cannot use dimensionSlice() here, because the points in question are a subset of all of the points (just those belonging to a particular cluster). How could dimensionSlice() be rewritten to be more generic? We will leave thinking about this as an exercise for the reader.

Now let's look at the method (and a helper) that will actually execute the algorithm.

Listing 6.10   KMeans.java continued

```
    // Check if two Lists of DataPoints are of equivalent DataPoints
    private boolean listsEqual(List<DataPoint> first, List<DataPoint> second)
    {
        if (first.size() != second.size()) {
            return false;
        }
        for (int i = 0; i < first.size(); i++) {
            for (int j = 0; j < first.get(0).numDimensions; j++) {
```

```
        if (first.get(i).dimensions.get(j).doubleValue() !=
second.get(i).dimensions.get(j).doubleValue()) {
                return false;
            }
        }
    }
    return true;
}

public List<Cluster> run(int maxIterations) {
    for (int iteration = 0; iteration < maxIterations; iteration++) {
        for (Cluster cluster : clusters) { // clear all clusters
            cluster.points.clear();
        }
        assignClusters();
        List<DataPoint> oldCentroids = new ArrayList<>(centroids());
        generateCentroids(); // find new centroids
        if (listsEqual(oldCentroids, centroids())) {
            System.out.println("Converged after " + iteration + "
iterations.");
            return clusters;
        }
    }
    return clusters;
}
```

run() is the purest expression of the original algorithm. The only change to the algorithm you may find unexpected is the removal of all points at the beginning of each iteration. If this were not to occur, the assignClusters() method, as written, would end up putting duplicate points in each cluster. listsEqual() is a helper that checks if two lists of DataPoints are holding the same points. This is useful for checking if there were no changes to the centroids between generations (indicating movement has ceased, and the algorithm should stop).

You can perform a quick test using test DataPoints and k set to 2.

Listing 6.11 KMeans.java continued

```
public static void main(String[] args) {
    DataPoint point1 = new DataPoint(List.of(2.0, 1.0, 1.0));
    DataPoint point2 = new DataPoint(List.of(2.0, 2.0, 5.0));
    DataPoint point3 = new DataPoint(List.of(3.0, 1.5, 2.5));
    KMeans<DataPoint> kmeansTest = new KMeans<>(2, List.of(point1,
point2, point3));
    List<KMeans<DataPoint>.Cluster> testClusters = kmeansTest.run(100);
    for (int clusterIndex = 0; clusterIndex < testClusters.size();
clusterIndex++) {
        System.out.println("Cluster " + clusterIndex + ": "
            + testClusters.get(clusterIndex).points);
    }
}

}
```

Because there is randomness involved, your results may vary. The expected result is something along these lines:

```
Converged after 1 iterations.
Cluster 0: [[2.0, 1.0, 1.0], [3.0, 1.5, 2.5]]
Cluster 1: [[2.0, 2.0, 5.0]]
```

6.3   *Clustering governors by age and longitude*

Every American state has a governor. In June 2017, those governors ranged in age from 42 to 79. If we take the United States from east to west, looking at each state by its longitude, perhaps we can find clusters of states with similar longitudes and similar-age governors. Figure 6.2 is a scatter plot of all 50 governors. The x-axis is state longitude, and the y-axis is governor age.

Are there any obvious clusters in figure 6.2? In this figure, the axes are not normalized. Instead, we are looking at raw data. If clusters were always obvious, there would be no need for clustering algorithms.

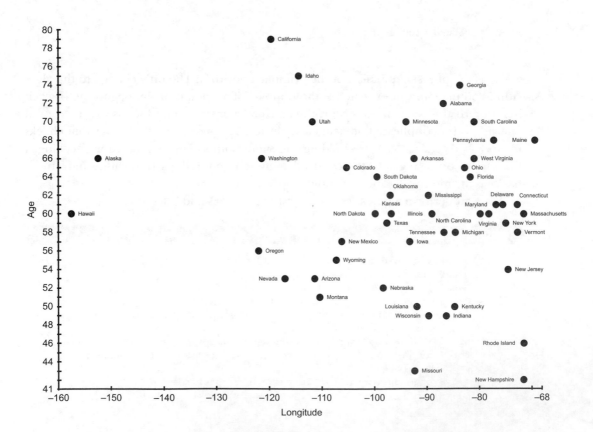

Figure 6.2   State governors, as of June 2017, plotted by state longitude and governor age

Let's try running this data set through k-means. First, we will need a way of representing an individual data point.

Listing 6.12   Governor.java

```java
package chapter6;

import java.util.ArrayList;
import java.util.List;

public class Governor extends DataPoint {
    private double longitude;
    private double age;
    private String state;

    public Governor(double longitude, double age, String state) {
        super(List.of(longitude, age));
        this.longitude = longitude;
        this.age = age;
        this.state = state;
    }

    @Override
    public String toString() {
        return state + ": (longitude: " + longitude + ", age: " + age + ")";
    }
}
```

A Governor has two named and stored dimensions: longitude and age. Other than that, Governor makes no modifications to the machinery of its superclass, DataPoint, other than an overridden toString() for pretty-printing. It would be pretty unreasonable to enter the following data manually, so check out the source code repository that accompanies this book.

Listing 6.13   Governor.java continued

```java
    public static void main(String[] args) {
        List<Governor> governors = new ArrayList<>();
        governors.add(new Governor(-86.79113, 72, "Alabama"));
        governors.add(new Governor(-152.404419, 66, "Alaska"));
        governors.add(new Governor(-111.431221, 53, "Arizona"));
        governors.add(new Governor(-92.373123, 66, "Arkansas"));
        governors.add(new Governor(-119.681564, 79, "California"));
        governors.add(new Governor(-105.311104, 65, "Colorado"));
        governors.add(new Governor(-72.755371, 61, "Connecticut"));
        governors.add(new Governor(-75.507141, 61, "Delaware"));
        governors.add(new Governor(-81.686783, 64, "Florida"));
        governors.add(new Governor(-83.643074, 74, "Georgia"));
        governors.add(new Governor(-157.498337, 60, "Hawaii"));
        governors.add(new Governor(-114.478828, 75, "Idaho"));
        governors.add(new Governor(-88.986137, 60, "Illinois"));
        governors.add(new Governor(-86.258278, 49, "Indiana"));
```

```
governors.add(new Governor(-93.210526, 57, "Iowa"));
governors.add(new Governor(-96.726486, 60, "Kansas"));
governors.add(new Governor(-84.670067, 50, "Kentucky"));
governors.add(new Governor(-91.867805, 50, "Louisiana"));
governors.add(new Governor(-69.381927, 68, "Maine"));
governors.add(new Governor(-76.802101, 61, "Maryland"));
governors.add(new Governor(-71.530106, 60, "Massachusetts"));
governors.add(new Governor(-84.536095, 58, "Michigan"));
governors.add(new Governor(-93.900192, 70, "Minnesota"));
governors.add(new Governor(-89.678696, 62, "Mississippi"));
governors.add(new Governor(-92.288368, 43, "Missouri"));
governors.add(new Governor(-110.454353, 51, "Montana"));
governors.add(new Governor(-98.268082, 52, "Nebraska"));
governors.add(new Governor(-117.055374, 53, "Nevada"));
governors.add(new Governor(-71.563896, 42, "New Hampshire"));
governors.add(new Governor(-74.521011, 54, "New Jersey"));
governors.add(new Governor(-106.248482, 57, "New Mexico"));
governors.add(new Governor(-74.948051, 59, "New York"));
governors.add(new Governor(-79.806419, 60, "North Carolina"));
governors.add(new Governor(-99.784012, 60, "North Dakota"));
governors.add(new Governor(-82.764915, 65, "Ohio"));
governors.add(new Governor(-96.928917, 62, "Oklahoma"));
governors.add(new Governor(-122.070938, 56, "Oregon"));
governors.add(new Governor(-77.209755, 68, "Pennsylvania"));
governors.add(new Governor(-71.51178, 46, "Rhode Island"));
governors.add(new Governor(-80.945007, 70, "South Carolina"));
governors.add(new Governor(-99.438828, 64, "South Dakota"));
governors.add(new Governor(-86.692345, 58, "Tennessee"));
governors.add(new Governor(-97.563461, 59, "Texas"));
governors.add(new Governor(-111.862434, 70, "Utah"));
governors.add(new Governor(-72.710686, 58, "Vermont"));
governors.add(new Governor(-78.169968, 60, "Virginia"));
governors.add(new Governor(-121.490494, 66, "Washington"));
governors.add(new Governor(-80.954453, 66, "West Virginia"));
governors.add(new Governor(-89.616508, 49, "Wisconsin"));
governors.add(new Governor(-107.30249, 55, "Wyoming"));
```

We will run k-means with k set to 2.

Listing 6.14   Governor.java continued

```
KMeans<Governor> kmeans = new KMeans<>(2, governors);
List<KMeans<Governor>.Cluster> govClusters = kmeans.run(100);
for (int clusterIndex = 0; clusterIndex < govClusters.size();
clusterIndex++) {
    System.out.printf("Cluster %d: %s%n", clusterIndex,
govClusters.get(clusterIndex).points);
    }
}


}
```

Because it starts with randomized centroids, every run of KMeans may potentially return different clusters. It takes some human analysis to see if the clusters are actually relevant. The following result is from a run that did have an interesting cluster:

```
Converged after 3 iterations.
Cluster 0: [Alabama: (longitude: -86.79113, age: 72.0), Arizona: (longitude:
-111.431221, age: 53.0), Arkansas: (longitude: -92.373123, age: 66.0),
Colorado: (longitude: -105.311104, age: 65.0), Connecticut: (longitude:
-72.755371, age: 61.0), Delaware: (longitude: -75.507141, age: 61.0),
Florida: (longitude: -81.686783, age: 64.0), Georgia: (longitude: -83.643074,
age: 74.0), Illinois: (longitude: -88.986137, age: 60.0), Indiana:
(longitude: -86.258278, age: 49.0), Iowa: (longitude: -93.210526, age: 57.0),
Kansas: (longitude: -96.726486, age: 60.0), Kentucky: (longitude: -84.670067,
age: 50.0), Louisiana: (longitude: -91.867805, age: 50.0), Maine: (longitude:
-69.381927, age: 68.0), Maryland: (longitude: -76.802101, age: 61.0),
Massachusetts: (longitude: -71.530106, age: 60.0), Michigan: (longitude:
-84.536095, age: 58.0), Minnesota: (longitude: -93.900192, age: 70.0),
Mississippi: (longitude: -89.678696, age: 62.0), Missouri: (longitude:
-92.288368, age: 43.0), Montana: (longitude: -110.454353, age: 51.0),
Nebraska: (longitude: -98.268082, age: 52.0), Nevada: (longitude:
-117.055374, age: 53.0), New Hampshire: (longitude: -71.563896, age: 42.0),
New Jersey: (longitude: -74.521011, age: 54.0), New Mexico: (longitude:
-106.248482, age: 57.0), New York: (longitude: -74.948051, age: 59.0), North
Carolina: (longitude: -79.806419, age: 60.0), North Dakota: (longitude:
-99.784012, age: 60.0), Ohio: (longitude: -82.764915, age: 65.0), Oklahoma:
(longitude: -96.928917, age: 62.0), Pennsylvania: (longitude: -77.209755,
age: 68.0), Rhode Island: (longitude: -71.51178, age: 46.0), South Carolina:
(longitude: 80.945007, age: 70.0), South Dakota: (longitude: -99.438828,
age: 64.0), Tennessee: (longitude: -86.692345, age: 58.0), Texas: (longitude:
-97.563461, age: 59.0), Vermont: (longitude: -72.710686, age: 58.0),
Virginia: (longitude: -78.169968, age: 60.0), West Virginia: (longitude:
-80.954453, age: 66.0), Wisconsin: (longitude: -89.616508, age: 49.0),
Wyoming: (longitude: -107.30249, age: 55.0)]
Cluster 1: [Alaska: (longitude: -152.404419, age: 66.0), California:
(longitude: -119.681564, age: 79.0), Hawaii: (longitude: -157.498337, age:
60.0), Idaho: (longitude: -114.478828, age: 75.0), Oregon: (longitude:
-122.070938, age: 56.0), Utah: (longitude: -111.862434, age: 70.0),
Washington: (longitude: -121.490494, age: 66.0)]
```

Cluster 1 represents the extreme Western states, all geographically next to each other (if you consider Alaska and Hawaii next to the Pacific coast states). They all have relatively old governors and hence formed an interesting cluster. Do folks on the Pacific Rim like older governors? We cannot determine anything conclusive from these clusters beyond a correlation. Figure 6.3 illustrates the result. Squares are cluster 1, and circles are cluster 0.

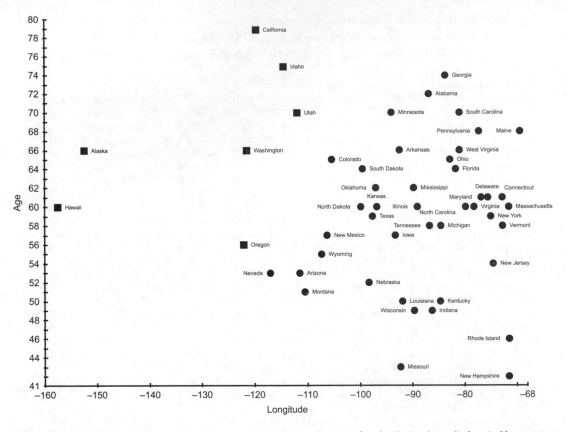

Figure 6.3   Data points in cluster 0 are designated by circles, and data points in cluster 1 are designated by squares.

> **TIP** It cannot be emphasized enough that your results with k-means using random initialization of centroids will vary. Be sure to run k-means multiple times with any data set.

6.4   *Clustering Michael Jackson albums by length*

Michael Jackson released 10 solo studio albums. In the following example, we will cluster those albums by looking at two dimensions: album length (in minutes) and number of tracks. This example is a nice contrast with the preceding governors example because it is easy to see the clusters in the original data set without even running kmeans. An example like this can be a good way of debugging an implementation of a clustering algorithm.

> **NOTE** Both of the examples in this chapter make use of two-dimensional data points, but k-means can work with data points of any number of dimensions.

The example is presented here in its entirety as one code listing. If you look at the album data in the following code listing before even running the example, it is clear that Michael Jackson made longer albums toward the end of his career. So the two clusters of albums should probably be divided between earlier albums and later albums. *HIStory: Past, Present, and Future, Book I* is an outlier and can also logically end up in its own solo cluster. An *outlier* is a data point that lies outside the normal limits of a data set.

Listing 6.15   Album.java

```java
package chapter6;

import java.util.ArrayList;
import java.util.List;

public class Album extends DataPoint {

    private String name;
    private int year;

    public Album(String name, int year, double length, double tracks) {
        super(List.of(length, tracks));
        this.name = name;
        this.year = year;
    }


    @Override
    public String toString() {
        return "(" + name + ", " + year + ")";
    }


    public static void main(String[] args) {
        List<Album> albums = new ArrayList<>();
        albums.add(new Album("Got to Be There", 1972, 35.45, 10));
        albums.add(new Album("Ben", 1972, 31.31, 10));
        albums.add(new Album("Music & Me", 1973, 32.09, 10));
        albums.add(new Album("Forever, Michael", 1975, 33.36, 10));
        albums.add(new Album("Off the Wall", 1979, 42.28, 10));
        albums.add(new Album("Thriller", 1982, 42.19, 9));
        albums.add(new Album("Bad", 1987, 48.16, 10));
        albums.add(new Album("Dangerous", 1991, 77.03, 14));
        albums.add(new Album("HIStory: Past, Present and Future, Book I", 1995,
    148.58, 30));
        albums.add(new Album("Invincible", 2001, 77.05, 16));
        KMeans<Album> kmeans = new KMeans<>(2, albums);
        List<KMeans<Album>.Cluster> clusters = kmeans.run(100);
        for (int clusterIndex = 0; clusterIndex < clusters.size();
    clusterIndex++) {
            System.out.printf("Cluster %d Avg Length %f Avg Tracks %f: %s%n",
            clusterIndex, clusters.get(clusterIndex).centroid.dimensions.get(0),
            clusters.get(clusterIndex).centroid.dimensions.get(1),
            clusters.get(clusterIndex).points);
        }
    }

}
```

Note that the attributes name and year are only recorded for labeling purposes and are not included in the actual clustering. Here is an example output:

```
Converged after 1 iterations.
Cluster 0 Avg Length -0.5458820039179509 Avg Tracks -0.5009878988684237:
[(Got to Be There, 1972), (Ben, 1972), (Music & Me, 1973), (Forever, Michael,
1975), (Off the Wall, 1979), (Thriller, 1982), (Bad, 1987)]
Cluster 1 Avg Length 1.2737246758085525 Avg Tracks 1.168971764026322:
[(Dangerous, 1991), (HIStory: Past, Present and Future, Book I, 1995),
(Invincible, 2001)]
```

The reported cluster averages are interesting. Note that the averages are z-scores. Cluster 1's three albums, Michael Jackson's final three albums, were about one standard deviation longer than the average of all ten of his solo albums.

6.5 *K-means clustering problems and extensions*

When k-means clustering is implemented using random starting points, it may completely miss useful points of division within the data. This often results in a lot of trial and error for the operator. Figuring out the right value for "k" (the number of clusters) is also difficult and error prone if the operator does not have good insight into how many groups of data should exist.

There are more sophisticated versions of k-means that can try to make educated guesses or do automatic trial and error regarding these problematic variables. One popular variant is k-means++, which attempts to solve the initialization problem by choosing centroids based on a probability distribution of distance to every point instead of pure randomness. An even better option for many applications is to choose good starting regions for each of the centroids based on information about the data that is known ahead of time—in other words, a version of k-means where the user of the algorithm chooses the initial centroids.

The runtime for k-means clustering is proportional to the number of data points, the number of clusters, and the number of dimensions of the data points. It can become unusable in its basic form when there are a high number of points that have a large number of dimensions. There are extensions that try to not do as much calculation between every point and every center by evaluating whether a point really has the potential to move to another cluster before doing the calculation. Another option for numerous-point or high-dimension data sets is to run just a sampling of the data points through k-means. This will approximate the clusters that the full k-means algorithm may find.

Outliers in a data set may result in strange results for k-means. If an initial centroid happens to fall near an outlier, it could form a cluster of one (as could potentially happen with the *HIStory* album in the Michael Jackson example). K-means may run better with outliers removed.

Finally, the mean is not always considered a good measure of the center. K-medians looks at the median of each dimension, and k-medoids uses an actual point in the data set as the middle of each cluster. There are statistical reasons beyond the scope of this book for choosing each of these centering methods, but common sense dictates that for a tricky problem it may be worth trying each of them and sampling the results. The implementations of each are not that different.

6.6 Real-world applications

Clustering is often the purview of data scientists and statistical analysts. It is used widely as a way to interpret data in a variety of fields. K-means clustering, in particular, is a useful technique when little is known about the structure of the data set.

In data analysis, clustering is an essential technique. Imagine a police department that wants to know where to put cops on patrol. Imagine a fast-food franchise that wants to figure out where its best customers are, to send promotions. Imagine a boat-rental operator that wants to minimize accidents by analyzing when they occur and who causes them. Now imagine how they could solve their problems using clustering.

Clustering helps with pattern recognition. A clustering algorithm may detect a pattern that the human eye misses. For instance, clustering is sometimes used in biology to identify groups of incongruous cells.

In image recognition, clustering helps to identify non-obvious features. Individual pixels can be treated as data points with their relationship to one another being defined by distance and color difference.

In political science, clustering is sometimes used to find voters to target. Can a political party find disgruntled voters concentrated in a single district that they should focus their campaign dollars on? What issues are similar voters likely to be concerned about?

6.7 Exercises

1   Create a function that can import data from a CSV file into `DataPoints`.
2   Create a function using a GUI framework (like AWT, Swing, or JavaFX) or a graphing library that creates a color-coded scatter plot of the results of any run of `KMeans` on a two-dimensional data set.
3   Create a new initializer for `KMeans` that takes initial centroid positions instead of assigning them randomly.
4   Research and implement the k-means++ algorithm

Fairly simple neural networks

7

When we hear about advances in artificial intelligence these days, they generally concern a particular subdiscipline known as *machine learning* (computers learning some new information without being explicitly told it). More often than not, those advances are being driven by a particular machine learning technique known as *neural networks*. Although they were invented decades ago, neural networks have been going through a kind of renaissance as improved hardware and newly discovered research-driven software techniques enable a new paradigm known as *deep learning*.

Deep learning has turned out to be a broadly applicable technique. It has been found useful in everything from hedge-fund algorithms to bioinformatics. Two deep learning applications that consumers have become familiar with are image recognition and speech recognition. If you have ever asked your digital assistant what the weather is or had a photo program recognize your face, there was probably some deep learning going on.

Deep learning techniques utilize the same building blocks as simpler neural networks. In this chapter, we will explore those blocks by building a simple neural network. It will not be state of the art, but it will give you a basis for understanding deep learning (which is based on more complex neural networks than we will build). Most practitioners of machine learning do not build neural networks from scratch. Instead, they use popular, highly optimized, off-the-shelf frameworks that do the heavy lifting. Although this chapter will not help you learn how to use any specific framework, and the network we will build will not be useful for a real-world application, it will help you understand how those frameworks work at a low level.

146

7.1   *Biological basis?*

The human brain is the most incredible computational device in existence. It cannot crunch numbers as fast as a microprocessor, but its ability to adapt to new situations, learn new skills, and be creative is unsurpassed by any known machine. Since the dawn of computers, scientists have been interested in modeling the brain's machinery. Each nerve cell in the brain is known as a *neuron*. Neurons in the brain are networked to one another via connections known as *synapses*. Electricity passes through synapses to power these networks of neurons—also known as *neural networks*.

> **NOTE** The preceding description of biological neurons is a gross oversimplification for analogy's sake. In fact, biological neurons have parts like axons, dendrites, and nuclei that you may remember from high school biology. And synapses are actually gaps between neurons where neurotransmitters are secreted to enable those electrical signals to pass.

Although scientists have identified the parts and functions of neurons, the details of how biological neural networks form complex thought patterns are still not well understood. How do they process information? How do they form original thoughts? Most of our knowledge of how the brain works comes from looking at it on a macro level. Functional magnetic resonance imaging (fMRI) scans of the brain show where blood flows when a human is doing a particular activity or thinking a particular thought (illustrated in figure 7.1). This and other macro techniques can lead to inferences about how the various parts are connected, but they do not explain the mysteries of how individual neurons aid in the development of new thoughts.

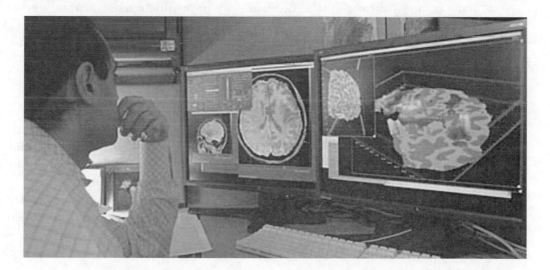

Figure 7.1   A researcher studies fMRI images of the brain. fMRI images do not tell us much about how individual neurons function or how neural networks are organized. (Source: National Institute of Mental Health)

Teams of scientists around the globe are racing to unlock the brain's secrets, but consider this: The human brain has approximately 100,000,000,000 neurons, and each of them may have connections with as many as tens of thousands of other neurons. Even for a computer with billions of logic gates and terabytes of memory, a single human brain would be impossible to model using today's technology. Humans will still likely be the most advanced general-purpose learning entities for the foreseeable future.

> **NOTE** A general-purpose learning machine that is equivalent to human beings in abilities is the goal of so-called *strong AI* (also known as *artificial general intelligence*). At this point in history, it is still the stuff of science fiction. *Weak AI* is the type of AI you see every day: computers intelligently solving specific tasks they were preconfigured to accomplish.

If biological neural networks are not fully understood, then how has modeling them been an effective computational technique? Although digital neural networks, known as *artificial neural networks*, are inspired by biological neural networks, inspiration is where the similarities end. Modern artificial neural networks do not claim to work like their biological counterparts. In fact, that would be impossible, because we do not completely understand how biological neural networks work to begin with.

7.2   *Artificial neural networks*

In this section, we will look at what is arguably the most common type of artificial neural network, a *feed-forward* network with *backpropagation*—the same type we will later be developing. *Feed-forward* means the signal is generally moving in one direction through the network. *Backpropagation* means we will determine errors at the end of each signal's traversal through the network and try to distribute fixes for those errors back through the network, especially affecting the neurons that were most responsible for them. There are many other types of artificial neural networks, and perhaps this chapter will pique your interest in exploring further.

7.2.1   *Neurons*

The smallest unit in an artificial neural network is a neuron. It holds a vector of weights, which are just floating-point numbers. A vector of inputs (also just floating-point numbers) is passed to the neuron. It combines those inputs with its weights using a dot product. It then runs an *activation function* on that product and spits the result out as its output. This action can be thought of as analogous to a real neuron firing.

An activation function is a transformer of the neuron's output. The activation function is almost always nonlinear, which allows neural networks to represent solutions to nonlinear problems. If there were no activation functions, the entire neural network would just be a linear transformation. Figure 7.2 shows a single neuron and its operation.

> **NOTE** There are some math terms in this section that you may not have seen since a precalculus or linear algebra class. Explaining what vectors or dot

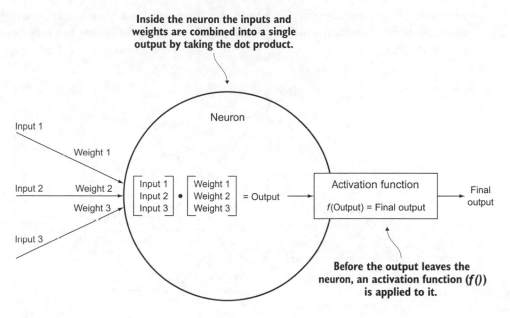

Figure 7.2 **A single neuron combines its weights with input signals to produce an output signal that is modified by an activation function.**

products are is beyond the scope of this chapter, but you will likely get an intuition of what a neural network does by following along in this chapter, even if you do not understand all of the math. Later in the chapter, there will be some calculus, including the use of derivatives and partial derivatives, but even if you do not understand all of the math, you should be able to follow the code. In fact, this chapter will not explain how to derive the formulas using calculus. Instead, it will focus on using the derivations.

7.2.2 *Layers*

In a typical feed-forward artificial neural network, neurons are organized in layers. Each layer consists of a certain number of neurons lined up in a row or column (depending on the diagram; the two are equivalent). In a feed-forward network, which is what we will be building, signals always pass in a single direction from one layer to the next. The neurons in each layer send their output signal to be used as input to the neurons in the next layer. Every neuron in each layer is connected to every neuron in the next layer.

The first layer is known as the *input layer*, and it receives its signals from some external entity. The last layer is known as the *output layer*, and its output typically must be interpreted by an external actor to get an intelligent result. The layers between the input and output layers are known as *hidden layers*. In simple neural networks like the one we will be building in this chapter, there is just one hidden layer, but deep learning networks have many. Figure 7.3 shows the layers working together in a simple network. Note how the outputs from one layer are used as the inputs to every neuron in the next layer.

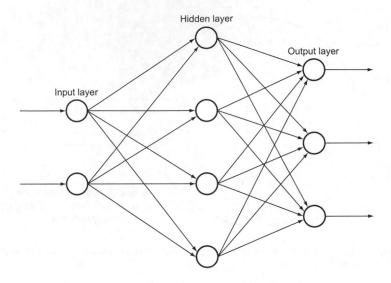

Figure 7.3   A simple neural network with one input layer of two neurons, one hidden layer of four neurons, and one output layer of three neurons. The number of neurons in each layer in this figure is arbitrary.

These layers just manipulate floating-point numbers. The inputs to the input layer are floating-point numbers, and the outputs from the output layer are floating-point numbers.

Obviously, these numbers must represent something meaningful. Imagine that the network was designed to classify small black-and-white images of animals. Perhaps the input layer has 100 neurons representing the grayscale intensity of each pixel in a 10 × 10 pixel animal image, and the output layer has 5 neurons representing the likelihood that the image is of a mammal, reptile, amphibian, fish, or bird. The final classification could be determined by the output neuron with the highest floating-point output. If the output numbers were 0.24, 0.65, 0.70, 0.12, and 0.21, respectively, the image would be determined to be an amphibian.

7.2.3   *Backpropagation*

The last piece of the puzzle, and the inherently most complex part, is backpropagation. Backpropagation finds the error in a neural network's output and uses it to modify the weights of neurons in an effort to reduce the error in subsequent runs. The neurons most responsible for the error are most heavily modified. But where does the error come from? How can we know the error? The error comes from a phase in the use of a neural network known as *training*.

> **TIP** There are steps written out (in English) for several mathematical formulas in this section. Pseudo formulas (not using proper notation) are in the accompanying figures. This approach will make the formulas readable for those uninitiated in (or out of practice with) mathematical notation. If the more formal notation (and the derivation of the formulas) interests you, check out chapter 18 of Norvig and Russell's *Artificial Intelligence.*[1]

Before they can be used, most neural networks must be trained. We must know the right outputs for some inputs so that we can use the difference between expected outputs and actual outputs to find errors and modify weights. In other words, neural networks know nothing until they are told the right answers for a certain set of inputs, so that they can prepare themselves for other inputs. Backpropagation only occurs during training.

> **NOTE** Because most neural networks must be trained, they are considered a type of *supervised* machine learning. Recall from chapter 6 that the k means algorithm and other cluster algorithms are considered a form of *unsupervised* machine learning because once they are started, no outside intervention is required. There are other types of neural networks than the one described in this chapter that do not require pretraining and are considered a form of unsupervised learning.

The first step in backpropagation is to calculate the error between the neural network's output for some input and the expected output. This error is spread across all of the neurons in the output layer. (Each neuron has an expected output and its actual output.) The derivative of the output neuron's activation function is then applied to what was output by the neuron before its activation function was applied. (We cache its preactivation function output.) This result is multiplied by the neuron's error to find its *delta*. This formula for finding the delta uses a partial derivative, and its calculus derivation is beyond the scope of this book, but we are basically figuring out how much of the error each output neuron was responsible for. See figure 7.4 for a diagram of this calculation.

Deltas must then be calculated for every neuron in the hidden layer(s) in the network. We must determine how much each neuron was responsible for the incorrect output in the output layer. The deltas in the output layer are used to calculate the deltas in the preceding hidden layer. For each previous layer, the deltas are calculated by taking the dot product of the next layer's weights with respect to the particular neuron in question and the deltas already calculated in the next layer. This dot product is multiplied by the derivative of the activation function applied to a neuron's last output (cached before the activation function was applied) to get the neuron's delta.

---

[1] Stuart Russell and Peter Norvig, *Artificial Intelligence: A Modern Approach*, 3rd ed. (Pearson, 2010).

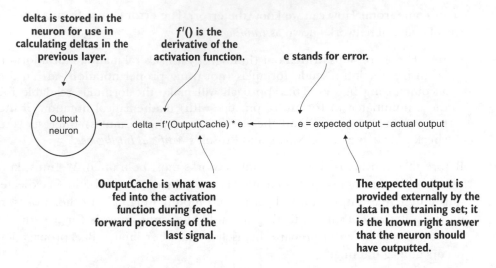

Figure 7.4   The mechanism by which an output neuron's delta is calculated during the backpropagation phase of training

Again, this formula is derived using a partial derivative, which you can read about in more mathematically focused texts.

Figure 7.5 shows the actual calculation of deltas for neurons in hidden layers. In a network with multiple hidden layers, neurons O1, O2, and O3 could be neurons in the next hidden layer instead of in the output layer.

Last, but most important, all of the weights for every neuron in the network must be updated. They can be updated by multiplying each individual weight's last input with the delta of the neuron and something called a *learning rate*, and adding that to the existing weight. This method of modifying the weight of a neuron is known as *gradient descent*. It is like climbing down a hill representing the error function of the neuron toward a point of minimal error. The delta represents the direction we want to climb, and the learning rate affects how fast we climb. It is hard to determine a good learning rate for an unknown problem without trial and error. Figure 7.6 shows how every weight in the hidden layer and output layer is updated.

Once the weights are updated, the neural network is ready to be trained again with another input and expected output. This process repeats until the network is deemed well trained by the neural network's user. This can be determined by testing it against inputs with known correct outputs.

Backpropagation is complicated. Do not worry if you do not yet grasp all of the details. The explanation in this section may not be enough. Ideally, implementing backpropagation will take your understanding to the next level. As we implement our neural network and backpropagation, keep in mind this overarching theme: backpropagation is a way of adjusting each individual weight in the network according to its responsibility for an incorrect output.

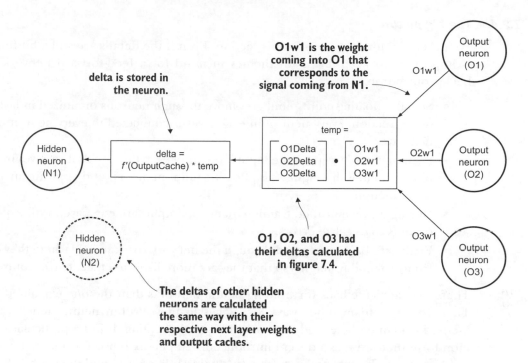

delta is stored in the neuron.

O1w1 is the weight coming into O1 that corresponds to the signal coming from N1.

O1, O2, and O3 had their deltas calculated in figure 7.4.

The deltas of other hidden neurons are calculated the same way with their respective next layer weights and output caches.

Figure 7.5 The weights of every hidden layer and output layer neuron are updated using the deltas calculated in the previous steps, the prior weights, the prior inputs, and a user-determined learning rate.

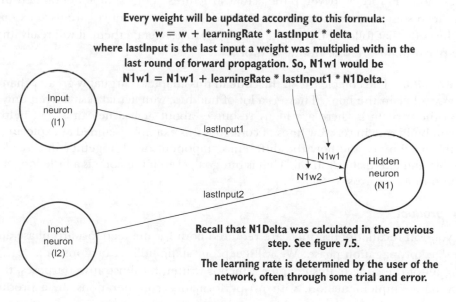

Every weight will be updated according to this formula:
$$w = w + learningRate * lastInput * delta$$
where lastInput is the last input a weight was multiplied with in the last round of forward propagation. So, N1w1 would be
$$N1w1 = N1w1 + learningRate * lastInput1 * N1Delta.$$

Recall that N1Delta was calculated in the previous step. See figure 7.5.

The learning rate is determined by the user of the network, often through some trial and error.

Figure 7.6 How a delta is calculated for a neuron in a hidden layer

7.2.4 *The big picture*

We covered a lot of ground in this section. Even if the details are still a bit fuzzy, it is important to keep the main themes in mind for a feed-forward network with backpropagation:

- Signals (floating-point numbers) move through neurons organized in layers in one direction. Every neuron in each layer is connected to every neuron in the next layer.
- Each neuron (except in the input layer) processes the signals it receives by combining them with weights (also floating-point numbers) and applying an activation function.
- During a process called training, network outputs are compared with expected outputs to calculate errors.
- Errors are backpropagated through the network (back toward where they came from) to modify weights so that they are more likely to create correct outputs.

There are more methods for training neural networks than the one explained here. There are also many other ways for signals to move within neural networks. The method explained here, and that we will be implementing, is just a particularly common form that serves as a decent introduction. Appendix B lists further resources for learning more about neural networks (including other types) and the math.

7.3 *Preliminaries*

Neural networks utilize mathematical mechanisms that require a lot of floating-point operations. Before we develop the actual structures of our simple neural network, we will need some mathematical primitives. These simple primitives are used extensively in the code that follows, so if you can find ways to accelerate them, it will really improve the performance of your neural network.

> **WARNING** The complexity of the code in this chapter is arguably greater than any other in the book. There is a lot of buildup, with actual results seen only at the very end. There are many resources about neural networks that help you build one in very few lines of code, but this example is aimed at exploring the machinery and how the different components work together in a readable and extensible fashion. That is our goal, even if the code is a little longer and more expressive.

7.3.1 *Dot product*

As you will recall, dot products are required both for the feed-forward phase and for the backpropagation phase. We will keep our static utility functions in a `Util` class. Like all of the code in this chapter, which is written for illustrative purposes, this is a very naive implementation, with no performance considerations. In a production library, vector instructions would be used, as discussed in section 7.6.

Listing 7.1   Util.java

```java
package chapter7;

import java.io.BufferedReader;
import java.io.IOException;
import java.io.InputStream;
import java.io.InputStreamReader;
import java.util.ArrayList;
import java.util.Arrays;
import java.util.Collections;
import java.util.List;
import java.util.stream.Collectors;

public final class Util {

    public static double dotProduct(double[] xs, double[] ys) {
        double sum = 0.0;
        for (int i = 0; i < xs.length; i++) {
            sum += xs[i] * ys[i];
        }
        return sum;
    }
}
```

7.3.2   *The activation function*

Recall that the activation function transforms the output of a neuron before the signal passes to the next layer (see figure 7.2). The activation function has two purposes: it allows the neural network to represent solutions that are not just linear transformations (as long as the activation function itself is not just a linear transformation), and it can keep the output of each neuron within a certain range. An activation function should have a computable derivative so that it can be used for backpropagation.

Sigmoid functions are a popular set of activation functions. One particularly popular sigmoid function (often just referred to as "the sigmoid function") is illustrated in figure 7.7 (referred to in the figure as $S(x)$), along with its equation and derivative ($S'(x)$). The result of the sigmoid function will always be a value between 0 and 1, which is useful for the network, as you will see. You will shortly see the formulas from the figure written out in code.

There are other activation functions, but we will use the sigmoid function. It and its derivative are easy to implement. Here is a straightforward conversion of the formulas in figure 7.7 into code.

Listing 7.2   Util.java continued

```java
// the classic sigmoid activation function
public static double sigmoid(double x) {
    return 1.0 / (1.0 + Math.exp(-x));
}
```

```java
public static double derivativeSigmoid(double x) {
    double sig = sigmoid(x);
    return sig * (1.0 - sig);
}
```

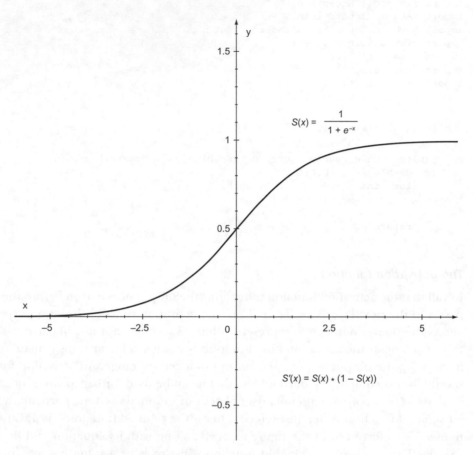

Figure 7.7   The sigmoid activation function (S(x)) will always return a value between 0 and 1. Note that its derivative is easy to compute as well (S'(x)).

7.4   *Building the network*

We will create classes to model all three organizational units in the network: neurons, layers, and the network itself. For the sake of simplicity, we will start from the smallest (neurons), move to the central organizing component (layers), and build up to the largest (the whole network). As we go from smallest component to largest component, we will encapsulate the previous level. Neurons only know about themselves. Layers know about the neurons they contain and other layers. And the network knows about all of the layers.

NOTE There are many long lines of code in this chapter that do not neatly fit in the column limits of a printed book. I strongly recommend downloading the source code for this chapter from the book's source code repository and following along on your computer screen as you read: https://github.com/ davecom/ClassicComputerScienceProblemsInJava.

7.4.1 Implementing neurons

Let's start with a neuron. An individual neuron will store many pieces of state, including its weights, its delta, its learning rate, a cache of its last output, and its activation function, along with the derivative of that activation function. Some of these elements could be more efficiently stored up a level (in the future Layer class), but they are included in the following Neuron class for illustrative purposes.

Listing 7.3 Neuron.java

```java
package chapter7;

import java.util.function.DoubleUnaryOperator;

public class Neuron {
    public double[] weights;
    public final double learningRate;
    public double outputCache;
    public double delta;
    public final DoubleUnaryOperator activationFunction;
    public final DoubleUnaryOperator derivativeActivationFunction;

    public Neuron(double[] weights, double learningRate, DoubleUnaryOperator
      activationFunction, DoubleUnaryOperator derivativeActivationFunction) {
        this.weights = weights;
        this.learningRate = learningRate;
        outputCache = 0.0;
        delta = 0.0;
        this.activationFunction = activationFunction;
        this.derivativeActivationFunction = derivativeActivationFunction;
    }

    public double output(double[] inputs) {
        outputCache = Util.dotProduct(inputs, weights);
        return activationFunction.applyAsDouble(outputCache);
    }

}
```

Most of these parameters are initialized in the constructor. Because delta and outputCache are not known when a Neuron is first created, they are just initialized to 0.0. Several of these variables (learningRate, activationFunction, derivative-ActivationFunction) look preset, so why are we making them configurable at the neuron level? If this Neuron class were to be used with other types of neural networks, it is possible that some of these values might differ from one neuron to another, so they are configurable for maximum flexibility. There are even neural networks that change the learning rate as the solution approaches, and that automatically try different activation functions. Since our variables are `final`, they could not change midstream, but making them non-`final` would be an easy code change.

The only other method, other than the constructor, is `output()`. `output()` takes the input signals (`inputs`) coming to the neuron and applies the formula discussed earlier in the chapter (see figure 7.2). The input signals are combined with the weights via a dot product, and this is cached in `outputCache`. Recall from the section on backpropagation that this value, obtained before the activation function is applied, is used to calculate delta. Finally, before the signal is sent on to the next layer (by being returned from `output()`), the activation function is applied to it.

That is it! An individual neuron in this network is fairly simple. It cannot do much beyond taking an input signal, transforming it, and sending it off to be processed further. It maintains several elements of state that are used by the other classes.

7.4.2 Implementing layers

A layer in our network will need to maintain three pieces of state: its neurons, the layer that preceded it, and an output cache. The output cache is similar to that of a neuron, but up one level. It caches the outputs (after activation functions are applied) of every neuron in the layer.

At creation time, a layer's main responsibility is to initialize its neurons. Our `Layer` class's constructor therefore needs to know how many neurons it should be initializing, what their activation functions should be, and what their learning rates should be. In this simple network, every neuron in a layer has the same activation function and learning rate.

Listing 7.4 Layer.java

```java
package chapter7;

import java.util.ArrayList;
import java.util.List;
import java.util.Optional;
import java.util.Random;
import java.util.function.DoubleUnaryOperator;

public class Layer {
    public Optional<Layer> previousLayer;
    public List<Neuron> neurons = new ArrayList<>();
    public double[] outputCache;

    public Layer(Optional<Layer> previousLayer, int numNeurons, double
      learningRate, DoubleUnaryOperator activationFunction, DoubleUnaryOperator
      derivativeActivationFunction) {
        this.previousLayer = previousLayer;
        Random random = new Random();
        for (int i = 0; i < numNeurons; i++) {
```

```
        double[] randomWeights = null;
        if (previousLayer.isPresent()) {
            randomWeights = random.doubles(previousLayer.get().neurons
.size()).toArray();
        }
        Neuron neuron = new Neuron(randomWeights, learningRate,
activationFunction, derivativeActivationFunction);
        neurons.add(neuron);
    }
    outputCache = new double[numNeurons];
}
```

As signals are fed forward through the network, the Layer must process them through every neuron. (Remember that every neuron in a layer receives the signals from every neuron in the previous layer.) outputs() does just that. outputs() also returns the result of processing them (to be passed by the network to the next layer) and caches the output. If there is no previous layer, that indicates the layer is an input layer, and it just passes the signals forward to the next layer.

Listing 7.5 Layer.java continued

```
public double[] outputs(double[] inputs) {
    if (previousLayer.isPresent()) {
        outputCache = neurons.stream().mapToDouble(n ->
n.output(inputs)).toArray();
    } else {
        outputCache = inputs;
    }
    return outputCache;
}
```

There are two distinct types of deltas to calculate in backpropagation: deltas for neurons in the output layer and deltas for neurons in hidden layers. The formulas are described in figures 7.4 and 7.5, and the following two methods are rote translations of those formulas. These methods will later be called by the network during backpropagation.

Listing 7.6 Layer.java continued

```
// should only be called on output layer
public void calculateDeltasForOutputLayer(double[] expected) {
    for (int n = 0; n < neurons.size(); n++) {
        neurons.get(n).delta =
neurons.get(n).derivativeActivationFunction.applyAsDouble(neurons.get(n)
.outputCache)
                * (expected[n] - outputCache[n]);
    }
}

// should not be called on output layer
public void calculateDeltasForHiddenLayer(Layer nextLayer) {
```

```
        for (int i = 0; i < neurons.size(); i++) {
            int index = i;
            double[] nextWeights = nextLayer.neurons.stream().mapToDouble(n ->
    n.weights[index]).toArray();
            double[] nextDeltas = nextLayer.neurons.stream().mapToDouble(n ->
    n.delta).toArray();
            double sumWeightsAndDeltas = Util.dotProduct(nextWeights,
    nextDeltas);
            neurons.get(i).delta = neurons.get(i).derivativeActivationFunction
            .applyAsDouble(neurons.get(i).outputCache) * sumWeightsAndDeltas;
        }
    }

}
```

7.4.3   Implementing the network

The network itself has only one piece of state: the layers that it manages. The Network class is responsible for initializing its constituent layers.

The constructor takes an int array describing the structure of the network. For example, the array {2, 4, 3} describes a network with 2 neurons in its input layer, 4 neurons in its hidden layer, and 3 neurons in its output layer. In this simple network, we will assume that all layers in the network will make use of the same activation function for their neurons and the same learning rate.

Listing 7.7   Network.java

```
package chapter7;

import java.util.ArrayList;
import java.util.List;
import java.util.Optional;
import java.util.function.DoubleUnaryOperator;
import java.util.function.Function;

public class Network<T> {
    private List<Layer> layers = new ArrayList<>();

    public Network(int[] layerStructure, double learningRate,
            DoubleUnaryOperator activationFunction, DoubleUnaryOperator
    derivativeActivationFunction) {
        if (layerStructure.length < 3) {
            throw new IllegalArgumentException("Error: Should be at least 3
    layers (1 input, 1 hidden, 1 output).");
        }
        // input layer
        Layer inputLayer = new Layer(Optional.empty(), layerStructure[0],
    learningRate, activationFunction, derivativeActivationFunction);
        layers.add(inputLayer);
        // hidden layers and output layer
        for (int i = 1; i < layerStructure.length; i++) {
            Layer nextLayer = new Layer(Optional.of(layers.get(i - 1)),
    layerStructure[i], learningRate, activationFunction,
    derivativeActivationFunction);
```

```
            layers.add(nextLayer);
        }
    }
```

NOTE The generic type, T, links the network to the type of the final classification categories from the data set. It is only used in the final method of the class, validate().

The outputs of the neural network are the result of signals running through all of its layers, one after another.

Listing 7.8   Network.java continued

```
    // Pushes input data to the first layer, then output from the first
    // as input to the second, second to the third, etc.
    private double[] outputs(double[] input) {
        double[] result = input;
        for (Layer layer : layers) {
            result = layer.outputs(result);
        }
        return result;
    }
```

The backpropagate() method is responsible for computing deltas for every neuron in the network. It uses the Layer methods calculateDeltasForOutputLayer() and calculateDeltasForHiddenLayer() in sequence. (Recall that in backpropagation, deltas are calculated backward.) It passes the expected values of output for a given set of inputs to calculateDeltasForOutputLayer(). That method uses the expected values to find the error used for delta calculation.

Listing 7.9   Network.java continued

```
    // Figure out each neuron's changes based on the errors of the output
    // versus the expected outcome
    private void backpropagate(double[] expected) {
        // calculate delta for output layer neurons
        int lastLayer = layers.size() - 1;
        layers.get(lastLayer).calculateDeltasForOutputLayer(expected);
        // calculate delta for hidden layers in reverse order
        for (int i = lastLayer - 1; i >= 0; i--) {
            layers.get(i).calculateDeltasForHiddenLayer(layers.get(i + 1));
        }
    }
```

backpropagate() is responsible for calculating all deltas, but it does not actually modify any of the network's weights. updateWeights() must be called after backpropagate() because weight modification depends on deltas. This method follows directly from the formula in figure 7.6.

Listing 7.10   Network.java continued

```java
// backpropagate() doesn't actually change any weights
// This function uses the deltas calculated in backpropagate() to
// actually make changes to the weights
private void updateWeights() {
    for (Layer layer : layers.subList(1, layers.size())) {
        for (Neuron neuron : layer.neurons) {
            for (int w = 0; w < neuron.weights.length; w++) {
                neuron.weights[w] = neuron.weights[w] + (neuron.learningRate
 * layer.previousLayer.get().outputCache[w] * neuron.delta);
            }
        }
    }
}
```

Neuron weights are modified at the end of each round of training. Training sets (inputs coupled with expected outputs) must be provided to the network. The `train()` method takes a list of arrays of doubles of inputs and a list of arrays of doubles of expected outputs. It runs each input through the network and then updates its weights by calling `backpropagate()` with the expected output (and `updateWeights()` after that). Try adding code in the following training function to print out the error rate as the network goes through a training set to see how the network gradually decreases its error rate as it rolls down the hill in gradient descent.

Listing 7.11   Network.java continued

```java
// train() uses the results of outputs() run over many inputs and compared
// against expecteds to feed backpropagate() and updateWeights()
public void train(List<double[]> inputs, List<double[]> expecteds) {
    for (int i = 0; i < inputs.size(); i++) {
        double[] xs = inputs.get(i);
        double[] ys = expecteds.get(i);
        outputs(xs);
        backpropagate(ys);
        updateWeights();
    }
}
```

Finally, after a network is trained, we need to test it. `validate()` takes inputs and expected outputs (not unlike `train()`), but uses them to calculate an accuracy percentage rather than perform training. It is assumed that the network is already trained. `validate()` also takes a function, `interpretOutput()`, that is used for interpreting the output of the neural network to compare it to the expected output. Perhaps the expected output is a string like "Amphibian" instead of a set of floating-point numbers. `interpretOutput()` must take the floating-point numbers it gets as output from the network and convert them into something comparable to the expected outputs. It is a custom function specific to a data set. `validate()` returns the number of correct classifications, the total number of samples tested, and the percentage of correct classifications. Those three values are wrapped inside the inner Results type.

Listing 7.12 Network.java continued

```java
public class Results {
    public final int correct;
    public final int trials;
    public final double percentage;

    public Results(int correct, int trials, double percentage) {
        this.correct = correct;
        this.trials = trials;
        this.percentage = percentage;
    }
}

// for generalized results that require classification
// this function will return the correct number of trials
// and the percentage correct out of the total
public Results validate(List<double[]> inputs, List<T> expecteds,
  Function<double[], T> interpret) {
    int correct = 0;
    for (int i = 0; i < inputs.size(); i++) {
        double[] input = inputs.get(i);
        T expected = expecteds.get(i);
        T result = interpret.apply(outputs(input));
        if (result.equals(expected)) {
            correct++;
        }
    }
    double percentage = (double) correct / (double) inputs.size();
    return new Results(correct, inputs.size(), percentage);
}
}
```

The neural network is done! It is ready to be tested with some actual problems. Although the architecture we built is general-purpose enough to be used for a variety of problems, we will concentrate on a popular kind of problem: classification.

7.5 *Classification problems*

In chapter 6 we categorized a data set with k-means clustering, using no preconceived notions about where each individual piece of data belonged. In clustering, we know we want to find categories of data, but we do not know ahead of time what those categories are. In a classification problem, we are also trying to categorize a data set, but there are preset categories. For example, if we were trying to classify a set of pictures of animals, we might decide ahead of time on categories like mammal, reptile, amphibian, fish, and bird.

There are many machine learning techniques that can be used for classification problems. Perhaps you have heard of support vector machines, decision trees, or naive

Bayes classifiers. Recently, neural networks have become widely deployed in the classification space. They are more computationally intensive than some of the other classification algorithms, but their ability to classify seemingly arbitrary kinds of data makes them a powerful technique. Neural network classifiers are behind much of the interesting image classification that powers modern photo software.

Why is there renewed interest in using neural networks for classification problems? Hardware has become fast enough that the extra computation involved, compared to other algorithms, makes the benefits worthwhile.

7.5.1 *Normalizing data*

The data sets that we want to work with generally require some "cleaning" before they are input into our algorithms. Cleaning may involve removing extraneous characters, deleting duplicates, fixing errors, and other menial tasks. The aspect of cleaning we will need to perform for the two data sets we are working with is normalization. In chapter 6 we did this via the zScoreNormalize() method in the KMeans class. Normalization is about taking attributes recorded on different scales and converting them to a common scale.

Every neuron in our network outputs values between 0 and 1 due to the sigmoid activation function. It sounds logical that a scale between 0 and 1 would make sense for the attributes in our input data set as well. Converting a scale from some range to a range between 0 and 1 is not challenging. For any value, V, in a particular attribute range with maximum (max) and minimum (min), the formula is just newV = (oldV - min) / (max - min). This operation is known as *feature scaling*. Here is a Java implementation to add to the Util class, as well as two utility methods for loading data from CSV files and finding the maximum number in an array that will be convenient for the rest of the chapter.

Listing 7.13   Util.java continued

```java
// Assume all rows are of equal length
// and feature scale each column to be in the range 0 - 1
public static void normalizeByFeatureScaling(List<double[]> dataset) {
    for (int colNum = 0; colNum < dataset.get(0).length; colNum++) {
        List<Double> column = new ArrayList<>();
        for (double[] row : dataset) {
            column.add(row[colNum]);
        }
        double maximum = Collections.max(column);
        double minimum = Collections.min(column);
        double difference = maximum - minimum;
        for (double[] row : dataset) {
            row[colNum] = (row[colNum] - minimum) / difference;
        }
    }
}
```

```java
// Load a CSV file into a List of String arrays
public static List<String[]> loadCSV(String filename) {
    try (InputStream inputStream = Util.class.getResourceAsStream(filename)) {
        InputStreamReader inputStreamReader = new
  InputStreamReader(inputStream);
        BufferedReader bufferedReader = new BufferedReader(inputStreamReader);
        return bufferedReader.lines().map(line -> line.split(","))
                .collect(Collectors.toList());
    }
    catch (IOException e) {
        e.printStackTrace();
        throw new RuntimeException(e.getMessage(), e);
    }
}


// Find the maximum in an array of doubles
public static double max(double[] numbers) {
    return Arrays.stream(numbers)
            .max()
            .orElse(Double.MIN_VALUE);
}

}
```

Look at the `dataset` parameter in `normalizeByFeatureScaling()`. It is a reference to a list of double arrays that will be modified in place. In other words, `normalizeBy-FeatureScaling()` does not receive a copy of the data set. It receives a reference to the original data set. This is a situation where we want to make changes to a value rather than receive back a transformed copy. Java is pass by value, but in this instance we are passing by value a reference, therefore getting a copy of a reference to the same list.

Note also that our program assumes that data sets are effectively two-dimensional lists of floating-point numbers arranged as lists of double arrays.

7.5.2 The classic iris data set

Just as there are classic computer science problems, there are classic data sets in machine learning. These data sets are used to validate new techniques and compare them to existing ones. They also serve as good starting points for people learning machine learning for the first time. Perhaps the most famous is the iris data set. Originally collected in the 1930s, the data set consists of 150 samples of iris plants (pretty flowers), split among three different species (50 of each). Each plant is measured on four different attributes: sepal length, sepal width, petal length, and petal width.

It is worth noting that a neural network does not care what the various attributes represent. Its model for training makes no distinction between sepal length and petal length in terms of importance. If such a distinction should be made, it is up to the user of the neural network to make appropriate adjustments.

The source code repository that accompanies this book contains a comma-separated values (CSV) file that features the iris data set.[2] The iris data set is from the University of California's UCI Machine Learning Repository.[3] A CSV file is just a text file with values separated by commas. It is a common interchange format for tabular data, including spreadsheets.

Here are a few lines from iris.csv:

```
5.1,3.5,1.4,0.2,Iris-setosa
4.9,3.0,1.4,0.2,Iris-setosa
4.7,3.2,1.3,0.2,Iris-setosa
4.6,3.1,1.5,0.2,Iris-setosa
5.0,3.6,1.4,0.2,Iris-setosa
```

Each line represents one data point. The four numbers represent the four attributes (sepal length, sepal width, petal length, and petal width), which, again, are arbitrary to us in terms of what they actually represent. The name at the end of each line represents the particular iris species. All five lines are for the same species because this sample was taken from the top of the file, and the three species are clumped together, with fifty lines each.

To read the CSV file from disk, we will use a few functions from the Java standard library. These are wrapped up in the `loadCSV()` method we earlier defined in the `Util` class. Beyond those few lines, the rest of the constructor for `IrisTest`, our class for actually running the classification, just rearranges the data from the CSV file to prepare it to be consumed by our network for training and validation.

Listing 7.14   IrisTest.java

```java
package chapter7;

import java.util.ArrayList;
import java.util.Arrays;
import java.util.Collections;
import java.util.List;

public class IrisTest {
    public static final String IRIS_SETOSA = "Iris-setosa";
    public static final String IRIS_VERSICOLOR = "Iris-versicolor";
    public static final String IRIS_VIRGINICA = "Iris-virginica";

    private List<double[]> irisParameters = new ArrayList<>();
    private List<double[]> irisClassifications = new ArrayList<>();
    private List<String> irisSpecies = new ArrayList<>();
```

---

[2] The repository is available from GitHub at https://github.com/davecom/ClassicComputerScienceProblems-InJava.

[3] M. Lichman, UCI Machine Learning Repository (Irvine, CA: University of California, School of Information and Computer Science, 2013), http://archive.ics.uci.edu/ml.

```
public IrisTest() {
    // make sure iris.csv is in the right place in your path
    List<String[]> irisDataset = Util.loadCSV("/chapter7/data/iris.csv");
    // get our lines of data in random order
    Collections.shuffle(irisDataset);
    for (String[] iris : irisDataset) {
        // first four items are parameters (doubles)
        double[] parameters = Arrays.stream(iris)
                .limit(4)
                .mapToDouble(Double::parseDouble)
                .toArray();
        irisParameters.add(parameters);
        // last item is species
        String species = iris[4];
        switch (species) {
            case IRIS_SETOSA :
                irisClassifications.add(new double[] { 1.0, 0.0, 0.0 });
                break;
            case IRIS_VERSICOLOR :
                irisClassifications.add(new double[] { 0.0, 1.0, 0.0 });
                break;
            default :
                irisClassifications.add(new double[] { 0.0, 0.0, 1.0 });
                break;
        }
        irisSpecies.add(species);
    }
    Util.normalizeByFeatureScaling(irisParameters);
}
```

`irisParameters` represents the collection of four attributes per sample that we are using to classify each iris. `irisClassifications` is the actual classification of each sample. Our neural network will have three output neurons, with each representing one possible species. For instance, a final set of outputs of {0.9, 0.3, 0.1} will represent a classification of iris-setosa, because the first neuron represents that species, and it is the largest number.

For training, we already know the right answers, so each iris has a premarked answer. For a flower that should be iris-setosa, the entry in `irisClassifications` will be {1.0, 0.0, 0.0}. These values will be used to calculate the error after each training step. `IrisSpecies` corresponds directly to what each flower should be classified as in English. An iris-setosa will be marked as "Iris-setosa" in the data set.

WARNING The lack of error-checking makes this code fairly dangerous. It is not suitable as is for production, but it is fine for testing.

Listing 7.15   IrisTest.java continued

```
public String irisInterpretOutput(double[] output) {
    double max = Util.max(output);
    if (max == output[0]) {
        return IRIS_SETOSA;
```

```
    } else if (max == output[1]) {
        return IRIS_VERSICOLOR;
    } else {
        return IRIS_VIRGINICA;
    }
}
```

`irisInterpretOutput()` is a utility function that will be passed to the network's `validate()` method to help identify correct classifications.

The network is finally ready to be created. Let's define a `classify()` method that will set up the network, train it, and run it.

Listing 7.16   IrisTest.java continued

```
public Network<String>.Results classify() {
    // 4, 6, 3 layer structure; 0.3 learning rate; sigmoid activation
function
    Network<String> irisNetwork = new Network<>(new int[] { 4, 6, 3 },
    0.3, Util::sigmoid, Util::derivativeSigmoid);
```

The `layerStructure` argument of the `Network` constructor specifies a network with three layers (one input layer, one hidden layer, and one output layer) with {4, 6, 3}. The input layer has four neurons, the hidden layer has six neurons, and the output layer has three neurons. The four neurons in the input layer map directly to the four parameters that are used to classify each specimen. The three neurons in the output layer map directly to the three different species that we are trying to classify each input within. The hidden layer's six neurons are more the result of trial and error than some formula. The same is true of `learningRate`. These two values (the number of neurons in the hidden layer and the learning rate) can be experimented with if the accuracy of the network is suboptimal.

Listing 7.17   IrisTest.java continued

```
    // train over the first 140 irises in the data set 50 times
    List<double[]> irisTrainers = irisParameters.subList(0, 140);
    List<double[]> irisTrainersCorrects = irisClassifications.subList(0, 140);
    int trainingIterations = 50;
    for (int i = 0; i < trainingIterations; i++) {
        irisNetwork.train(irisTrainers, irisTrainersCorrects);
    }
```

We train on the first 140 irises out of the 150 in the data set. Recall that the lines read from the CSV file were shuffled. This ensures that every time we run the program, we will be training on a different subset of the data set. Note that we train over the 140 irises 50 times. Modifying this value will have a large effect on how long it takes your neural network to train. Generally, the more training, the more accurately the neural network will perform, although there is a risk of what is known as *overfitting*. The final test will be to verify the correct classification of the final 10 irises from the data set. We do this at the end of classify(), and we run the network from main().

```
Listing 7.18   IrisTest.java continued

        // test over the last 10 of the irises in the data set
        List<double[]> irisTesters = irisParameters.subList(140, 150);
        List<String> irisTestersCorrects = irisSpecies.subList(140, 150);
        return irisNetwork.validate(irisTesters, irisTestersCorrects,
    this::irisInterpretOutput);
    }

    public static void main(String[] args) {
        IrisTest irisTest = new IrisTest();
        Network<String>.Results results = irisTest.classify();
        System.out.println(results.correct + " correct of " + results.trials
    + " = " + results.percentage * 100 + "%");
    }

}
```

All of the work leads up to this final question: out of 10 randomly chosen irises from the data set, how many can our neural network correctly classify? Because there is randomness in the starting weights of each neuron, different runs may give you different results. You can try tweaking the learning rate, the number of hidden neurons, and the number of training iterations to make your network more accurate.

Ultimately, you should see a result that is close to this:

```
9 correct of 10 - 90.0%
```

7.5.3 Classifying wine

We are going to test our neural network with another data set, one based on the chemical analysis of wine cultivars from Italy.[4] There are 178 samples in the data set. The machinery of working with it will be much the same as with the iris data set, but the layout of the CSV file is slightly different. Here is a sample:

```
1,14.23,1.71,2.43,15.6,127,2.8,3.06,.28,2.29,5.64,1.04,3.92,1065
1,13.2,1.78,2.14,11.2,100,2.65,2.76,.26,1.28,4.38,1.05,3.4,1050
1,13.16,2.36,2.67,18.6,101,2.8,3.24,.3,2.81,5.68,1.03,3.17,1185
1,14.37,1.95,2.5,16.8,113,3.85,3.49,.24,2.18,7.8,.86,3.45,1480
1,13.24,2.59,2.87,21,118,2.8,2.69,.39,1.82,4.32,1.04,2.93,735
```

The first value on each line will always be an integer from 1 to 3 representing one of three cultivars that the sample may be a kind of. But notice how many more parameters there are for classification. In the iris data set, there were just 4. In this wine data set, there are 13.

---

[4] See footnote 3.

Our neural network model will scale just fine. We simply need to increase the number of input neurons. WineTest.java is analogous to IrisTest.java, but there are some minor changes to account for the different layouts of the respective files.

Listing 7.19 WineTest.java

```java
package chapter7;

import java.util.ArrayList;
import java.util.Arrays;
import java.util.Collections;
import java.util.List;

public class WineTest {
    private List<double[]> wineParameters = new ArrayList<>();
    private List<double[]> wineClassifications = new ArrayList<>();
    private List<Integer> wineSpecies = new ArrayList<>();

    public WineTest() {
        // make sure wine.csv is in the right place in your path
        List<String[]> wineDataset = Util.loadCSV("/chapter7/data/wine.csv");
        // get our lines of data in random order
        Collections.shuffle(wineDataset);
        for (String[] wine : wineDataset) {
            // last thirteen items are parameters (doubles)
            double[] parameters = Arrays.stream(wine)
                    .skip(1)
                    .mapToDouble(Double::parseDouble)
                    .toArray();
            wineParameters.add(parameters);
            // first item is species
            int species = Integer.parseInt(wine[0]);
            switch (species) {
                case 1 :
                    wineClassifications.add(new double[] { 1.0, 0.0, 0.0 });
                    break;
                case 2 :
                    wineClassifications.add(new double[] { 0.0, 1.0, 0.0 });
                    break;
                default :
                    wineClassifications.add(new double[] { 0.0, 0.0, 1.0 });
                    break;
            }
            wineSpecies.add(species);
        }
        Util.normalizeByFeatureScaling(wineParameters);
    }
```

wineInterpretOutput() is analogous to irisInterpretOutput(). Because we do not have names for the wine cultivars, we are just working with the integer assignment in the original data set.

```
Listing 7.20   WineTest.java continued

    public Integer wineInterpretOutput(double[] output) {
        double max = Util.max(output);
        if (max == output[0]) {
            return 1;
        } else if (max == output[1]) {
            return 2;
        } else {
            return 3;
        }
    }
}
```

The layer configuration for the wine classification network needs 13 input neurons, as was already mentioned (one for each parameter). It also needs 3 output neurons. There are three cultivars of wine, just as there were three species of iris. Interestingly, the network works well with fewer neurons in the hidden layer than in the input layer. One possible intuitive explanation for this is that some of the input parameters are not actually helpful for classification, and it is useful to cut them out during processing. This is not, in fact, exactly how having fewer neurons in the hidden layer works, but it is an interesting intuitive idea.

```
Listing 7.21   WineTest.java continued

public Network<Integer>.Results classify() {
    // 13, 7, 3 layer structure; 0.9 learning rate, sigmoid activation func
    Network<Integer> wineNetwork = new Network<>(new int[] { 13, 7, 3 }, 0.9,
      Util::sigmoid, Util::derivativeSigmoid);
```

Once again, it can be interesting to experiment with a different number of hidden-layer neurons or a different learning rate.

```
Listing 7.22   WineTest.java continued

    // train over the first 150 wines in the data set 50 times
    List<double[]> wineTrainers = wineParameters.subList(0, 150);
    List<double[]> wineTrainersCorrects = wineClassifications.subList(0,
      150);
    int trainingIterations = 10;
    for (int i = 0; i < trainingIterations; i++) {
        wineNetwork.train(wineTrainers, wineTrainersCorrects);
    }
```

We will train over the first 150 samples in the data set, leaving the last 28 for validation. We will train 10 times over the samples, significantly less than the 50 for the iris data set. For whatever reason (perhaps innate qualities of the data set or tuning of parameters like the learning rate and number of hidden neurons), this data set requires less training to achieve significant accuracy than the iris data set.

Listing 7.23   WineTest.java continued

```
    // test over the last 28 of the wines in the data set
    List<double[]> wineTesters = wineParameters.subList(150, 178);
    List<Integer> wineTestersCorrects = wineSpecies.subList(150, 178);
    return wineNetwork.validate(wineTesters, wineTestersCorrects,
  this::wineInterpretOutput);
}

public static void main(String[] args) {
    WineTest wineTest = new WineTest();
    Network<Integer>.Results results = wineTest.classify();
    System.out.println(results.correct + " correct of " + results.trials
 + " = " + results.percentage * 100 + "%");
}

}
```

With a little luck, your neural network should be able to classify the 28 samples quite accurately:

```
27 correct of 28 = 96.42857142857143%
```

7.6   *Speeding up neural networks*

Neural networks require a lot of vector/matrix math. Essentially, this means taking a list of numbers and doing an operation on all of them at once. Libraries for optimized, performant vector/matrix math are increasingly important as machine learning continues to permeate our society. Many of these libraries take advantage of GPUs, because GPUs are optimized for this role. (Vectors/matrices are at the heart of computer graphics.) An older library specification you may have heard of is BLAS (Basic Linear Algebra Subprograms). A BLAS implementation underlies many numerical libraries, including the Java library ND4J.

Beyond the GPU, CPUs have extensions that can speed up vector/matrix processing. BLAS implementations often include functions that make use of *single instruction, multiple data* (SIMD) instructions. SIMD instructions are special microprocessor instructions that allow multiple pieces of data to be processed at once. They are sometimes known as *vector instructions*.

Different microprocessors include different SIMD instructions. For example, the SIMD extension to the G4 (a PowerPC architecture processor found in early '00s Macs) was known as AltiVec. ARM microprocessors, like those found in iPhones, have an extension known as NEON. And modern Intel microprocessors include SIMD extensions known as MMX, SSE, SSE2, and SSE3. Luckily, you do not need to know the differences. A well-turned numerical library will automatically choose the right instructions for computing efficiently on the underlying architecture that your program is running on.

It is no surprise, then, that real-world neural network libraries (unlike our toy library in this chapter) use specialized types as their base data structure instead of Java standard library lists or arrays. But they go even further. Popular neural network libraries like TensorFlow and PyTorch not only make use of SIMD instructions, but also make extensive use of GPU computing. Because GPUs are explicitly designed for fast vector computations, this accelerates neural networks by an order of magnitude compared with running on a CPU alone.

Let's be clear: *You would never want to naively implement a neural network for production using just the Java standard library as we did in this chapter.* Instead, you should use a well-optimized, SIMD- and GPU-enabled library like TensorFlow. The only exceptions would be a neural network library designed for education or one that had to run on an embedded device without SIMD instructions or a GPU.

7.7   *Neural network problems and extensions*

Neural networks are all the rage right now, thanks to advances in deep learning, but they have some significant shortcomings. The biggest problem is that a neural network solution to a problem is something of a black box. Even when neural networks work well, they do not give the user much insight into how they solve the problem. For instance, the iris data set classifier we worked on in this chapter does not clearly show how much each of the four parameters in the input affects the output. Was sepal length more important than sepal width for classifying each sample?

It is possible that careful analysis of the final weights for the trained network could provide some insight, but such analysis is nontrivial and does not provide the kind of insight that, say, linear regression does in terms of the meaning of each variable in the function being modeled. In other words, a neural network may solve a problem, but it does not explain how the problem is solved.

Another problem with neural networks is that to become accurate, they often require very large data sets. Imagine an image classifier for outdoor landscapes. It may need to classify thousands of different types of images (forests, valleys, mountains, streams, steppes, and so on). It will potentially need millions of training images. Not only are such large data sets hard to come by, but also, for some applications they may be completely nonexistent. It tends to be large corporations and governments that have the data-warehousing and technical facilities for collecting and storing such massive data sets.

Finally, neural networks are computationally expensive. Just training on a moderately sized data set can bring your computer to its knees. And it's not just naive neural network implementations—with any computational platform where neural networks are used, it is the sheer number of calculations that have to be performed in training the network, more than anything else, that takes so much time. Many tricks abound to make neural networks more performant (like using SIMD instructions or GPUs), but ultimately, training a neural network requires a lot of floating-point operations.

One nice realization is that training is much more computationally expensive than actually using the network. Some applications do not require ongoing training. In those instances, a trained network can just be dropped into an application to solve a problem. For example, the first version of Apple's Core ML framework did not even support training. It only supported helping app developers run pretrained neural network models in their apps. An app developer creating a photo app could download a freely licensed image-classification model, drop it into Core ML, and start using performant machine learning in an app instantly.

In this chapter, we only worked with a single type of neural network: a feed-forward network with backpropagation. As has been mentioned, many other kinds of neural networks exist. Convolutional neural networks are also feed-forward, but they have multiple different types of hidden layers, different mechanisms for distributing weights, and other interesting properties that make them especially well designed for image classification. In recurrent neural networks, signals do not just travel in one direction. They allow feedback loops and have proven useful for continuous input applications like handwriting recognition and voice recognition.

A simple extension to our neural network that would make it more performant would be the inclusion of bias neurons. A *bias neuron* is like a dummy neuron in a layer that allows the next layer's output to represent more functions by providing a constant input (still modified by a weight) into it. Even simple neural networks used for real-world problems usually contain bias neurons. If you add bias neurons to our existing network, you will likely find that it requires less training to achieve a similar level of accuracy.

7.8   *Real-world applications*

Although they were first imagined in the middle of the 20th century, artificial neural networks did not become commonplace until the last decade. Their widespread application was held back by a lack of sufficiently performant hardware. Today, artificial neural networks have become the most explosive growth area in machine learning because they work!

Artificial neural networks have enabled some of the most exciting user-facing computing applications in decades. These include practical voice recognition (practical in terms of sufficient accuracy), image recognition, and handwriting recognition. Voice recognition is present in typing aids like Dragon NaturallySpeaking and digital assistants like Siri, Alexa, and Cortana. A specific example of image recognition is Facebook's automatic tagging of people in a photo using facial recognition. In recent versions of iOS, you can search words within your notes, even if they are handwritten, by employing handwriting recognition.

An older recognition technology that can be powered by neural networks is OCR (optical character recognition). OCR is used every time you scan a document and it comes back as selectable text instead of an image. OCR enables toll booths to read license plates and envelopes to be quickly sorted by the postal service.

In this chapter you have seen neural networks used successfully for classification problems. Similar applications that neural networks work well in are recommendation systems. Think of Netflix suggesting a movie you might like to watch or Amazon suggesting a book you might want to read. There are other machine learning techniques that work well for recommendation systems too (Amazon and Netflix do not necessarily use neural networks for these purposes; the details of their systems are likely proprietary), so neural networks should only be selected after all options have been explored.

Neural networks can be used in any situation where an unknown function needs to be approximated. This makes them useful for prediction. Neural networks can be employed to predict the outcome of a sporting event, election, or the stock market (and they are). Of course, their accuracy is a product of how well they are trained, and that has to do with how large a data set relevant to the unknown-outcome event is available, how well the parameters of the neural network are tuned, and how many iterations of training are run. With prediction, like most neural network applications, one of the hardest parts is deciding on the structure of the network itself, which is often ultimately determined by trial and error.

7.9 *Exercises*

1 Use the neural network framework developed in this chapter to classify items in another data set.

2 Try running the examples with a different activation function. (Remember to also find its derivative.) How does the change in activation function affect the accuracy of the network? Does it require more or less training?

3 Take the problems in this chapter and re-create their solutions using a popular neural network framework like TensorFlow.

4 Rewrite the `Network`, `Layer`, and `Neuron` classes using a third-party Java numerical library to accelerate the execution of the neural network developed in this chapter.

Adversarial search

A two-player, zero-sum, perfect information game is one in which both opponents have all of the information about the state of the game available to them, and any gain in advantage for one is a loss of advantage for the other. Such games include tic-tac-toe, Connect Four, checkers, and chess. In this chapter, we will study how to create an artificial opponent that can play such games with great skill. In fact, the techniques discussed in this chapter, coupled with modern computing power, can create artificial opponents that play simple games of this class perfectly and that can play complex games beyond the ability of any human opponent.

8.1   *Basic board game components*

As with most of our more complex problems in this book, we will try to make our solution as generic as possible. In the case of adversarial search, that means making our search algorithms non-game-specific. Let's start by defining some simple interfaces that define all of the ways to access state that our search algorithms will need. Later, we can implement those interfaces for the specific games we are interested in developing (tic-tac-toe and Connect Four) and feed the implementations into the search algorithms to make them "play" the games. Here are those interfaces.

Listing 8.1   Piece.java

```java
package chapter8;

public interface Piece {
    Piece opposite();
}
```

`Piece` is an interface for a piece on the board in a game. It will also double as our turn indicator. This is why the `opposite` method is needed. We need to know whose turn follows a given turn.

> **TIP** Because tic-tac-toe and Connect Four only have one kind of piece, a single `Piece` implementation can double as a turn indicator in this chapter. For a more complex game, like chess, that has different kinds of pieces, turns can be indicated by an integer or a Boolean. Alternatively, just the "color" attribute of a more complex `Piece` type could be used to indicate turn.

Listing 8.2 Board.java

```java
package chapter8;

import java.util.List;

public interface Board<Move> {
    Piece getTurn();

    Board<Move> move(Move location);

    List<Move> getLegalMoves();

    boolean isWin();

    default boolean isDraw() {
        return !isWin() && getLegalMoves().isEmpty();
    }

    double evaluate(Piece player);
}
```

`Board` describes the interface for a class that is the actual maintainer of positional state. For any given game that our search algorithms will compute, we need to be able to answer four questions:

- Whose turn is it?
- What legal moves can be played in the current position?
- Is the game won?
- Is the game drawn?

That last question, about draws, is actually a combination of the previous two questions for many games. If the game is not won but there are no legal moves, then it is a draw. This is why our interface, `Board`, can already have a concrete default implementation of the `isDraw()` method. In addition, there are a couple of actions we need to be able to take:

- Make a move to go from the current position to a new position.
- Evaluate the position to see which player has an advantage.

Each of the methods and properties in `Board` is a proxy for one of the preceding questions or actions. The `Board` interface could also be called Position in game parlance, but we will use that nomenclature for something more specific in each of our subclasses.

`Board` has a generic type, `Move`. The `Move` type will represent a move in a game. In this chapter, it can just be an integer. In games like tic-tac-toe and Connect Four, an integer can represent a move by indicating a square or column where a piece should be placed. In more complex games, more than an integer may be needed to describe a move. Making `Move` generic allows `Board` to represent a wider variety of games.

8.2   Tic-tac-toe

Tic-tac-toe is a simple game, but it can be used to illustrate the same minimax algorithm that can be applied in advanced strategy games like Connect Four, checkers, and chess. We will build a tic-tac-toe AI that plays perfectly using minimax.

> **NOTE**   This section assumes that you are familiar with the game tic-tac-toe and its standard rules. If not, a quick search on the web should get you up to speed.

8.2.1   Managing tic-tac-toe state

Let's develop some structures to keep track of the state of a tic-tac-toe game as it progresses.

First, we need a way of representing each square on the tic-tac-toe board. We will use an enum called `TTTPiece`, an implementer of `Piece`. A tic-tac-toe piece can be `X`, `O`, or empty (represented by `E` in the enum).

Listing 8.3   TTTPiece.java

```java
package chapter8;

public enum TTTPiece implements Piece {
    X, O, E; // E is Empty

    @Override
    public TTTPiece opposite() {
        switch (this) {
        case X:
            return TTTPiece.O;
        case O:
            return TTTPiece.X;
        default: // E, empty
            return TTTPiece.E;
        }
    }

    @Override
    public String toString() {
        switch (this) {
        case X:
            return "X";
```

```
        case O:
            return "O";
        default: // E, empty
            return " ";
        }

    }

}
```

The enum `TTTPiece` has a method, `opposite`, that returns another `TTTPiece`. This will be useful for flipping from one player's turn to the other player's turn after a tic-tac-toe move. To represent moves, we will just use an integer that corresponds to a square on the board where a piece is placed. As you will recall, `Move` was a generic type in `Board`. We will specify that `Move` is an `Integer` when we define `TTTBoard`.

A tic-tac-toe board has nine positions organized in three rows and three columns. For simplicity, these nine positions can be represented using a one-dimensional array. Which squares receive which numeric designation (a.k.a., index in the array) is arbitrary, but we will follow the scheme outlined in figure 8.1.

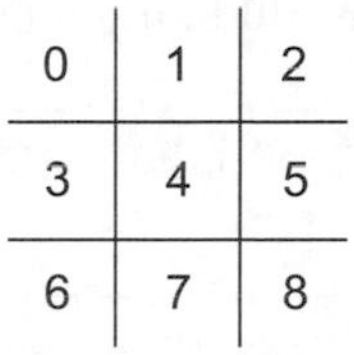

0	1	2
3	4	5
6	7	8

Figure 8.1 The one-dimensional array indices that correspond to each square in the tic-tac-toe board

The main holder of state will be the class `TTTBoard`. `TTTBoard` keeps track of two different pieces of state: the position (represented by the aforementioned one-dimensional list) and the player whose turn it is.

Listing 8.4 TTTBoard.java

```
package chapter8;

import java.util.ArrayList;
import java.util.Arrays;
import java.util.List;

public class TTTBoard implements Board<Integer> {
    private static final int NUM_SQUARES = 9;
    private TTTPiece[] position;
    private TTTPiece turn;

    public TTTBoard(TTTPiece[] position, TTTPiece turn) {
        this.position = position;
        this.turn = turn;
    }
```

```
public TTTBoard() {
    // by default start with blank board
    position = new TTTPiece[NUM_SQUARES];
    Arrays.fill(position, TTTPiece.E);
    // X goes first
    turn = TTTPiece.X;
}

@Override
public Piece getTurn() {
    return turn;
}
```

A default board is one where no moves have yet been made (an empty board). The no-parameter constructor for TTTBoard initializes such a position, with X to move (the usual first player in tic-tac-toe). getTurn() indicates whose turn it is in the current position, X or O.

TTTBoard is an informally immutable data structure; TTTBoards should not be modified. Instead, every time a move needs to be played, a new TTTBoard with the position changed to accommodate the move will be generated. This will later be helpful in our search algorithm. When the search branches, we will not inadvertently change the position of a board from which potential moves are still being analyzed.

Listing 8.5   TTTBoard.java continued

```
@Override
public TTTBoard move(Integer location) {
    TTTPiece[] tempPosition = Arrays.copyOf(position, position.length);
    tempPosition[location] = turn;
    return new TTTBoard(tempPosition, turn.opposite());
}
```

A legal move in tic-tac-toe is any empty square. getLegalMoves() looks for any empty squares on the board and returns a list of them.

Listing 8.6   TTTBoard.java continued

```
@Override
public List<Integer> getLegalMoves() {
    ArrayList<Integer> legalMoves = new ArrayList<>();
    for (int i = 0; i < NUM_SQUARES; i++) {
        // empty squares are legal moves
        if (position[i] == TTTPiece.E) {
            legalMoves.add(i);
        }
    }
    return legalMoves;
}
```

There are many ways to scan the rows, columns, and diagonals of a tic-tac-toe board to check for wins. The following implementation of the method isWin(), along with its helper method, checkPos(), does so with a hardcoded, seemingly endless amalgamation of &&, ||, and ==. It is not the prettiest code, but it does the job in a straightforward manner.

Listing 8.7   TTTBoard.java continued

```java
@Override
public boolean isWin() {
    // three row, three column, and then two diagonal checks
    return
        checkPos(0, 1, 2) || checkPos(3, 4, 5) || checkPos(6, 7, 8)
        || checkPos(0, 3, 6) || checkPos(1, 4, 7) || checkPos(2, 5, 8)
        || checkPos(0, 4, 8) || checkPos(2, 4, 6);
}

private boolean checkPos(int p0, int p1, int p2) {
    return position[p0] == position[p1] && position[p0] == position[p2]
            && position[p0] != TTTPiece.E;
}
```

If all of a row's, column's, or diagonal's squares are not empty, and they contain the same piece, the game has been won.

A game is drawn if it is not won and there are no more legal moves left; that property was already covered by the Board interface's default method isDraw(). Finally, we need a way of evaluating a particular position and pretty-printing the board.

Listing 8.8   TTTBoard.java continued

```java
@Override
public double evaluate(Piece player) {
    if (isWin() && turn == player) {
        return -1;
    } else if (isWin() && turn != player) {
        return 1;
    } else {
        return 0.0;
    }
}

@Override
public String toString() {
    StringBuilder sb = new StringBuilder();
    for (int row = 0; row < 3; row++) {
        for (int col = 0; col < 3; col++) {
            sb.append(position[row * 3 + col].toString());
            if (col != 2) {
                sb.append("|");
            }
        }
        sb.append(System.lineSeparator());
        if (row != 2) {
            sb.append("-----");
```

```
            sb.append(System.lineSeparator());
        }
    }
    return sb.toString();
}

}
```

For most games, an evaluation of a position needs to be an approximation, because we cannot search the game to the very end to find out with certainty who wins or loses depending on what moves are played. But tic-tac-toe has a small enough search space that we can search from any position to the very end. Therefore, the `evaluate()` method can simply return one number if the player wins, a worse number for a draw, and an even worse number for a loss.

8.2.2 *Minimax*

Minimax is a classic algorithm for finding the best move in a two-player, zero-sum game with perfect information, like tic-tac-toe, checkers, or chess. It has been extended and modified for other types of games as well. Minimax is typically implemented using a recursive function in which each player is designated either the maximizing player or the minimizing player.

The maximizing player aims to find the move that will lead to maximal gains. However, the maximizing player must account for moves by the minimizing player. After each attempt to maximize the gains of the maximizing player, minimax is called recursively to find the opponent's reply that minimizes the maximizing player's gains. This continues back and forth (maximizing, minimizing, maximizing, and so on) until a base case in the recursive function is reached. The base case is a terminal position (a win or a draw) or a maximal search depth.

Minimax will return an evaluation of the starting position for the maximizing player. For the `evaluate()` method of the `TTTBoard` class, if the best possible play by both sides will result in a win for the maximizing player, a score of 1 will be returned. If the best play will result in a loss, –1 is returned. A 0 is returned if the best play is a draw.

These numbers are returned when a base case is reached. They then bubble up through all of the recursive calls that led to the base case. For each recursive call to maximize, the best evaluations one level further down bubble up. For each recursive call to minimize, the worst evaluations one level further down bubble up. In this way, a decision tree is built. Figure 8.2 illustrates such a tree that facilitates bubbling up for a game with two moves left.

For games that have a search space too deep to reach a terminal position (such as checkers and chess), minimax is stopped after a certain depth (the number of moves deep to search, sometimes called *ply*). Then the evaluation function kicks in, using heuristics to score the state of the game. The better the game is for the originating player, the higher the score that is awarded. We will come back to this concept with Connect Four, which has a much larger search space than tic-tac-toe.

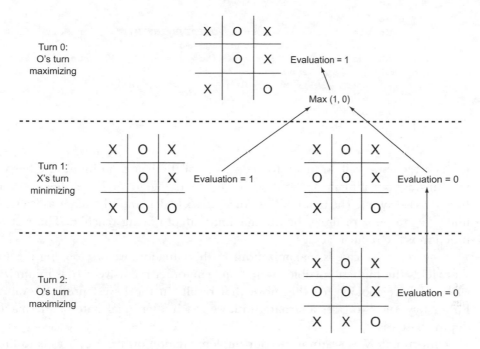

Figure 8.2 A minimax decision tree for a tic-tac-toe game with two moves left. To maximize the likelihood of winning, the initial player, O, will choose to play O in the bottom center. Arrows indicate the positions from which a decision is made.

Here is minimax() in its entirety.

Listing 8.9 Minimax.java

```java
package chapter8;

public class Minimax {
    // Find the best possible outcome for originalPlayer
    public static <Move> double minimax(Board<Move> board, boolean
      maximizing, Piece originalPlayer, int maxDepth) {
        // Base case-terminal position or maximum depth reached
        if (board.isWin() || board.isDraw() || maxDepth == 0) {
            return board.evaluate(originalPlayer);
        }
        // Recursive case-maximize your gains or minimize opponent's gains
        if (maximizing) {
            double bestEval = Double.NEGATIVE_INFINITY; // result above
            for (Move move : board.getLegalMoves()) {
                double result = minimax(board.move(move), false,
  originalPlayer, maxDepth - 1);
                bestEval = Math.max(result, bestEval);
            }
            return bestEval;
```

```
        } else { // minimizing
            double worstEval = Double.POSITIVE_INFINITY; // result below
            for (Move move : board.getLegalMoves()) {
                double result = minimax(board.move(move), true,
    originalPlayer, maxDepth - 1);
                worstEval = Math.min(result, worstEval);
            }
            return worstEval;
        }
    }
```

In each recursive call, we need to keep track of the board position, whether we are maximizing or minimizing, and who we are trying to evaluate the position for (originalPlayer). The first few lines of minimax() deal with the base case: a terminal node (a win, loss, or draw) or the maximum depth being reached. The rest of the function is the recursive cases.

One recursive case is maximization. In this situation, we are looking for a move that yields the highest possible evaluation. The other recursive case is minimization, where we are looking for the move that results in the lowest possible evaluation. Either way, the two cases alternate until we reach a terminal state or the maximum depth (base case).

Unfortunately, we cannot use our implementation of minimax() as is to find the best move for a given position. It returns an evaluation (a double value). It does not tell us what best first move led to that evaluation.

Instead, we will create a helper function, findBestMove(), that loops through calls to minimax() for each legal move in a position to find the move that evaluates to the highest value. You can think of findBestMove() as the first maximizing call to minimax(), but with us keeping track of those initial moves.

Listing 8.10   Minimax.java continued

```
    // Find the best possible move in the current position
    // looking up to maxDepth ahead
    public static <Move> Move findBestMove(Board<Move> board, int maxDepth) {
        double bestEval = Double.NEGATIVE_INFINITY;
        Move bestMove = null; // won't stay null for sure
        for (Move move : board.getLegalMoves()) {
            double result = minimax(board.move(move), false, board.getTurn(),
    maxDepth);
            if (result > bestEval) {
                bestEval = result;
                bestMove = move;
            }
        }
        return bestMove;
    }
}
```

We now have everything ready to find the best possible move for any tic-tac-toe position.

8.2.3   *Testing minimax with tic-tac-toe*

Tic-tac-toe is such a simple game that it's easy for us, as humans, to figure out the definite correct move in a given position. This makes it possible to easily develop unit tests. In the following code snippet, we will challenge our minimax algorithm to find the correct next move in three different tic-tac-toe positions. The first is easy and only requires it to think to the next move for a win. The second requires a block; the AI must stop its opponent from scoring a victory. The last is a little bit more challenging and requires the AI to think two moves into the future.

> **WARNING** At the beginning of this book I promised you that all examples would use only the Java standard library. And, unfortunately for this next snippet of code, I have stuck to my promise. In reality, unit testing is best done using a mature framework like JUnit, instead of rolling your own, as we do here. But this example is interesting for its illustration of reflection.

Listing 8.11   TTTMinimaxTests.java

```java
package chapter8;

import java.lang.annotation.Retention;
import java.lang.annotation.RetentionPolicy;
import java.lang.reflect.Method;

// Annotation for unit tests
@Retention(RetentionPolicy.RUNTIME)
@interface UnitTest {
    String name() default "";
}

public class TTTMinimaxTests {

    // Check if two values are equal and report back
    public static <T> void assertEquality(T actual, T expected) {
        if (actual.equals(expected)) {
            System.out.println("Passed!");
        } else {
            System.out.println("Failed!");
            System.out.println("Actual: " + actual.toString());
            System.out.println("Expected: " + expected.toString());
        }
    }

    @UnitTest(name = "Easy Position")
    public void easyPosition() {
        TTTPiece[] toWinEasyPosition = new TTTPiece[] {
                TTTPiece.X, TTTPiece.O, TTTPiece.X,
                TTTPiece.X, TTTPiece.E, TTTPiece.O,
                TTTPiece.E, TTTPiece.E, TTTPiece.O };
        TTTBoard testBoard1 = new TTTBoard(toWinEasyPosition, TTTPiece.X);
        Integer answer1 = Minimax.findBestMove(testBoard1, 8);
        assertEquality(answer1, 6);
    }
```

```java
@UnitTest(name = "Block Position")
public void blockPosition() {
    TTTPiece[] toBlockPosition = new TTTPiece[] {
            TTTPiece.X, TTTPiece.E, TTTPiece.E,
            TTTPiece.E, TTTPiece.E, TTTPiece.O,
            TTTPiece.E, TTTPiece.X, TTTPiece.O };
    TTTBoard testBoard2 = new TTTBoard(toBlockPosition, TTTPiece.X);
    Integer answer2 = Minimax.findBestMove(testBoard2, 8);
    assertEquality(answer2, 2);
}


@UnitTest(name = "Hard Position")
public void hardPosition() {
    TTTPiece[] toWinHardPosition = new TTTPiece[] {
            TTTPiece.X, TTTPiece.E, TTTPiece.E,
            TTTPiece.E, TTTPiece.E, TTTPiece.O,
            TTTPiece.O, TTTPiece.X, TTTPiece.E };
    TTTBoard testBoard3 = new TTTBoard(toWinHardPosition, TTTPiece.X);
    Integer answer3 = Minimax.findBestMove(testBoard3, 8);
    assertEquality(answer3, 1);
}


// Run all methods marked with the UnitTest annotation
public void runAllTests() {
    for (Method method : this.getClass().getMethods()) {
        for (UnitTest annotation :
 method.getAnnotationsByType(UnitTest.class)) {
            System.out.println("Running Test " + annotation.name());
            try {
                method.invoke(this);
            } catch (Exception e) {
                e.printStackTrace();
            }
            System.out.println("_____");
        }
    }
}


public static void main(String[] args) {
    new TTTMinimaxTests().runAllTests();
}
}
```

As was mentioned in the preceding note, it's probably not a good idea to roll your own unit testing framework instead of using something like JUnit. That said, it's also not that hard, thanks to Java's reflection capabilities. Each method represent-ing a test is annotated with a custom annotation called UnitTest, defined at the top of the file. The method runAllTests() looks for all methods with that annotation and runs them along with some helpful printouts. assertEquality() checks if two items are equal, and if they're not, prints them out. While it might not be a good idea to define your own unit testing framework, it is interesting to see how one could work. To take our framework to the next level, we would probably define a base class that includes `runAllTests()` and `assertEquality()` that other testing classes could extend.

All three of the tests should pass when you run TTTMinimaxTests.java.

TIP It does not take much code to implement minimax, and it will work for many more games than just tic-tac-toe. If you plan to implement minimax for another game, it is important to set yourself up for success by creating data structures that work well for the way minimax is designed, like the `Board` class. A common mistake for students learning minimax is to use a modifiable data structure that gets changed by a recursive call to minimax and then cannot be rewound to its original state for additional calls.

8.2.4 *Developing a tic-tac-toe AI*

With all of these ingredients in place, it is trivial to take the next step and develop a full artificial opponent that can play an entire game of tic-tac-toe. Instead of evaluating a test position, the AI will just evaluate the position generated by each opponent's move. In the following short code snippet, the tic-tac-toe AI plays against a human opponent who goes first.

Listing 8.12 TicTacToe.java

```java
package chapter8;

import java.util.Scanner;

public class TicTacToe {

    private TTTBoard board = new TTTBoard();
    private Scanner scanner = new Scanner(System.in);

    private Integer getPlayerMove() {
        Integer playerMove = -1;
        while (!board.getLegalMoves().contains(playerMove)) {
            System.out.println("Enter a legal square (0-8):");
            Integer play = scanner.nextInt();
            playerMove = play;
        }
        return playerMove;
    }

    private void runGame() {
        // main game loop
        while (true) {
            Integer humanMove = getPlayerMove();
            board = board.move(humanMove);
            if (board.isWin()) {
                System.out.println("Human wins!");
                break;
            } else if (board.isDraw()) {
                System.out.println("Draw!");
```

```
                break;
            }
            Integer computerMove = Minimax.findBestMove(board, 9);
            System.out.println("Computer move is " + computerMove);
            board = board.move(computerMove);
            System.out.println(board);
            if (board.isWin()) {
                System.out.println("Computer wins!");
                break;
            } else if (board.isDraw()) {
                System.out.println("Draw!");
                break;
            }
        }
    }

    public static void main(String[] args) {
        new TicTacToe().runGame();
    }

}
```

By setting the maxDepth parameter of findBestMove() to 9 (it could be 8, really), this tic-tac-toe AI will always see to the very end of the game. (The maximum number of moves in tic-tac-toe is nine, and the AI goes second.) Therefore, it should play perfectly every time. A perfect game is one in which both opponents play the best possible move every turn. The result of a perfect game of tic-tac-toe is a draw. With this in mind, you should never be able to beat the tic-tac-toe AI. If you play your best, it will be a draw. If you make a mistake, the AI will win. Try it out yourself. You should not be able to beat it. Here's an example run of our program:

```
Enter a legal square (0-8):
4
Computer move is 0
O| |
-----
 |X|
-----
 | |

Enter a legal square (0-8):
2
Computer move is 6
O| |X
-----
 |X|
-----
O| |

Enter a legal square (0-8):
3
```

```
Computer move is 5
O| |X
-----
X|X|O
-----
O| |

Enter a legal square (0-8):
1
Computer move is 7
O|X|X
-----
X|X|O
-----
O|O|

Enter a legal square (0-8):
8
Draw!
```

8.3   Connect Four

In Connect Four,[1] two players alternate dropping different-colored pieces in a seven-column, six-row vertical grid. Pieces fall from the top of the grid to the bottom until they hit the bottom or another piece. In essence, the player's only decision each turn is which of the seven columns to drop a piece into. The player cannot drop it into a full column. The first player that has four pieces of their color next to one another with no breaks in a row, column, or diagonal wins. If no player achieves this, and the grid is completely filled, the game is a draw.

8.3.1   Connect Four game machinery

Connect Four, in many ways, is similar to tic-tac-toe. Both games are played on a grid and require the player to line up pieces to win. But because the Connect Four grid is larger and has many more ways to win, evaluating each position is significantly more complex.

Some of the following code will look very familiar, but the data structures and the evaluation method are quite different from tic-tac-toe. Both games are built using classes that implement the same base `Piece` and `Board` interfaces you saw at the beginning of the chapter, making `minimax()` usable for both games.

Listing 8.13   C4Piece.java

```java
package chapter8;

public enum C4Piece implements Piece {
    B, R, E; // E is Empty
```

---

[1] Connect Four is a trademark of Hasbro, Inc. It is used here only in a descriptive and positive manner.

```
    @Override
    public C4Piece opposite() {
        switch (this) {
        case B:
            return C4Piece.R;
        case R:
            return C4Piece.B;
        default: // E, empty
            return C4Piece.E;
        }
    }

    @Override
    public String toString() {
        switch (this) {
        case B:
            return "B";
        case R:
            return "R";
        default: // E, empty
            return " ";
        }
    }

}
```

The C4Piece class is almost identical to the TTTPiece class. We will also have a convenience class, C4Location for keeping track of a location on the board's grid (a col-
umn/row pair). Connect Four is a column-oriented game, so we implement all of its
grid code in the unusual format of column first.

Listing 8.14   C4Location.java

```
package chapter8;

public final class C4Location {
    public final int column, row;

    public C4Location(int column, int row) {
        this.column = column;
        this.row = row;
    }
}
```

Next, we turn to the heart of our Connect Four implementation, the C4Board class.
This class defines some static constants and one static method. The static method
generateSegments() returns a list of arrays of grid locations (C4Locations). Each
array in the list contains four grid locations. We call each of these arrays of four grid
locations a *segment*. If any segment from the board is all the same color, that color has
won the game.

Being able to quickly search all of the segments on the board is useful for both checking whether a game is over (someone has won) and for evaluating a position. Hence, you will notice in the next code snippet that we cache the segments for the board as a class variable called SEGMENTS in the C4Board class.

Listing 8.15 C4Board.java

```java
package chapter8;

import java.util.ArrayList;
import java.util.Arrays;
import java.util.List;

public class C4Board implements Board<Integer> {
    public static final int NUM_COLUMNS = 7;
    public static final int NUM_ROWS = 6;
    public static final int SEGMENT_LENGTH = 4;
    public static final ArrayList<C4Location[]> SEGMENTS = generateSegments();

    // generate all of the segments for a given board
    // this static method is only run once
    private static ArrayList<C4Location[]> generateSegments() {
        ArrayList<C4Location[]> segments = new ArrayList<>();
        // vertical
        for (int c = 0; c < NUM_COLUMNS; c++) {
            for (int r = 0; r <= NUM_ROWS - SEGMENT_LENGTH; r++) {
                C4Location[] bl = new C4Location[SEGMENT_LENGTH];
                for (int i = 0; i < SEGMENT_LENGTH; i++) {
                    bl[i] = new C4Location(c, r + i);
                }
                segments.add(bl);
            }
        }
        // horizontal
        for (int c = 0; c <= NUM_COLUMNS - SEGMENT_LENGTH; c++) {
            for (int r = 0; r < NUM_ROWS; r++) {
                C4Location[] bl = new C4Location[SEGMENT_LENGTH];
                for (int i = 0; i < SEGMENT_LENGTH; i++) {
                    bl[i] = new C4Location(c + i, r);
                }
                segments.add(bl);
            }
        }
        // diagonal from bottom left to top right
        for (int c = 0; c <= NUM_COLUMNS - SEGMENT_LENGTH; c++) {
            for (int r = 0; r <= NUM_ROWS - SEGMENT_LENGTH; r++) {
                C4Location[] bl = new C4Location[SEGMENT_LENGTH];
                for (int i = 0; i < SEGMENT_LENGTH; i++) {
                    bl[i] = new C4Location(c + i, r + i);
                }
                segments.add(bl);
            }
        }
```

```
        // diagonal from bottom right to top left
        for (int c = NUM_COLUMNS - SEGMENT_LENGTH; c >= 0; c--) {
            for (int r = SEGMENT_LENGTH - 1; r < NUM_ROWS; r++) {
                C4Location[] bl = new C4Location[SEGMENT_LENGTH];
                for (int i = 0; i < SEGMENT_LENGTH; i++) {
                    bl[i] = new C4Location(c + i, r - i);
                }
                segments.add(bl);
            }
        }

        return segments;
    }
```

We store the current position in a two-dimensional array of C4Piece called position. In most cases, two-dimensional arrays are indexed row first. But thinking about the Connect Four board as a group of seven columns is conceptually powerful and makes writing the rest of the C4Board class slightly easier. For example, the accompanying array, columnCount, keeps track of how many pieces are in any given column at a time. And this makes generating legal moves easy, since each move is essentially a selection of a non-filled column.

The next four methods are fairly similar to their tic-tac-toe equivalents.

Listing 8.16   C4Board.java continued

```
private C4Piece[][] position; // column first, then row
private int[] columnCount; // number of pieces in each column
private C4Piece turn;

public C4Board() {
    // note that we're doing columns first
    position = new C4Piece[NUM_COLUMNS][NUM_ROWS];
    for (C4Piece[] col : position) {
        Arrays.fill(col, C4Piece.E);
    }
    // ints by default are initialized to 0
    columnCount = new int[NUM_COLUMNS];
    turn = C4Piece.B; // black goes first
}

public C4Board(C4Piece[][] position, C4Piece turn) {
    this.position = position;
    columnCount = new int[NUM_COLUMNS];
    for (int c = 0; c < NUM_COLUMNS; c++) {
        int piecesInColumn = 0;
        for (int r = 0; r < NUM_ROWS; r++) {
            if (position[c][r] != C4Piece.E) {
                piecesInColumn++;
            }
        }
        columnCount[c] = piecesInColumn;
    }
```

```
        this.turn = turn;
    }

    @Override
    public Piece getTurn() {
        return turn;
    }

    @Override
    public C4Board move(Integer location) {
        C4Piece[][] tempPosition = Arrays.copyOf(position, position.length);
        for (int col = 0; col < NUM_COLUMNS; col++) {
            tempPosition[col] = Arrays.copyOf(position[col],
 position[col].length);
        }
        tempPosition[location][columnCount[location]] = turn;
        return new C4Board(tempPosition, turn.opposite());
    }

    @Override
    public List<Integer> getLegalMoves() {
        List<Integer> legalMoves = new ArrayList<>();
        for (int i = 0; i < NUM_COLUMNS; i++) {
            if (columnCount[i] < NUM_ROWS) {
                legalMoves.add(i);
            }
        }
        return legalMoves;
    }
```

A private helper method, countSegment(), returns the number of black or red pieces in a particular segment. It is followed by the win-checking method, isWin(), which looks at all of the segments in the board and determines a win by using countSegment() to see if any segments have four of the same color.

Listing 8.17 C4Board.java continued

```
    private int countSegment(C4Location[] segment, C4Piece color) {
        int count = 0;
        for (C4Location location : segment) {
            if (position[location.column][location.row] == color) {
                count++;
            }
        }
        return count;
    }

    @Override
    public boolean isWin() {
        for (C4Location[] segment : SEGMENTS) {
            int blackCount = countSegment(segment, C4Piece.B);
            int redCount = countSegment(segment, C4Piece.R);
            if (blackCount == SEGMENT_LENGTH || redCount == SEGMENT_LENGTH) {
                return true;
```

```
        }
    }
    return false;
}
```

Like `TTTBoard`, `C4Board` can use the `Board` interface's `isDraw()` default method without modification.

Finally, to evaluate a position, we will evaluate all of its representative segments, one segment at a time, and sum those evaluations to return a result. A segment that has both red and black pieces will be considered worthless. A segment that has two of the same color and two empties will be considered a score of 1. A segment with three of the same color will be scored 100. Finally, a segment with four of the same color (a win) is scored 1,000,000. These `evaluate` numbers are arbitrary in absolute terms but their importance lies in their relative weight to one another. If the segment is the opponent's segment, we will negate its score. `evaluateSegment()` is a private helper method that evaluates a single segment using the preceding formula. The composite score of all segments using `evaluateSegment()` is generated by `evaluate()`.

Listing 8.18   C4Board.java continued

```java
    private double evaluateSegment(C4Location[] segment, Piece player) {
        int blackCount = countSegment(segment, C4Piece.B);
        int redCount = countSegment(segment, C4Piece.R);
        if (redCount > 0 && blackCount > 0) {
            return 0.0; // mixed segments are neutral
        }
        int count = Math.max(blackCount, redCount);
        double score = 0.0;
        if (count == 2) {
            score = 1.0;
        } else if (count == 3) {
            score = 100.0;
        } else if (count == 4) {
            score = 1000000.0;
        }
        C4Piece color = (redCount > blackCount) ? C4Piece.R : C4Piece.B;
        if (color != player) {
            return -score;
        }
        return score;
    }

    @Override
    public double evaluate(Piece player) {
        double total = 0.0;
        for (C4Location[] segment : SEGMENTS) {
            total += evaluateSegment(segment, player);
        }
        return total;
    }
```

```
    @Override
    public String toString() {
        StringBuilder sb = new StringBuilder();
        for (int r = NUM_ROWS - 1; r >= 0; r--) {
            sb.append("|");
            for (int c = 0; c < NUM_COLUMNS; c++) {
                sb.append(position[c][r].toString());
                sb.append("|");
            }
            sb.append(System.lineSeparator());
        }
        return sb.toString();
    }

}
```

8.3.2   A Connect Four AI

Amazingly, the same minimax() and findBestMove() functions we developed for tic-tac-toe can be used unchanged with our Connect Four implementation. In the following code snippet, there are only a couple of changes from the code for our tic-tac-toe AI. The big difference is that maxDepth is now set to 5. That enables the computer's thinking time per move to be reasonable. In other words, our Connect Four AI looks at (evaluates) positions up to five moves in the future.

Listing 8.19   ConnectFour.java

```
package chapter8;

import java.util.Scanner;

public class ConnectFour {

    private C4Board board = new C4Board();
    private Scanner scanner = new Scanner(System.in);

    private Integer getPlayerMove() {
        Integer playerMove = 1;
        while (!board.getLegalMoves().contains(playerMove)) {
            System.out.println("Enter a legal column (0-6):");
            Integer play = scanner.nextInt();
            playerMove = play;
        }
        return playerMove;
    }

    private void runGame() {
        // main game loop
        while (true) {
            Integer humanMove = getPlayerMove();
            board = board.move(humanMove);
            if (board.isWin()) {
                System.out.println("Human wins!");
                break;
```

```
        } else if (board.isDraw()) {
            System.out.println("Draw!");
            break;
        }
        Integer computerMove = Minimax.findBestMove(board, 5);
        System.out.println("Computer move is " + computerMove);
        board = board.move(computerMove);
        System.out.println(board);
        if (board.isWin()) {
            System.out.println("Computer wins!");
            break;
        } else if (board.isDraw()) {
            System.out.println("Draw!");
            break;
        }
    }
}

public static void main(String[] args) {
    new ConnectFour().runGame();
}

}
```

Try playing the Connect Four AI. You will notice that it takes a few seconds to generate each move, unlike the tic-tac-toe AI. It will probably still beat you unless you're carefully thinking about your moves. It at least will not make any completely obvious mistakes. We can improve its play by increasing the depth that it searches, but each computer move will take exponentially longer to compute. Here's the first few moves of a game against our AI:

```
Enter a legal column (0-6):
3
Computer move is 3
| | | | | | | |
| | | | | | | |
| | | | | | | |
| | | | | | | |
| | | |R| | | |
| | | |B| | | |

Enter a legal column (0-6):
4
Computer move is 5
| | | | | | | |
| | | | | | | |
| | | | | | | |
| | | | | | | |
| | | |R| | | |
| | | |B|B|R| |

Enter a legal column (0-6):
4
```

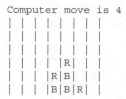

```
Computer move is 4
| | | | | | | |
| | | | | | | |
| | | | | | | |
| | | | |R| | |
| | | |R|B| | |
| | | |B|B|R| |
```

TIP Did you know Connect Four has been "solved" by computer scientists? To solve a game means to know the best move to play in any position. The best first move in Connect Four is to place your piece in the center column.

8.3.3 *Improving minimax with alpha-beta pruning*

Minimax works well, but we are not getting a very deep search at present. There is a small extension to minimax, known as *alpha-beta pruning*, that can improve search depth by excluding positions in the search that will not result in improvements over positions already searched. This magic is accomplished by keeping track of two values between recursive minimax calls: alpha and beta. *Alpha* represents the evaluation of the best maximizing move found up to this point in the search tree, and *beta* represents the evaluation of the best minimizing move found so far for the opponent. If beta is ever less than or equal to alpha, it's not worth further exploring this branch of the search, because a better or equivalent move has already been found than will be found farther down this branch. This heuristic decreases the search space significantly.

Here is alphabeta() as just described. It should be put into our existing Minimax.java file.

Listing 8.20 Minimax.java continued

```java
// Helper that sets alpha and beta for the first call
public static <Move> double alphabeta(Board<Move> board, boolean
    maximizing, Piece originalPlayer, int maxDepth) {
    return alphabeta(board, maximizing, originalPlayer, maxDepth,
    Double.NEGATIVE_INFINITY, Double.POSITIVE_INFINITY);
}

// Evaluates a Board b
private static <Move> double alphabeta(Board<Move> board, boolean
    maximizing, Piece originalPlayer, int maxDepth,
        double alpha,
        double beta) {
    // Base case - terminal position or maximum depth reached
    if (board.isWin() || board.isDraw() || maxDepth == 0) {
        return board.evaluate(originalPlayer);
    }

    // Recursive case - maximize your gains or minimize the opponent's
    if (maximizing) {
        for (Move m : board.getLegalMoves()) {
            alpha = Math.max(alpha, alphabeta(board.move(m), false,
originalPlayer, maxDepth - 1, alpha, beta));
```

```
                    if (beta <= alpha) { // check cutoff
                        break;
                    }
                }
                return alpha;
            } else { // minimizing
                for (Move m : board.getLegalMoves()) {
                    beta = Math.min(beta, alphabeta(board.move(m), true,
            originalPlayer, maxDepth - 1, alpha, beta));
                    if (beta <= alpha) { // check cutoff
                        break;
                    }
                }
                return beta;
            }

        }
```

Now you can make two very small changes to take advantage of our new function. Change `findBestMove()` in Minimax.java to use `alphabeta()` instead of `minimax()`, and change the search depth in ConnectFour.java to 7 from 5. With these changes, your average Connect Four player will not be able to beat our AI. On my computer, using `minimax()` at a depth of 7, our Connect Four AI takes about 20 seconds per move, whereas using `alphabeta()` at the same depth takes just a couple seconds. That's one tenth of the time! That is quite an incredible improvement.

8.4   *Minimax improvements beyond alpha-beta pruning*

The algorithms presented in this chapter have been deeply studied, and many improvements have been found over the years. Some of those improvements are game-specific, such as "bitboards" in chess decreasing the time it takes to generate legal moves, but most are general techniques that can be utilized for any game.

One common technique is *iterative deepening*. In iterative deepening, first the search function is run to a maximum depth of 1. Then it is run to a maximum depth of 2. Then it is run to a maximum depth of 3, and so on. When a specified time limit is reached, the search is stopped. The result from the last completed depth is returned.

The examples in this chapter were hardcoded to a certain depth. This is okay if the game is played without a game clock and time limits or if we do not care how long the computer takes to think. Iterative deepening enables an AI to take a fixed amount of time to find its next move instead of a fixed amount of search depth with a variable amount of time to complete it.

Another potential improvement is *quiescence search*. In this technique, the minimax search tree will be further expanded along routes that cause large changes in position (captures in chess, for instance), rather than routes that have relatively "quiet" positions. In this way, ideally the search will not waste computing time on boring positions that are unlikely to gain the player a significant advantage.

The two best ways to improve upon minimax search is to search to a greater depth in the allotted amount of time or improve upon the evaluation function used to assess a position. Searching more positions in the same amount of time requires spending less time on each position. This can come from finding code efficiencies or using faster hardware, but it can also come at the expense of the latter improvement technique—improving the evaluation of each position. Using more parameters or heuristics to evaluate a position may take more time, but it can ultimately lead to a better engine that needs less search depth to find a good move.

Some evaluation functions used for minimax search with alpha-beta pruning in chess have dozens of heuristics. Genetic algorithms have even been used to tune these heuristics. How much should the capture of a knight be worth in a game of chess? Should it be worth as much as a bishop? These heuristics can be the secret sauce that separates a great chess engine from one that is just good.

8.5 *Real-world applications*

Minimax, combined with further extensions like alpha-beta pruning, is the basis of most modern chess engines. It has been applied to a wide variety of strategy games with great success. In fact, most of the board game artificial opponents that you play on your computer probably use some form of minimax.

Minimax (with its extensions, like alpha-beta pruning) has been so effective in chess that it led to the famous 1997 defeat of the human chess world champion, Gary Kasparov, by Deep Blue, a chess-playing computer made by IBM. The match was a highly anticipated and game-changing event. Chess was seen as a domain of the highest intellectual caliber. The fact that a computer could exceed human ability in chess meant, to some, that artificial intelligence should be taken seriously.

Two decades later, the vast majority of chess engines still are based on minimax. Today's minimax-based chess engines far exceed the strength of the world's best human chess players. New machine learning techniques are starting to challenge pure minimax-based (with extensions) chess engines, but they have yet to definitively prove their superiority in chess.

The higher the branching factor for a game, the less effective minimax will be. The branching factor is the average number of potential moves in a position for some game. This is why recent advances in computer play of the board game Go have required exploration of other domains, like machine learning. A machine learning–based Go AI has now defeated the best human Go player. The branching factor (and therefore the search space) for Go is simply overwhelming for minimax-based algorithms that attempt to generate trees containing future positions. But Go is the exception rather than the rule. Most traditional board games (checkers, chess, Connect Four, Scrabble, and the like) have search spaces small enough that minimax-based techniques can work well.

If you are implementing a new board game artificial opponent or even an AI for a turn-based purely computer-oriented game, minimax is probably the first algorithm you should reach for. Minimax can also be used for economic and political simulations, as well as experiments in game theory. Alpha-beta pruning should work with any form of minimax.

8.6   *Exercises*

1 Add unit tests to tic-tac-toe to ensure that the methods `getLegalMoves()`, `isWin()`, and `isDraw()` work correctly.

2 Create minimax unit tests for Connect Four.

3 The code in TicTacToe.java and ConnectFour.java is almost identical. Refactor it into two methods that can be used for either game.

4 Change ConnectFour.java to have the computer play against itself. Does the first player or the second player win? Is it the same player every time?

5 Can you find a way (through profiling the existing code or otherwise) to optimize the evaluation method in ConnectFour.java to enable a higher search depth in the same amount of time?

6 Use the `alphabeta()` function developed in this chapter together with a Java library for legal chess move generation and maintenance of chess game state to develop a chess AI.

Miscellaneous problems

Throughout this book we have covered a myriad of problem-solving techniques relevant to modern software development tasks. To study each technique, we have explored famous computer science problems. But not every famous problem fits the mold of the prior chapters. This chapter is a gathering point for famous problems that did not quite fit into any other chapter. Think of these problems as a bonus: more interesting problems with less scaffolding around them.

9.1 *The knapsack problem*

The knapsack problem is an optimization problem that takes a common computational need—finding the best use of limited resources given a finite set of usage options—and spins it into a fun story. A thief enters a home with the intent to steal. He has a knapsack, and he is limited in what he can steal by the capacity of the knapsack. How does he figure out what to put into the knapsack? The problem is illustrated in figure 9.1.

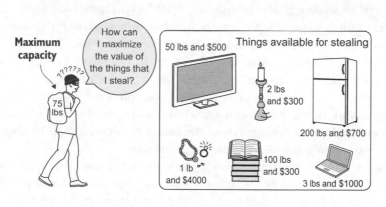

Figure 9.1 The burglar must decide what items to steal because the capacity of the knapsack is limited.

If the thief could take any amount of any item, he could simply divide each item's value by its weight to figure out the most valuable items for the available capacity. But to make the scenario more realistic, let's say that the thief cannot take half of an item (such as 2.5 televisions). Instead, we will come up with a way to solve the 0/1 variant of the problem, so-called because it enforces another rule: the thief may only take one or none of each item.

First, let's define an inner class, Item, to hold our items.

Listing 9.1   Knapsack.java

```java
package chapter9;

import java.util.ArrayList;
import java.util.List;

public final class Knapsack {

    public static final class Item {
        public final String name;
        public final int weight;
        public final double value;

        public Item(String name, int weight, double value) {
            this.name = name;
            this.weight = weight;
            this.value = value;
        }
    }
}
```

If we tried to solve this problem using a brute-force approach, we would look at every combination of items available to be put in the knapsack. For the mathematically inclined, this is known as a *powerset*, and a powerset of a set (in our case, the set of items) has 2^N different possible subsets, where *N* is the number of items. Therefore, we would need to analyze 2^N combinations ($O(2^N)$). This is okay for a small number of items, but it is untenable for a large number. Any approach that solves a problem using an exponential number of steps is an approach we want to avoid.

Instead, we will use a technique known as *dynamic programming*, which is similar in concept to memoization (chapter 1). Instead of solving a problem outright with a brute-force approach, in dynamic programming one solves subproblems that make up the larger problem, stores those results, and utilizes those stored results to solve the larger problem. As long as the capacity of the knapsack is considered in discrete steps, the problem can be solved with dynamic programming.

For instance, to solve the problem for a knapsack with a 3-pound capacity and three items, we can first solve the problem for a 1-pound capacity and one possible item, 2-pound capacity and one possible item, and 3-pound capacity and one possible item. We can then use the results of that solution to solve the problem for 1-pound capacity and two possible items, 2-pound capacity and two possible items, and 3-pound capacity and two possible items. Finally, we can solve for all three possible items.

All along the way we will fill in a table that tells us the best possible solution for each combination of items and capacity. Our function will first fill in the table and then figure out the solution based on the table.[1]

Listing 9.2   Knapsack.java continued

```java
public static List<Item> knapsack(List<Item> items, int maxCapacity) {
    // build up dynamic programming table
    double[][] table = new double[items.size() + 1][maxCapacity + 1];
    for (int i = 0; i < items.size(); i++) {
        Item item = items.get(i);
        for (int capacity = 1; capacity <= maxCapacity; capacity++) {
            double prevItemValue = table[i][capacity];
            if (capacity >= item.weight) { // item fits in knapsack
                double valueFreeingWeightForItem = table[i][capacity -
item.weight];
                // only take if more valuable than previous item
                table[i + 1][capacity] = Math.max(valueFreeingWeightForItem
+ item.value, prevItemValue);
            } else { // no room for this item
                table[i + 1][capacity] = prevItemValue;
            }
        }
    }
    // figure out solution from table
    List<Item> solution = new ArrayList<>();
    int capacity = maxCapacity;
    for (int i = items.size(); i > 0; i--) { // work backwards
        // was this item used?
        if (table[i - 1][capacity] != table[i][capacity]) {
            solution.add(items.get(i - 1));
            // if the item was used, remove its weight
            capacity -= items.get(i - 1).weight;
        }
    }
    return solution;
}
```

The inner loop of the first part of this function will execute $N * C$ times, where N is the number of items and C is the maximum capacity of the knapsack. Therefore, the algorithm performs in $O(N * C)$ time, a significant improvement over the brute-force approach for a large number of items. For instance, for the 11 items that follow, a brute-force algorithm would need to examine 2^11, or 2,048, combinations. The preceding

---

[1] I studied several resources to write this solution, the most authoritative of which was *Algorithms* (Addison-Wesley, 1988), 2nd ed., by Robert Sedgewick (p. 596). I looked at several examples of the 0/1 knapsack problem on Rosetta Code, most notably the Python dynamic programming solution (http://mng.bz/kx8C), which this function is largely a port of, originally from the Swift version of the book. (It went from Python to Swift, back to Python again, and then to Java.)

dynamic programming function will execute 825 times, because the maximum capacity of the knapsack in question is 75 arbitrary units (11 * 75). This difference would grow exponentially with more items.

Let's look at the solution in action.

Listing 9.3   Knapsack.java continued

```java
public static void main(String[] args) {
    List<Item> items = new ArrayList<>();
    items.add(new Item("television", 50, 500));
    items.add(new Item("candlesticks", 2, 300));
    items.add(new Item("stereo", 35, 400));
    items.add(new Item("laptop", 3, 1000));
    items.add(new Item("food", 15, 50));
    items.add(new Item("clothing", 20, 800));
    items.add(new Item("jewelry", 1, 4000));
    items.add(new Item("books", 100, 300));
    items.add(new Item("printer", 18, 30));
    items.add(new Item("refrigerator", 200, 700));
    items.add(new Item("painting", 10, 1000));
    List<Item> toSteal = knapsack(items, 75);
    System.out.println("The best items for the thief to steal are:");
    System.out.printf("%-15.15s %-15.15s %-15.15s%n", "Name", "Weight",
    "Value");
    for (Item item : toSteal) {
        System.out.printf("%-15.15s %-15.15s %-15.15s%n", item.name,
    item.weight, item.value);
    }
}

}
```

If you inspect the results printed to the console, you will see that the optimal items to take are the painting, jewelry, clothing, laptop, stereo, and candlesticks. Here's some sample output showing the most valuable items for the thief to steal, given the limited-capacity knapsack:

```
The best items for the thief to steal are:
Name            Weight          Value
painting        10              1000.0
jewelry         1               4000.0
clothing        20              800.0
laptop          3               1000.0
stereo          35              400.0
candlesticks    2               300.0
```

To get a better idea of how this all works, let's look at some of the particulars of the knapsack() method:

```java
for (int i = 0; i < items.size(); i++) {
    Item item = items.get(i);
    for (int capacity = 1; capacity <= maxCapacity; capacity++) {
```

For each possible number of items, we loop through all of the capacities in a linear fashion, up to the maximum capacity of the knapsack. Notice that I say "each possible number of items" instead of each item. When i equals 2, it does not just represent item 2. It represents the possible combinations of the first two items for every explored capacity. item is the next item that we are considering stealing:

```
double prevItemValue = table[i][capacity];
if (capacity >= item.weight) { // item fits in knapsack
```

prevItemValue is the value of the last combination of items at the current capacity being explored. For each possible combination of items, we consider whether adding in the latest "new" item is even possible.

If the item weighs more than the knapsack capacity we are considering, we simply copy over the value for the last combination of items that we considered for the capacity in question:

```
else { // no room for this item
    table[i + 1][capacity] = prevItemValue;
}
```

Otherwise, we consider whether adding in the "new" item will result in a higher value than the last combination of items at that capacity that we considered. We do this by adding the value of the item to the value already computed in the table for the previous combination of items at a capacity equal to the item's weight, subtracted from the current capacity we are considering. If this value is higher than the last combination of items at the current capacity, we insert it; otherwise, we insert the last value:

```
double valueFreeingWeightForItem = table[i][capacity - item.weight];
// only take if more valuable than previous item
table[i + 1][capacity] = Math.max(valueFreeingWeightForItem + item.value,
    prevItemValue);
```

That concludes building up the table. To actually find which items are in the solution, though, we need to work backward from the highest capacity and the final explored combination of items:

```
for (int i = items.size(); i > 0; i--) { // work backwards
    // was this item used?
    if (table[i - 1][capacity] != table[i][capacity]) {
```

We start from the end and loop through our table from right to left, checking whether there was a change in the value inserted into the table at each stop. If there was, that means we added the new item that was considered in a particular combination because the combination was more valuable than the prior one. Therefore, we add that item to the solution. Also, capacity is decreased by the weight of the item, which can be thought of as moving up the table:

```
solution.add(items.get(i - 1));
// if the item was used, remove its weight
capacity -= items.get(i - 1).weight;
```

> **NOTE** Throughout both the buildup of the table and the solution search, you may have noticed some manipulation of iterators and table size by 1. This is done for convenience from a programmatic perspective. Think about how the problem is built from the bottom up. When the problem begins, we are dealing with a zero-capacity knapsack. If you work your way up from the bottom in a table, it will become clear why we need the extra row and column.

Are you still confused? Table 9.1 is the table the `knapsack()` function builds. It would be quite a large table for the preceding problem, so instead, let's look at a table for a knapsack with 3-pound capacity and three items: matches (1 pound), flashlight (2 pounds), and book (1 pound). Assume those items are valued at $5, $10, and $15, respectively.

Table 9.1 An example of a knapsack problem of three items

	0 lb.	1 lb.	2 lb.	3 lb.
Matches (1 lb., $5)	0	5	5	5
Flashlight (2 lbs., $10)	0	5	10	15
Book (1 lb., $15)	0	15	20	25

As you look across the table from left to right, the weight is increasing (how much you are trying to fit in the knapsack). As you look down the table from top to bottom, the number of items you are attempting to fit is increasing. On the first row, you are only trying to fit the matches. On the second row, you fit the most valuable combination of the matches and the flashlight that the knapsack can hold. On the third row, you fit the most valuable combination of all three items.

As an exercise to facilitate your understanding, try filling in a blank version of this table yourself, using the algorithm described in the `knapsack()` method with these same three items. Then use the algorithm at the end of the function to read back the right items from the table. This table corresponds to the `table` variable in the function.

9.2 *The Traveling Salesman Problem*

The Traveling Salesman Problem is one of the most classic and talked-about problems in all of computing. A salesman must visit all of the cities on a map exactly once, returning to his start city at the end of the journey. There is a direct connection from every city to every other city, and the salesman may visit the cities in any order. What is the shortest path for the salesman?

The problem can be thought of as a graph problem (chapter 4), with the cities being the vertices and the connections between them being the edges. Your first instinct might be to find the minimum spanning tree, as described in chapter 4. Unfortunately, the solution to the Traveling Salesman Problem is not so simple. The minimum spanning tree is the way to connect all of the cities with the least amount of road, but it does not provide the shortest path for visiting all of them exactly once.

Although the problem, as posed, appears fairly simple, there is no algorithm that can solve it quickly for an arbitrary number of cities. What do I mean by "quickly"? I mean that the problem is what is known as *NP hard.* An NP-hard (non-deterministic polynomial hard) problem is a problem for which no polynomial time algorithm is known. (The time it takes is a polynomial function of the size of the input.) As the number of cities that the salesman needs to visit increases, the difficulty of solving the problem grows exceptionally quickly. It is much harder to solve the problem for 20 cities than 10. It is impossible (to the best of current knowledge), in a reasonable amount of time, to solve the problem perfectly (optimally) for millions of cities.

> **NOTE** The naive approach to the Traveling Salesman Problem is $O(n!)$. Why this is the case is discussed in section 9.2.2. We suggest reading section 9.2.1 before reading 9.2.2, though, because the implementation of a naive solution to the problem will make its complexity obvious.

9.2.1   *The naive approach*

The naive approach to the problem is simply to try every possible combination of cities. Attempting the naive approach will illustrate the difficulty of the problem and this approach's unsuitability for brute-force attempts at larger scales.

OUR SAMPLE DATA

In our version of the Traveling Salesman Problem, the salesman is interested in visiting five of the major cities of Vermont. We will not specify a starting (and therefore ending) city. Figure 9.2 illustrates the five cities and the driving distances between them. Note that there is a distance listed for the route between every pair of cities.

Perhaps you have seen driving distances in table form before. In a driving-distance table, one can easily look up the distance between any two cities. Table 9.2 lists the driving distances for the five cities in the problem.

Table 9.2   Driving distances between cities in Vermont

	Rutland	Burlington	White River Junction	Bennington	Brattleboro
Rutland	0	67	46	55	75
Burlington	67	0	91	122	153
White River Junction	46	91	0	98	65
Bennington	55	122	98	0	40
Brattleboro	75	153	65	40	0

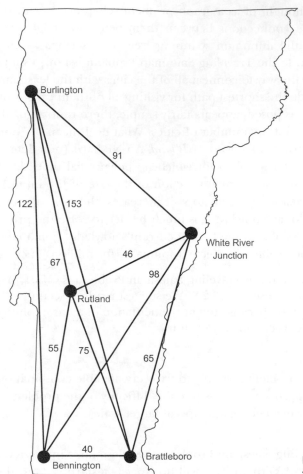

Figure 9.2   Five cities in Vermont and the driving distances between them

We will need to codify both the cities and the distances between them for our problem. To make the distances between cities easy to look up, we will use a map of maps, with the outer set of keys representing the first of a pair and the inner set of keys representing the second. This will be the type `Map<String, Map<String, Integer>>`, and it will allow lookups like `vtDistances.get("Rutland").get("Burlington")`, which should return 67. We will use the `vtDistances` map when we actually solve the problem for Vermont, but first, let's do some setup. Our class holds the map and has a utility method we will use later for doing a swap of the items at two locations within an array.

Listing 9.4   TSP.java

```java
package chapter9;

import java.util.ArrayList;
import java.util.Arrays;
```

```java
import java.util.List;
import java.util.Map;

public class TSP {
    private final Map<String, Map<String, Integer>> distances;

    public TSP(Map<String, Map<String, Integer>> distances) {
        this.distances = distances;
    }

    public static <T> void swap(T[] array, int first, int second) {
        T temp = array[first];
        array[first] = array[second];
        array[second] = temp;
    }
```

FINDING ALL PERMUTATIONS

The naive approach to solving the Traveling Salesman Problem requires generating every possible permutation of the cities. There are many permutation-generation algorithms; they are simple enough to ideate that you could almost certainly come up with one on your own.

One common approach is backtracking. You first saw backtracking in chapter 3 in the context of solving a constraint-satisfaction problem. In constraint-satisfaction problem solving, backtracking is used after a partial solution is found that does not satisfy the problem's constraints. In such a case, you revert to an earlier state and continue the search along a different path than that which led to the incorrect partial solution.

To find all of the permutations of the items in an array (eventually, our cities), we will also use backtracking. After we make a swap between elements and go down a path of further permutations, we will backtrack to the state before the swap was made so we can make a different swap and go down a different path.

Listing 9.5 TSP.java continued

```java
    private static <T> void allPermutationsHelper(T[] permutation, List<T[]>
        permutations, int n) {
        // Base case - we found a new permutation, add it and return
        if (n <= 0) {
            permutations.add(permutation);
            return;
        }
        // Recursive case - find more permutations by doing swaps
        T[] tempPermutation = Arrays.copyOf(permutation, permutation.length);
        for (int i = 0; i < n; i++) {
            swap(tempPermutation, i, n - 1); // move element at i to end
            // move everything else around, holding the end constant
            allPermutationsHelper(tempPermutation, permutations, n - 1);
            swap(tempPermutation, i, n - 1); // backtrack
        }
    }
```

This recursive function is labeled a "helper" because it will actually be called by another function that takes fewer arguments. The parameters of allPermutationsHelper() are the starting permutation we are working with, the permutations generated so far, and the number of remaining items to swap around.

A common pattern for recursive functions that need to keep multiple items of state across calls is to have a separate outward-facing function with fewer parameters that is easier to use. allPermutations() is that simpler function.

Listing 9.6   TSP.java continued

```java
private static <T> List<T[]> permutations(T[] original) {
    List<T[]> permutations = new ArrayList<>();
    allPermutationsHelper(original, permutations, original.length);
    return permutations;
}
```

allPermutations() takes just a single argument: the array for which the permutations should be generated. It calls allPermutationsHelper() to find those permutations. This saves the user of allPermutations() from having to provide the parameters permutations and n to allPermutationsHelper().

The backtracking approach to finding all permutations presented here is fairly efficient. Finding each permutation requires just two swaps within the array. However, it is possible to find all the permutations of an array with just one swap per permutation. One efficient algorithm that accomplishes that task is Heap's algorithm (not to be confused with the heap data structure—Heap, in this case, is the name of the inventor of the algorithm).[2] This difference in efficiency may be important for very large data sets (which is not what we are dealing with here).

BRUTE-FORCE SEARCH

We can now generate all of the permutations of the city list, but this is not quite the same as a Traveling Salesman Problem path. Recall that in the Traveling Salesman Problem, the salesman must return, at the end, to the same city that he started in. We can easily add the distance from the last city the salesman visited to the first city visited when we calculate which path is the shortest, and we will do that shortly.

We are now ready to try testing the paths we have permuted. A brute-force search approach painstakingly looks at every path in a list of paths and uses the distance between the two cities in the lookup table (distances) to calculate each path's total distance. It prints both the shortest path and that path's total distance.

Listing 9.7   TSP.java continued

```java
public int pathDistance(String[] path) {
    String last = path[0];
    int distance = 0;
```

---

[2] Robert Sedgewick, "Permutation Generation Methods" (Princeton University), http://mng.bz/87Te.

```
        for (String next : Arrays.copyOfRange(path, 1, path.length)) {
            distance += distances.get(last).get(next);
            // distance to get back from last city to first city
            last = next;
        }
        return distance;
    }

    public String[] findShortestPath() {
        String[] cities = distances.keySet().toArray(String[]::new);
        List<String[]> paths = permutations(cities);
        String[] shortestPath = null;
        int minDistance = Integer.MAX_VALUE; // arbitrarily high
        for (String[] path : paths) {
            int distance = pathDistance(path);
            // distance from last to first must be added
            distance += distances.get(path[path.length - 1]).get(path[0]);
            if (distance < minDistance) {
                minDistance = distance;
                shortestPath = path;
            }
        }
        // add first city on to end and return
        shortestPath = Arrays.copyOf(shortestPath, shortestPath.length + 1);
        shortestPath[shortestPath.length - 1] = shortestPath[0];
        return shortestPath;
    }

    public static void main(String[] args) {
        Map<String, Map<String, Integer>> vtDistances = Map.of(
                "Rutland", Map.of(
                        "Burlington", 67,
                        "White River Junction", 46,
                        "Bennington", 55,
                        "Brattleboro", 75),
                "Burlington", Map.of(
                        "Rutland", 67,
                        "White River Junction", 91,
                        "Bennington", 122,
                        "Brattleboro", 153),
                "White River Junction", Map.of(
                        "Rutland", 46,
                        "Burlington", 91,
                        "Bennington", 98,
                        "Brattleboro", 65),
                "Bennington", Map.of(
                        "Rutland", 55,
                        "Burlington", 122,
                        "White River Junction", 98,
                        "Brattleboro", 40),
                "Brattleboro", Map.of(
                        "Rutland", 75,
                        "Burlington", 153,
                        "White River Junction", 65,
                        "Bennington", 40));
```

```
        TSP tsp = new TSP(vtDistances);
        String[] shortestPath = tsp.findShortestPath();
        int distance = tsp.pathDistance(shortestPath);
        System.out.println("The shortest path is " +
Arrays.toString(shortestPath) + " in " +
            distance + " miles.");
    }
}
```

We finally can brute-force the cities of Vermont, finding the shortest path to reach all five. The output should look something like the following, and the best path is illustrated in figure 9.3.

```
The shortest path is [White River Junction, Burlington, Rutland, Bennington,
    Brattleboro, White River Junction] in 318 miles.
```

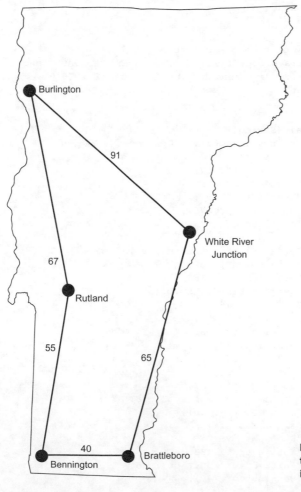

Figure 9.3 **The shortest path for the salesman to visit all five cities in Vermont is illustrated.**

9.2.2 Taking it to the next level

There is no easy answer to the Traveling Salesman Problem. Our naive approach quickly becomes infeasible. The number of permutations generated is n factorial ($n!$), where n is the number of cities in the problem. If we were to include just one more city (six instead of five), the number of evaluated paths would grow by a factor of six. Then it would be seven times harder to solve the problem for just one more city after that. This is not a scalable approach!

In the real world, the naive approach to the Traveling Salesman Problem is seldom used. Most algorithms for instances of the problem with a large number of cities are approximations. They try to solve the problem for a near-optimal solution. The near-optimal solution may be within a small known band of the perfect solution. (For example, perhaps they will be no more than 5% less efficient.)

Two techniques that have already appeared in this book have been used to attempt the Traveling Salesman Problem on large data sets. Dynamic programming, which we used in the knapsack problem earlier in this chapter, is one approach. Another is genetic algorithms, as described in chapter 5. Many journal articles have been published attributing genetic algorithms to near-optimal solutions for the traveling salesman with large numbers of cities.

9.3 Phone number mnemonics

Before there were smartphones with built-in address books, telephones included letters on each of the keys on their number pads. The reason for these letters was to provide easy mnemonics by which to remember phone numbers. In the United States, typically the 1 key would have no letters, 2 would have ABC, 3 DEF, 4 GHI, 5 JKL, 6 MNO, 7 PQRS, 8 TUV, 9 WXYZ, and 0 no letters. For example, 1-800-MY-APPLE corresponds to the phone number 1-800-69-27753. Once in a while you will still find these mnemonics in advertisements, so the numbers on the keypad have made their way into modern smartphone apps, as evidenced by figure 9.4.

How does one come up with a new mnemonic for a phone number? In the 1990s there was popular shareware to help with the effort. These pieces of software would

Figure 9.4 The Phone app in iOS retains the letters on keys that its telephone forebears contained.

generate every ordered combination of a phone number's letters and then look through a dictionary to find words that were contained in the combinations. They would then show the combinations with the most complete words to the user. We will do the first half of the problem. The dictionary lookup will be left as an exercise.

In the last problem, when we looked at permutation generation, we generated our answers by taking an existing permutation and swapping to get a different permutation. You can think about it like starting with a finished product and working backwards. For this problem, instead of swapping positions in an existing solution to generate a new one, we will generate each solution from the ground up, starting with an empty string. We will do this by looking at the letters that potentially match each numeral in the phone number and continually adding more options to the end as we go to each successive numeral. This is a kind of Cartesian product.

What's a Cartesian product? In set theory, a Cartesian product is the set of all combinations of the members from one set with each of the members in another set. For example, if one set contains the letters "A" and "B," and another set contains the letters "C" and "D," then the Cartesian product would be the set "AC," "AD," "BC," and "BD." "A" was combined with every letter it could in the second set, and "B" was combined with every letter it could in the second set. If our phone number were 234, we would need to find the Cartesian product of "A," "B," "C" with "D," "E," and "F." Once we found that result, we would need to take it and find its Cartesian product with "G," "H," "I." And that product of a product would be our answer.

We will not be working with sets. We will be working with arrays. It is just more convenient for our data representation.

First, we will define a mapping of numerals to potential letters and a constructor.

Listing 9.8 PhoneNumberMnemonics.java

```java
package chapter9;

import java.util.ArrayList;
import java.util.Arrays;
import java.util.Map;
import java.util.Scanner;

public class PhoneNumberMnemonics {
    Map<Character, String[]> phoneMapping = Map.of(
            '1', new String[] { "1" },
            '2', new String[] { "a", "b", "c" },
            '3', new String[] { "d", "e", "f" },
            '4', new String[] { "g", "h", "i" },
            '5', new String[] { "j", "k", "l" },
            '6', new String[] { "m", "n", "o" },
            '7', new String[] { "p", "q", "r", "s" },
            '8', new String[] { "t", "u", "v" },
            '9', new String[] { "w", "x", "y", "z" },
            '0', new String[] { "0", });
    private final String phoneNumber;
```

```java
public PhoneNumberMnemonics(String phoneNumber) {
    this.phoneNumber = phoneNumber;
}
```

The next method performs a Cartesian product of two `String` arrays by simply adding every item in the first array to every item in the second array and aggregating those results.

Listing 9.9 PhoneNumberMnemonics.java continued

```java
public static String[] cartesianProduct(String[] first, String[] second)
{
    ArrayList<String> product = new ArrayList<>(first.length * second.length);
    for (String item1 : first) {
        for (String item2 : second) {
            product.add(item1 + item2);
        }
    }
    return product.toArray(String[]::new);
}
```

Now we can find all of the possible mnemonics for a phone number. `getMnemonics()` does this by successively taking the Cartesian product of each previous product (starting with an array of one empty string) and the array of letters representing the next numeral. `main()` runs `getMnemonics()` for any phone number provided by the user.

Listing 9.10 PhoneNumberMnemonics.java continued

```java
public String[] getMnemonics() {
    String[] mnemonics = { "" };
    for (Character digit : phoneNumber.toCharArray()) {
        String[] combo = phoneMapping.get(digit);
        if (combo != null) {
            mnemonics = cartesianProduct(mnemonics, combo);
        }
    }
    return mnemonics;
}

public static void main(String[] args) {
    System.out.println("Enter a phone number:");
    Scanner scanner = new Scanner(System.in);
    String phoneNumber = scanner.nextLine();
    scanner.close();
    System.out.println("The possible mnemonics are:");
    PhoneNumberMnemonics pnm = new PhoneNumberMnemonics(phoneNumber);
    System.out.println(Arrays.toString(pnm.getMnemonics()));
}

}
```

It turns out that the phone number 1440787 can also be written as 1GH0STS. That is easier to remember.

9.4 *Real-world applications*

Dynamic programming, as used with the knapsack problem, is a widely applicable technique that can make seemingly intractable problems solvable by breaking them into constituent smaller problems and building up a solution from those parts. The knapsack problem itself is related to other optimization problems where a finite amount of resources (the capacity of the knapsack) must be allocated among a finite but exhaustive set of options (the items to steal). Imagine a college that needs to allocate its athletic budget. It does not have enough money to fund every team, and it has some expectation of how much alumni donations each team will bring in. It can run a knapsack-like problem to optimize the budget's allocation. Problems like this are common in the real world.

The Traveling Salesman Problem is an everyday occurrence for shipping and distribution companies like UPS and FedEx. Package delivery companies want their drivers to travel the shortest routes possible. Not only does this make the drivers' jobs more pleasant, but it also saves fuel and maintenance costs. We all travel for work or for pleasure, and finding optimal routes when visiting many destinations can save resources. But the Traveling Salesman Problem is not just for routing travel; it comes up in almost any routing scenario that requires singular visits to nodes. Although a minimum spanning tree (chapter 4) may minimize the amount of wire needed to connect a neighborhood, it does not tell us the optimal amount of wire if every house must be forward-connected to just one other house as part of a giant circuit that returns to its origination. The Traveling Salesman Problem does.

Permutation and combination generation techniques like the ones used in the naive approach to the Traveling Salesman Problem and the phone number mnemonics problem are useful for testing all sorts of brute-force algorithms. For instance, if you were trying to crack a short password and you knew its length, you could generate every possible permutation of the characters that could potentially be in the password. Practitioners of such large-scale permutation-generation tasks would be wise to use an especially efficient permutation-generation algorithm like Heap's algorithm.

9.5 *Exercises*

1 Reprogram the naive approach to the Traveling Salesman Problem using the graph framework from chapter 4.

2 Implement a genetic algorithm, as described in chapter 5, to solve the Traveling Salesman Problem. Start with the simple data set of Vermont cities described in this chapter. Can you get the genetic algorithm to arrive at the optimal solution in a short amount of time? Then attempt the problem with an increasingly large number of cities. How well does the genetic algorithm hold up? You can

find a large number of data sets specifically made for the Traveling Salesman Problem by searching the web. Develop a testing framework for checking the efficiency of your method.

3 Use a dictionary with the phone number mnemonics program and return only permutations that contain valid dictionary words.

Interview with
Brian Goetz

Brian Goetz is one of the leading figures in the Java world. As Java Language Architect at Oracle, he helps steer the direction of the language's evolution and its supporting libraries. He has led the language through several important modernizations, including Project Lambda. Brian has a long career in software engineering and is the author of the best-selling book *Java Concurrency in Practice* (Addison-Wesley Professional, 2006).

This interview was conducted on August 25, 2020, at Brian's home in Williston, Vermont. The transcript has been edited and condensed for clarity.

1 How did you first get started in computing?

I started as a hobbyist around 1978, when I was 13 or 14. I had access to a timeshare computing system through the local school, and my older brother who had been through the same program ahead of me brought me books and stuff to read, and I was just absolutely hooked. I was completely fascinated by this system that was governed by a complex but understandable set of rules. And so, I spent as much time as I could after school in the computer room, at school, learning everything I could. And at the time, it was a very polyglot time for programming. There wasn't a dominant language the way there has been for probably the last 25 years. Everybody was expected to know multiple programming languages. I taught myself BASIC, Fortran, COBOL, APL, and assembly language. I saw how each of these was a different tool for a different problem. I was completely self-taught because there wasn't really any formal education available at the time. My degree is not in computer science, it's in mathematics, because at the time a lot of schools didn't even have a computer science department. And I think that mathematical orientation has stood me in very good stead.

2 Was there one programming language when you were first learning that had a very big influence on you?

When I was first learning, there wasn't really. I was just swapping it all in. The dominant languages at the time were Fortran, COBOL, and BASIC for different categories of problems. But later, when I was a graduate student, I had the opportunity to take the Structure and Interpretation of Computer Programs class at MIT where I learned Scheme, and this was where all the light bulbs came on. At that point, I had already been programming for almost 10 years, and I had already encountered a lot of interesting problems. This was the first time I saw that there was an overarching theory that could connect a lot of the observations I had made. For me, I was very lucky to take that class as a graduate student rather than as a freshman, because the freshmen were just completely overwhelmed by the volume of material being thrown at them. Having more experience allowed me to see the underlying beauty and structure, without being distracted by the details. If I had to pick a moment where the beauty of computing really became obvious to me, it was that class.

3 How did you develop your software engineering and computer science skill sets after college?

I think the same way almost everyone else does—mostly by doing. In typical professional engineering situations, more often than not you get thrown in the deep end of the pool with a problem to solve, and you have to figure it out on your own. You have an array of tools at your disposal, but it's not always obvious what the right one to use is, and there's a process of trial and error where you try things. You see what works and what stops working when the problem reaches a certain threshold of complexity. Hopefully, there's some inductive reasoning process that's going on alongside that, by which you can figure out why something worked, and when it might work again, or might not. Earlier in my career, I had a number of fairly typical software engineering jobs; I worked for a research laboratory, I worked for a small software company that made networking software. I learned by doing and experimenting, like most developers do today.

4 How did your career lead you to become the Java Language Architect?

By a fairly strange and circuitous path! For the first half of my career, I was mostly an ordinary programmer. At some point, I made this transition to being sort of halfway between programming and education, giving presentations and writing articles and eventually a book. I always tried to choose topics that had been confusing to me on the theory that they might also be confusing to others—and I tried to present them in an understandable light. I discovered I had a talent for bridging the gap between the technical details and the intuitive mental models, and that culminated in writing *Java*

Concurrency in Practice, which at this point was almost 15 years ago! And from there I went to work at Sun in a role that was more about technology evangelism than development, explaining to people, "How does the JVM work?" "What does a dynamic compiler do?" "Why is dynamic compilation potentially better than static compilation?" I was trying to demystify the technology and debunk the myths surrounding it. Once I was in there, I got to see how the engineering process worked on the Java team, and at some point the opportunity to contribute in a more substantial way arose. If I had to give people a road map for how to get there, I don't know how I would draw it. It was definitely not a straight line.

5   What does it mean to be the Java Language Architect?

In the simplest terms, I have to decide in what direction the Java programming model moves. And there are, of course, many, many options here—and many people who would happily give me advice! I'm sure each of the nine million Java developers has an idea or two for a language feature. And of course we can't do all of them, or even many of them. So we have to pick very, very carefully. My job is to balance the need to keep moving forward, so Java stays relevant, with the need for Java to stay "Java." And relevance has many dimensions: relevant to the problems that we want to solve; relevant to the hardware we run on; relevant to the interests, orientations, and even fashions of programmers. We have to evolve, but we also can't move so quickly that we lose people. If we were to make a radical overnight change, people would say, "This isn't the Java I know," and they would go do something else. And so, we have to pick both the direction and a rate to move forward, such that we're able to stay relevant to the problems people want to solve without making people feel uncomfortable.

For me, that means getting into the shoes of Java developers and understanding where their pain points are. Then we try to move the language in a way that works with them and obviates the pain points that they're experiencing, but not necessarily in the same way they imagined they needed. There's an old saying attributed to Henry Ford: "If I asked my customers what they wanted, they would tell me 'faster horses.'" Programmers are very much prone to say "you should add this feature," and the art is in listening to that suggestion and understanding the kind of pain they are in that leads them to think that this would be the right solution. By comparing that to the things we've heard from other developers, perhaps we can see what's really missing that will actually address people's pain, make them more productive, make programs safer, and more efficient.

6   How does the process of evolving the Java language work? How is it decided that new features should be added to the language?

It's actually fairly rare that a feature is invented out of whole cloth. The reality is, almost every "new" idea has been kicking around the programming world for decades. Invariably, when someone comes to me with a feature idea, I can see a connection to something that was done in some other language long ago. A big part of the process is waiting for the right time to expose a new concept, and fitting it in a way that is consistent with the rest of the language. There's no shortage of feature ideas, and in every language you find lots of features that people in those communities like. The real game is to get underneath them and ask, "What does having this feature enable you to do that you can't do otherwise? How does it make your programs safer? How would it permit better type checking? How does it make your programs less error prone, more expressive, and so on?"

It's a fairly subjective process; if we're looking to alleviate people's pain, we have to make subjective calls about which kinds of pain are more important to alleviate now. You can look at the big features that have been added to Java in the past: In the mid-2000s, we saw generics, and that was an obvious gap. At that time the language screamed out for parametric polymorphism. They wanted to have it in 1995, but they didn't know how to do it in a way that made sense for the language. And they didn't want to graft C++ templates onto Java, which would've been terrible. It took almost another 10 years to figure out how to add parametric polymorphism and data abstraction to Java in a way that feels natural. And I think they did a fantastic job. We did the same thing with behavioral abstraction when we did lambdas more recently. Again, all the hard work there was not in the theory. The theory of lambda expressions has been well understood since the 1930s. The hard part was, how do you make it fit into Java so that it doesn't look nailed on the side? The ultimate measure of success is when you finally deliver something after three or five or seven years, and people say, "What took you so long? That's so obvious." Well, the version we had in the first year would not look so easy or obvious. We don't want to inflict that on people, so we have to take our time.

7 How do you know, when considering a feature, that it's not just fashion and it's something important that developers really need?

That is a really good question, because there have been some real near misses. In the early 2000s, there was a big call to add XML literals to the Java language, and I consider that to be a bullet that was dodged. Not all languages dodged that bullet.

I can't give you an algorithm for it; often, you just have to sit and think about it for a long time and see what the connections to the rest of the language look like. We've all seen languages that bolt a feature on the side to solve a particular problem, but that problem may not be a problem for all time. If you're willing to sit and be patient and think about it over and over again before you make a decision, very often you can get a sense of when something is just the flavor of the week.

8 What additions to Java are you most proud of during your tenure as Java Language Architect?

I was the specifications lead for adding lambdas to Java. Not only was that an enormous change, but it signaled a change for how the language would be evolved going forward. It was, in some sense, a make or break thing, because in the time leading up to that, Sun was fairly distracted by slowly going out of business, and we had not been able to evolve the platform at the rate that we would have liked. It was pretty clear at the time that Java was falling behind, and this was our big chance to prove to the world that it was possible for Java to remain relevant and fun to program in; that we could continue to teach this old dog some fancy new tricks.

The main challenge of adding lambdas to Java was making it not look like it was tacked on the side, but integrated into the whole as if it had always been there. There were no shortage of suggestions for how to do it—nearly all of which were "do it like this other language does it." All of these would have been unsatisfying. We might have gotten there a year or two faster, but we would not have gotten a result that worked as well, and we'd be stuck with it for a long time. What I'm really proud of is how we managed to figure out how to integrate it into the language at multiple levels so that it looked like it belonged there. It works very cleanly with the generic type system. We had to overhaul a number of other aspects of the language in order to make it work—we had to overhaul type inference and its interaction with overload selection. If you ask people what features were added in Java 8, that would never be on anybody's list. But that was a huge part of the work—it was under the waterline, but it was the foundation that was needed to make it so that you could write the code that you wanted to write, and it just naturally worked.

We also had to start to address the problem of compatible API evolution. One of the huge risks we faced in Java 8 was that the way you would write a library with lambdas is very different from how you would in a language without lambdas. We didn't want to make the language better and then be in the situation where, all of a sudden, all our libraries look 20 years older. We had to address the question of how we were going to evolve the libraries in a compatible way so they could take advantage of these new library design idioms. That led to the ability to compatibly add methods to interfaces, which was an essential part to keeping the libraries we had relevant, so that on day one, the language and the libraries were ready for a newer style of programming.

9 A question I get asked by a lot of students is how much should they use lambdas? Can they overuse them in their code?

I come at this perhaps from a different perspective than a lot of students, because most of the code that I write are libraries that are intended to be used by a lot of people. The bar for writing a library like that, like the streams API, is very high because you have to get it right the first time. The compatibility bar for changing it is very high. The way I tend to think about abstracting over behavior is when you're crossing a boundary between user code and library code, the main thing that lambdas allow you to do is to design APIs that could be parameterized not just with data, but with behavior, because lambdas let us treat behavior as data. So I am focused on the interaction between the client and this library and the natural flow of control. When does it make sense for the client to be pulling all the strings, versus when does it make sense for the client to hand some behavior to the library that it will call at the appropriate time? I'm not sure my experiences translate directly to the experience of your students. But one thing that will surely be a key to success here is being able to recognize where the boundaries are in your code, and where the divisions of responsibility lie. Whether those are strictly demarcated in separately compiled modules or carefully documented APIs, or whether they're just conventions for how we organize our code, this is something we want to stay aware of.

We use these boundaries in our code for a reason—so that we can manage the complexity through divide-and-conquer. Every time you're designing one of these boundaries, you're designing a little protocol interaction, and you should be thinking about the roles of the participants on each side, what information they are exchanging, and what that interchange looks like.

10 You spoke earlier about a period of stagnation for Java. When was that, and why did it happen?

I would say the Java 6–7 timeframe was the dark ages for Java. Not coincidentally, this was the time at which Scala started to gain some traction, in part because I think the ecosystem was saying, "Well, we may need to find another horse to back if Java doesn't get up and run." Thankfully, it did get up and run, and it's been running ever since.

11 And now we're seeing a pretty rapid evolution of the language. How has the philosophy changed?

In the big picture, it hasn't changed that much, but in the details, it's changed quite a lot. Starting after Java 9, we moved to a six-month time-boxed release cadence rather than a multiyear feature-boxed cadence. And there were all kinds of good reasons for doing that, but one of them was that there were a lot of good, smaller ideas that always got crowded out when we were planning multiyear releases with big release drivers. The shorter release cadence has allowed us to have a better mix of big and small features. In these six-month releases, a lot of them have smaller language features, like local variable type inference. They didn't necessarily only take six months to do; they may still have taken a year or two, but we now have more opportunities to deliver something once it's ready. In addition to smaller features, you'll also see bigger feature arcs like pattern matching that may play out in increments over a multiyear period. The earlier parts can give us a sense of the direction of where the language is going.

There are also clusters of related features which may be delivered individually. For example, pattern matching, records, and sealed types work together to support a more data-oriented model of programming. And that's not an accident. That's based on observing what kind of pain people are having using Java's static type system to model the data that they're working with. And how have programs changed in the last 10 years? They've gotten smaller. People are writing smaller units of functionality and deploying them as (say) microservices. So more of the code is closer to the boundary where it's going to be getting data in from some partner, whether it's JSON or XML or

YAML over a socket connection, that it's then going to turn into some Java data model, operate on, and then do the reverse. We wanted to make it easier to model data as data, since people are doing it more. So this cluster of features is designed to work together in that way. And you can see similar clusters of features in a lot of other languages, just with different names. In ML you would call them algebraic data types because records are product types and sealed classes are sum types, and you do polymorphism over algebraic data types with pattern matching. These are individual features that maybe Java developers haven't seen before because they haven't programmed in Scala or ML or Haskell. They may be new to Java, but they are not new concepts, and they have been proven to work together to enable a style of programming that's relevant to the problems people are solving today.

12   I'm wondering if there's one upcoming feature in Java that you are most excited about.

I'm really excited about the bigger picture for pattern matching because, as I've worked on it, I realized that it has been a missing piece of the object model from Java all along, and we just hadn't noticed. Java offers good tools for encapsulation, but it only goes one way: you invoke a constructor with some data and that gives you an object, which then is very cagey about giving up its state. And the ways in which it gives up its state are generally via some ad hoc API that's hard to reason about programmatically. But there is a large category of classes that are just modeling plain old data. The notion of a deconstruction pattern is really just the dual of a concept that we've had from day one, which is the constructor. The constructor takes state and turns it into an object. What's the reverse of that? How do you deconstruct an object into the state that you started with (or could restart with)? That's exactly what pattern matching lets you do. It turns out that there are an awful lot of problems for which the solution with pattern matching is just much more straightforward, elegant, and most importantly composable, than doing it the ad hoc way.

I bring that up because despite all we've learned about advances in programming language theory in the last 50 years, my one-sentence summary of the history of programming languages is, "We have one good trick that works." And that trick is composition. That's the only thing that works to manage complexity. And so, as a language designer, you want to be looking for techniques that allow developers to work with composition rather than against it.

13   Why is it important to know problem-solving techniques from the realm of computer science?

To stand on the shoulders of giants! There are so many problems that have already been solved by someone else, often at great effort and expense and with many false starts. If you don't know how to recognize that you're staring at a problem that has probably been solved by somebody before, you're going to be tempted to reinvent their solution—and you're probably not going to do it as well.

I saw a funny comic the other day about how mathematics works. When something new is being discovered, at first no one believes that it's even true, and it takes years to figure out the details. It may take years more to get the rest of the mathematical community to agree that this actually makes sense. And then at the other end, you spend 45 minutes on it in a lecture, and when a student doesn't understand it, the professor asks, "We spent all class on that yesterday, how could you not get it?" A lot of the concepts that we see as lecture-sized units of understanding in class are the result of years of someone bashing their head against the problem. The problems that we solve are hard enough that we need every bit of help we can get. If we can decompose the problem so that some part can be solved by an existing technique, that is hugely freeing. It means you don't have to reinvent a solution, and especially not a bad solution. You don't have to rediscover all the ways in which the obvious solution isn't quite right. You can just lean on an existing solution and focus on the part of your problem that is unique.

14 Sometimes students have trouble envisioning how the data structure and algorithm problems they learn will actually come up in real-world software development. Can you tell us how often computer science problems actually come up in software engineering?

This reminds me of a conversation I had when I went back to visit my thesis advisor some 10–15 years after graduation. He asked me two questions. The first was, "Do you use the math that you learned in your work here?" And I said, "Well, to be honest, not very often." The second was, "But do you use the thinking and analysis skills that you learned when studying math?" And I said, "Absolutely, every day." And he smiled with the pride of a job well done.

For example, take red-black trees. How do they work? Most of the time, I shouldn't have to care. If you need one, every language has an excellent prewritten, well tested, high-performance library that you can just use. The important skill is not being able to recreate this library, but knowing how to spot when you can use it profitably to solve a bigger problem, whether it is the right tool, how this will fit into the time or space complexity of your overall solution, and so on. These are skills that you use all the time. It can be hard, when you're in the middle of a data structures class, to see the forest through the trees. You can spend a lot of time in class working through the mechanics of a red-black tree, and this might be important, but it's something you'll likely never have to do again. And hopefully you won't get asked to do it in an interview, because I think that's a terrible interview question! But you should know what the time complexity of a tree lookup could be, what the conditions on the key distribution would have to be in order to achieve that complexity, and so on. That's the kind of thinking that real-world developers are called on to apply every day.

15 Can you give us an example of a time in which you or another engineer were able to parlay knowledge from computer science to better attack an engineering problem?

In my own work, it's kind of funny, because the theory is a very important underpinning to a lot of what we do. But the theory also stops short of being able to solve the problem for you in real-world language design. For example, Java is not a pure language, so in theory there's nothing to be learned from monads. But of course there's a lot to be learned from monads. So when I'm looking at a possible feature, there is a lot of theory I can lean on. That gives me an intuition, but I'm going to have to fill in the last mile myself. The same thing with type systems. Most of type theory doesn't deal with effects like throwing exceptions. Well, Java has exceptions. That doesn't mean that type theory is useless. There's a lot of type theory I can lean on in evolving the Java language. But I have to recognize that the theory is going to get me only so far, and I'm going to need to pave the last mile on my own.

Finding that balance is hard. But it's critical, because it's all too easy to say, "Oh, the theory won't help me," and then you're reinventing wheels.

16 What areas of computer science are important in language development?

Type theory is the obvious one. Most languages have a type system, and some of them have more than one. Java, for example, has one type system at static compilation time, and a different type system at run time. There is even a third type system for verification time. These type systems have to be consistent, of course, but they have different degrees of precision and granularity. So type theory is, of course, important. There is a lot of formal work on program semantics that is useful to be aware of, but not necessarily something that gets applied in everyday language design. But I don't think any reasonable project goes by without opening the type theory books and reading dozens of papers.

17 If somebody out there is interested in eventually getting involved in language design, is there something you recommend they study or that they do in their career so that they could be in a position like yours someday?

Obviously, in order to be involved in language design, you have to understand the tools that language developers use. You have to understand compilers, and type systems, and all the details from computational theory: finite automata, context-free grammars, and so on. It is a prerequisite to understand all of that stuff. It's also really important to have programmed in a number of different languages, and specifically different kinds of languages, to see the different ways in which they approach problems, the different assumptions they make, the different tools that they reserve for the language versus what they put in the user's hands, and so on. I think you have to have a pretty broad perspective on programming in order to be able to succeed in language design. You also need to have a "systems thinking" perspective. When you add a feature to a language, it changes how people will program in that language, and it changes the set of directions you can go in the future. You have to be able to see not only how a feature will be used, but also abused, and whether the new equilibrium is actually better than the old, or whether it just moves the problem to a different place.

In fact, I'd give some of that advice—specifically, to go out and learn different kinds of programming languages—to everyone, regardless of whether they are interested in programming languages or not. Learning more than one programming paradigm will make them better programmers; when they approach a problem, they'll more easily see multiple ways to attack it. I'd especially recommend learning a functional language, because it will give you a different and useful perspective on how to construct programs and will stretch your brain (in good ways).

18   What mistakes do you often see Java programmers make, that they could perhaps avoid by better exploiting the language's features?

I think the biggest one is not doing the work to understand how generics work. There are a few non-obvious concepts in generics, but not that many, and they're not all that hard once you set yourself to it. And generics are the underpinnings of other features, such as lambdas, as well as the key to understanding a lot of libraries. But a lot of developers treat it as an exercise in "What do I have to do to make the red squiggles go away?" rather than as leverage.

19   What do you think is one of the biggest shifts that is going to happen in the next 5 to 10 years for working programmers?

I suspect it will be the integration of traditional computational problem solving with machine learning. Right now, programming and machine learning are completely separate areas. The current techniques for machine learning have been sort of lying dormant for 40 years. All the work on neural networks was done in the '60s and '70s. But we didn't have the computational power or the data to train them until now. We have those things now, and all of a sudden it's become relevant. You're seeing machine learning applied to things like handwriting recognition, speech recognition, fraud detection, and all of these things that we used to try to solve (not very well) with rule-based systems or heuristics. But the problem is that the tools we use for machine learning and the styles of thinking we apply for machine learning are completely different from the way we write traditional programs. I think this is going to be a big challenge for the programmers of the next 20 years. How are they going to bridge these two different types of thinking in these two different tool sets in order to solve problems that will increasingly require both sets of skills?

20   What do you think some of the largest evolutionary changes in programming languages over the next decade will be?

I think we're seeing the broad shape of a trend now, which is the convergence between object-oriented and functional languages. Twenty years ago, languages were strictly separated into functional languages, procedural languages, and object-oriented languages, and they each had their own philosophy of how to model the world. But each of those models was deficient in some way because it was only modeling part of the world. What we've seen over the last decade or so, starting with languages like Scala and F#, and now languages like C# and Java, is that many of the concepts that originally took root in functional programming are finding their way into the more broad-spectrum languages, and I think that trend will only continue. Some people like to joke that all the languages are converging to $MY_FAVORITE_LANGUAGE. There's some truth to that joke, in that functional languages are acquiring more tools for data encapsulation, and object-oriented languages are acquiring more tools for functional composition. And there's an obvious reason, which is that these are both useful sets of tools. Each excels at one kind of problem or another, and we are called on to solve problems that have both aspects. So I think what we're going to see over the next 10 years is an increased convergence of concepts that were traditionally considered object-oriented and concepts that were traditionally considered functional.

21   I think there are many examples of influences from the functional programming world on Java. Can you give us a few of those?

The most obvious one is lambda expressions. And, you know, it's not really fair to call them a functional programming concept because the lambda calculus predates computers by several decades. It is a natural model for describing and composing behavior. It makes just as much sense in a language like Java or C# as it does in Haskell or ML. So that's clearly one. Another similar one is pattern matching, which again most people associate with functional languages, because that's probably the first place they saw it, but actually, pattern matching goes way back to languages like SNOBOL from the '70s, which was a text-processing language. Pattern matching actually fits into the object model very cleanly. It's not a pure functional concept. It just happens that the functional languages noticed that it was useful a little bit before we did. A lot of these concepts that we associate with functional languages make perfect sense in object-oriented languages as well.

22   Java is by many measures one of the most popular programming languages in the world. What do you think has caused it to be so successful, and why do you think it will continue to be successful going forward?

As with any success, there's a little bit of luck, and I think you should always acknowledge the role that luck has played in your success, because to do otherwise is not being honest. I think in many ways Java came around at just about the right time. At that time, the world was on the cusp of deciding whether to leap from C to C++. C was the dominant language at the time, for better or worse, and C++ offered on the one hand better abstractive power than C, and on the other hand ungodly complexity. So you can imagine that the world was poised on a cliff, saying, "Do we really want to make this jump?" And Java came along and said, "I can give you most of what C++ is promising you without nearly as much complexity." And everyone said, "Yes, please, we want that!" It was the right thing at the right time. It picked up on a number of old ideas that had been kicking around the computing world for years, including garbage collection and building concurrency into the programming model, that had not been used before in serious commercial languages. All of these things were relevant to the problems people were solving in the '90s.

James Gosling has a quote where he describes Java as the "wolf in sheep's clothing." People needed garbage collection, they needed an integrated concurrency model that was better than pthreads, but they didn't want the languages that these things traditionally came with because they came with all sorts of other things that scared the heck out of them. Java, on the other hand, looked like C. In fact, they went out of their way to make the syntax look like C. It was familiar, and then they could sneak some cool stuff along with it that you only noticed much later. One of the things that the creators of Java did was design the entire language runtime with the anticipation that just-in-time compilation was coming but wasn't quite there. The first version of Java in 1995 was strictly interpreted. It was slow, but every design decision about the language and the class file format and the runtime structure was made with the know-how to make this fast. Eventually it became fast enough, and in some cases, even faster than C (though some people still don't believe this is possible). So there was some right-place, right-time luck, and a lot of brilliant vision for where the technology was going and what people really needed, that got Java going. But that's just what happened at the start—to keep Java number one, with competitors itching to eat Java's lunch, we needed something more. And I think the thing that has kept us going, even through the dark times we discussed, is the relentless commitment to compatibility.

Making incompatible changes is breaking your promises. It invalidates the investment that your customers have made in their code. Whenever you break someone's code, you're almost handing them an opportunity to go rewrite it in some other language, and Java has never done that. The Java code that you wrote 5, 10, 15, 20, 25 years ago still works. That means that we evolve a little bit more slowly. But it means that the investment you've made not only in code but in your understanding of how the language works is preserved. We don't break our promises, and we don't hurt our users in that way. The challenge is how to balance moving forward with that kind of commitment to compatibility. And I think that's our secret weapon. We figured out how to do that in the last 25 years, and we've gotten pretty good at it. That's what enables us to add generics, and lambda expressions, and modules, and pattern matching, and other things that may seem foreign to Java without making them look bolted on—because we figured out how to do this.

23 **Go gets a lot of credit for its integrated concurrency model, but Java already had synchronization primitives, keywords, and a threading model built into the language back in 1995. Why do you think it doesn't get more credit for this?**

I think part of it is that a lot of the real cleverness is under the waterline where people don't see it. When something just works, it often doesn't get the credit. So that might be part of it. I'm not a big fan of Go for a couple of reasons. Everyone thinks that the concurrency model is Go's secret weapon, but I think their concurrency model is actually quite error prone. That is, you have coroutines with a very basic message-passing mechanism (channels). But in almost all cases, the things on one side or the other of the channel are going to have some shared mutable state guarded with locks. And that means that you have the union of the mistakes you can make with message passing and the mistakes you can make with shared-state concurrency, combined with the fact that Go's concurrency primitives for shared-state concurrency are dramatically weaker than those in Java. (For example, their locks aren't reentrant, which means that you can't compose any behaviors that use locks. It means that you often have to write two versions of the same thing—one to be called with lock held, one not to be called with the lock held.) I think what people will discover is that Go's concurrency model, not unlike Reactive, is going to be a transitional technology that looked attractive for a while, but something better is going to come along, and I think people will desert it quite quickly. (Of course, that might just be my bias showing.)

24   What does your work look like on a day-to-day basis as the Java Language Architect?

It's actually all over the map. Any given day, I could be doing pure research on language evolution and how far-off features will connect up. I could be prototyping the implementation of something to see how the moving parts fit together. I could be writing up a direction statement for the team: "Here's where I think we are in the process of solving this problem, here's what I think we have figured out, here are the problems that are left." I might be speaking at conferences, talking to users, trying to understand what their pain points are, and to some degree, selling the message of where we're going in the future. Any given day could be any of those things. Some of those things are very much in the moment, some are forward looking, some are backward looking, some are community facing, some are internal facing. Every day is different!

Right now, one of the projects that I'm involved in, that we've been working on for several years, is an upgrade to the generic type system to support primitives and primitive-like aggregates. This is something that touches the language, the compiler, the translation strategy, the class file format, and the JVM. In order to be able to credibly say that we have a story here, all of those pieces have to line up. So on any given day I might be working at the intersection of two of those things to see if the story is lining up properly or not. This is a process that can take years!

25   What words of advice do you have for self-taught programmers trying to improve their skill set, students, or experienced developers going back and reviewing material to improve their computer science skills?

One of the most valuable ways to understand a technology is to put it in historical context. Ask, "How does this technology relate to whatever came before it for solving the same problem?" Because most developers don't always get to pick what technology they're using to solve a problem. If you were a developer in 2000 and you took a job, they would tell you, "We use this database, we use this application container, we use this IDE, we use this language. Now go program." All of these choices were already made for you, and you might be overwhelmed by the complexity of how they all fit together. But every one of those pieces that you're working with exists in a historical context, and it is the product of somebody's better idea for solving a problem we solved in a different way yesterday. Very often you can get a better understanding of how a given piece of technology works by understanding what didn't work about the previous iteration of the technology, what made someone say, "Let's not do it that way. Let's do it this way." Because the history of computing is so compressed, most of that material is still available, and you can go back and read what was written about in the version 1.0 release. The designers will tell you why they invented it and what problems they were frustrated by that they couldn't solve with yesterday's technology. That technique is tremendously useful for understanding both what it's for and the limitations that you're going to run into.

Brian can be followed on Twitter @BrianGoetz.

appendix A
Glossary

This appendix defines a selection of key terms from throughout the book.

activation function   A function that transforms the output of a *neuron* in an *artificial neural network*, generally to render it capable of handling nonlinear transformations or to ensure its output value is clamped within some range (chapter 7).

acyclic   A *graph* with no *cycles* (chapter 4).

admissible heuristic   A *heuristic* for the A* search algorithm that never overestimates the cost to reach the goal (chapter 2).

artificial neural network   A simulation of a biological *neural network* using computational tools to solve problems not easily reduced into forms amenable to traditional algorithmic approaches. Note that the operation of an *artificial neural network* generally strays significantly from its biological counterpart (chapter 7).

auto-memoization   A version of *memoization* implemented at the language level, in which the results of function calls without side effects are stored for lookup upon further identical calls (chapter 1).

backpropagation   A technique used for *training neural network* weights according to a set of inputs with known-correct outputs. Partial derivatives are used to calculate each weight's "responsibility" for the error between actual results and expected results. These *deltas* are used to update the weights for future runs (chapter 7).

backtracking   Returning to an earlier decision point (to go a different direction than was last pursued) after hitting a wall in a search problem (chapter 3).

bit string   A data structure that stores a sequence of 1s and 0s represented using a single bit of memory for each. This is sometimes referred to as a *bit vector* or *bit array* (chapter 1).

centroid   The center point in a *cluster*. Typically, each dimension of this point is the mean of the rest of the points in that dimension (chapter 6).

chromosome   In a genetic algorithm, each individual in the *population* is referred to as a *chromosome* (chapter 5).

cluster   See *clustering* (chapter 6).

clustering   An *unsupervised learning* technique that divides a data set into groups of related points, known as *clusters* (chapter 6).

codon   A combination of three *nucleotides* that form an amino acid (chapter 2).

compression   Encoding data (changing its form) to require less space (chapter 1).

connected   A graph property that indicates there is a *path* from any *vertex* to any other *vertex* (chapter 4).

constraint   A requirement that must be fulfilled in order for a constraint-satisfaction problem to be solved (chapter 3).

crossover   In a genetic algorithm, combining individuals from the *population* to create offspring that are a mixture of the parents and that will be a part of the next *generation* (chapter 5).

CSV   A text interchange format in which rows of data sets have their values separated by commas, and the rows themselves are generally separated by newline characters. *CSV* stands for *comma-separated values*. CSV is a common export format from spreadsheets and databases (chapter 7).

cycle   A *path* in a *graph* that visits the same *vertex* twice without *backtracking* (chapter 4).

decompression   Reversing the process of *compression*, returning the data to its original form (chapter 1).

deep learning   Something of a buzzword, deep learning can refer to any of several techniques that use advanced machine learning algorithms to analyze big data. Most commonly, deep learning refers to using multilayer *artificial neural networks* to solve problems using large data sets (chapter 7).

delta   A value that is representative of a gap between the expected value of a weight in a *neural network* and its actual value. The expected value is determined through the use of *training* data and *backpropagation* (chapter 7).

digraph   See *directed graph* (chapter 4).

directed graph   Also known as a *digraph*, a directed graph is a *graph* in which *edges* may only be traversed in one direction (chapter 4).

domain   The possible values of a *variable* in a constraint-satisfaction problem (chapter 3).

dynamic programming   Instead of solving a large problem outright using a brute-force approach, in dynamic programming the problem is broken up into smaller subproblems that are each more manageable (chapter 9).

edge   A connection between two *vertices* (nodes) in a *graph* (chapter 4).

exclusive or   See *XOR* (chapter 1).

feed-forward   A type of *neural network* in which signals propagate in one direction (chapter 7).

fitness function   A function that evaluates the effectiveness of a potential solution to a problem (chapter 5).

generation   One round in the evaluation of a genetic algorithm; also used to refer to the *population* of individuals active in a round (chapter 5).

genetic programming   Programs that modify themselves using the *selection*, *crossover*, and *mutation* operators to find solutions to programming problems that are non-obvious (chapter 5).

gradient descent   The method of modifying an *artificial neural network*'s weights using the *deltas* calculated during *backpropagation* and the *learning rate* (chapter 7).

graph   An abstract mathematical construct that is used for modeling a real-world problem by dividing the problem into a set of *connected* nodes. The nodes are known as *vertices*, and the connections are known as *edges* (chapter 4).

greedy algorithm   An algorithm that always selects the best immediate choice at any decision point, hopeful that it will lead to the globally optimal solution (chapter 4).

heuristic   An intuition about the way to solve a problem that points in the right direction (chapter 2).

hidden layer   Any layers between the *input layer* and the *output layer* in a *feed-forward artificial neural network* (chapter 7).

infinite loop   A loop that does not terminate (chapter 1).

infinite recursion   A set of recursive calls that does not terminate but instead continues to make additional recursive calls. Analogous to an *infinite loop*. Usually caused by the lack of a base case (chapter 1).

input layer   The first layer of a *feed-forward artificial neural network* that receives its input from some kind of external entity (chapter 7).

learning rate   A value, usually a constant, used to adjust the rate at which weights are modified in an *artificial neural network*, based on calculated *deltas* (chapter 7).

memoization   A technique in which the results of computational tasks are stored for later retrieval from memory, saving additional computation time to re-create the same results (chapter 1).

minimum spanning tree   A *spanning tree* that connects all vertices using the minimum total weight of *edges* (chapter 4).

mutate   In a genetic algorithm, randomly changing some property of an individual before it is included in the next *generation* (chapter 5).

natural selection   The evolutionary process by which well-adapted organisms succeed and poorly adapted organisms fail. Given a limited set of resources in the environment, the organisms best suited to leverage those resources will survive and propagate. Over several *generations*, this leads to helpful traits for survival being propagated among a *population*, hence being naturally selected by the constraints of the environment (chapter 5).

neural network   A network of multiple *neurons* that act in concert to process information. *Neurons* are often thought about as being organized in layers (chapter 7).

neuron   An individual nerve cell, such as those in the human brain (chapter 7), or the smallest computation unit in an artificial neural network.

normalization   The process of making different types of data comparable (chapter 6).

NP-hard   A problem that belongs to a class of problems for which there is no known polynomial time algorithm to solve (chapter 9).

nucleotide   One instance of one of the four bases of DNA: adenine (A), cytosine (C), guanine (G), and thymine (T) (chapter 2).

output layer   The last layer in a *feed-forward artificial neural network* that is used for determining the result of the network for a given input and problem (chapter 7).

path   A set of *edges* that connects two vertices in a *graph* (chapter 4).

ply   A turn (often thought of as a move) in a two-player game (chapter 8).

population   In a genetic algorithm, the population is the collection of individuals (each representing a potential solution to the problem) competing to solve the problem (chapter 5).

priority queue   A data structure that pops items based on a "priority" ordering. For instance, a priority queue may be used with a collection of emergency calls in order to respond to the highest-priority calls first (chapter 2).

queue   An abstract data structure that enforces the ordering FIFO (First-In-First-Out). A queue implementation provides at least the operations push and pop for adding and removing elements, respectively (chapter 2).

recursive function   A function that calls itself (chapter 1).

selection   The process of selecting individuals in a *generation* of a genetic algorithm for reproduction to create individuals for the next *generation* (chapter 5).

sigmoid function   One of a set of popular *activation functions* used in *artificial neural networks*. The eponymous sigmoid function always returns a value between 0 and 1. It is also useful for ensuring that results beyond just linear transformations can be represented by the network (chapter 7).

SIMD instructions   Microprocessor instructions optimized for doing calculations using vectors, also sometimes known as vector instructions. *SIMD* stands for *single instruction, multiple data* (chapter 7).

spanning tree   A *tree* that connects every *vertex* in a *graph* (chapter 4).

stack   An abstract data structure that enforces the Last-In-First-Out (LIFO) ordering. A stack implementation provides at least the operations push and pop for adding and removing elements, respectively (chapter 2).

supervised learning   Any machine-learning technique in which the algorithm is somehow guided toward correct results using outside resources (chapter 7).

synapses   Gaps between *neurons* in which neurotransmitters are released to allow for the conduction of electrical current. In layman's terms, these are the connections between *neurons* (chapter 7).

training   A phase in which an *artificial neural network* has its weights adjusted by using *backpropagation* with known-correct outputs for some given inputs (chapter 7).

tree   A *graph* that has only one *path* between any two vertices. A tree is *acyclic* (chapter 4).

unsupervised learning   Any machine-learning technique that does not use foreknowledge to reach its conclusions—in other words, a technique that is not guided but instead runs on its own (chapter 6).

variable   In the context of a constraint-satisfaction problem, a variable is some parameter that must be solved for as part of the problem's solution. The possible values of the variable are its *domain*. The requirements for a solution are one or more *constraints* (chapter 3).

vertex   A single node in a *graph* (chapter 4).

XOR   A logical bitwise operation that returns `true` when either of its operands is true but not when both are true or neither is true. The abbreviation stands for *exclusive or*. In Java, the ^ operator is used for XOR (chapter 1).

z-score   The number of standard deviations a data point is away from the mean of a data set (chapter 6).

appendix B
More resources

Where should you go next? This book covered a wide swath of topics, and this appendix will connect you with great resources that will help you explore them further.

Java

As was stated in the introduction, *Classic Computer Science Problems in Java* assumes you have at least an intermediate knowledge of the Java language. Java has evolved quite a bit over the past few years. Here is a title that can help you get up to speed on the latest developments in the Java language, and that will help take your intermediate Java skills to the next level:

- Raoul-Gabriel Urma, Mario Fusco, Alan Mycroft, *Modern Java in Action* (Manning, 2018), www.manning.com/books/modern-java-in-action.
  - Covers lambdas, streams, and modern functional mechanisms in Java
  - Examples use the latest LTS (long-term-support) version of Java, Java 11
  - Covers wide variety of modern Java topics, which will help many developers who learned Java in the pre-Java 8 era

Data structures and algorithms

To quote this book's introduction, "This is not a data structures and algorithms textbook." There is little use of big-O notation in this book, and there are no mathematical proofs. This is more of a hands-on tutorial to important computational problem-solving techniques, and there is value in having a real textbook too. Not only will it provide you with a more formal explanation of why certain techniques work, but it will also serve as a useful reference. Online resources are great, but sometimes it is good to have information that has been meticulously vetted by academics and publishers.

- Thomas Cormen, Charles Leiserson, Ronald Rivest, and Clifford Stein, *Introduction to Algorithms*, 3rd ed. (MIT Press, 2009), https://mitpress.mit.edu/books/introduction-algorithms-third-edition.
  - This is one of the most-cited texts in computer science—so definitive that it is often just referred to by the initials of its authors: CLRS.
  - Comprehensive and rigorous in its coverage.
  - Its teaching style is sometimes seen as less approachable than other texts, but it is still an excellent reference.
  - Pseudocode is provided for most algorithms.
  - A fourth edition is being developed, and because this book is expensive, it may be worth looking into when the fourth edition is due to be released.
- Robert Sedgewick and Kevin Wayne, *Algorithms*, 4th ed. (Addison-Wesley Professional, 2011), http://algs4.cs.princeton.edu/home/.
  - An approachable yet comprehensive introduction to algorithms and data structures
  - Well organized with full examples of all algorithms in Java
  - Popular in college algorithm classes
- Steven Skiena, *The Algorithm Design Manual*, 2nd ed. (Springer, 2011), www.algorist.com.
  - Different in its approach from other textbooks in this discipline
  - Offers less code but more descriptive discussion of appropriate uses of each algorithm
  - Offers a "choose your own adventure"-like guide to a wide range of algorithms
- Aditya Bhargava, *Grokking Algorithms* (Manning, 2016), www.manning.com/books/grokking-algorithms.
  - A graphical approach to teaching basic algorithms, with cute cartoons to boot
  - Not a reference textbook, but instead a guide to learning some basic selected topics for the first time
  - Very intuitive analogies and easy-to-understand prose
  - Example code is in Python

Artificial intelligence

Artificial intelligence is changing our world. In this book, you not only were introduced to some traditional artificial intelligence search techniques like A* and mini-max, but also to techniques from its exciting subdiscipline, machine learning, like k-means and neural networks. Learning more about artificial intelligence is not only interesting, but also will ensure you are prepared for the next wave of computing.

- Stuart Russell and Peter Norvig, *Artificial Intelligence: A Modern Approach*, 3rd ed. (Pearson, 2009), http://aima.cs.berkeley.edu.
  - The definitive textbook on AI, often used in college courses
  - Wide in its breadth

- Excellent source code repositories (implemented versions of the pseudo-code in the book) available online
- Stephen Lucci and Danny Kopec, *Artificial Intelligence in the 21st Century*, 2nd ed. (Mercury Learning and Information, 2015), http://mng.bz/1N46.
  - An approachable text for those looking for a more down-to-earth and color-ful guide than Russell and Norvig
  - Interesting vignettes on practitioners and many references to real-world applications
- Andrew Ng, "Machine Learning" course (Stanford University), www.coursera .org/learn/machine-learning/.
  - A free online course that covers many of the fundamental algorithms in machine learning
  - Taught by a world-renowned expert
  - Often referenced as a great starting point in the field by practitioners

Functional programming

Java can be programmed in a functional style, but it wasn't really designed for that. Delving into the reaches of functional programming is possible in Java itself, but it can also be helpful to work in a purely functional language and then take some of the ideas you learn from that experience back to Java.

- Harold Abelson and Gerald Jay Sussman with Julie Sussman, *Structure and Inter-pretation of Computer Programs* (MIT Press, 1996), https://mitpress.mit.edu/sicp/.
  - A classic introduction to functional programming often used in introductory computer science college classes
  - Teaches in Scheme, an easy-to-pick-up, purely functional language
  - Available online for free
- Michał Płachta, *Grokking Functional Programming* (Manning, 2021), www.manning .com/books/grokking-functional-programming.
  - A graphical and friendly introduction to functional programming
- Pierre-Yves Saumont, *Functional Programming in Java* (Manning, 2017), www .manning.com/books/functional-programming-in-java.
  - Gives a basic introduction to some functional programming utilities in the Java standard library
  - Shows you how to use Java in a functional way

index